LUKE 1–9

A Commentary in the Wesleyan Tradition

*New Beacon Bible Commentary

LUKE 1–9
A Commentary in the Wesleyan Tradition

David A. Neale

BEACON HILL PRESS
OF KANSAS CITY

Copyright 2011
by Beacon Hill Press of Kansas City

ISBN 978-0-8341-2408-0

Printed in the United States of America

Cover Design: J.R. Caines
Interior Design: Sharon Page

Library of Congress Cataloging-in-Publication Data

Neale, David A.
    Luke 1-9 / David A. Neale.
    p. cm. — (New Beacon Bible commentary)
    Includes bibliographical references.
    ISBN 978-0-8341-2408-0 (pbk.)
    1. Bible. N.T. Luke I-IX—Commentaries. I. Title. II. Title: Luke one through nine.
    BS2595.53.N43 2011
    226.4'07—dc22

                                                                            2011000005

10 9 8 7 6 5 4 3 2 1

DEDICATION

To Christine

COMMENTARY EDITORS

CONTENTS

TABLE OF SIDEBARS

GENERAL EDITORS' PREFACE

The purpose of the New Beacon Bible Commentary is to make available to pastors and students in the twenty-first century a biblical commentary that reflects the best scholarship in the Wesleyan theological tradition. The commentary project aims to make this scholarship accessible to a wider audience to assist them in their understanding and proclamation of Scripture as God's Word.

Writers of the volumes in this series not only are scholars within the Wesleyan theological tradition and experts in their field but also have special interest in the books assigned to them. Their task is to communicate clearly the critical consensus and the full range of other credible voices who have commented on the Scriptures. Though scholarship and scholarly contribution to the understanding of the Scriptures are key concerns of this series, it is not intended as an academic dialogue within the scholarly community. Commentators of this series constantly aim to demonstrate in their work the significance of the Bible as the church's book and the contemporary relevance and application of the biblical message. The project's overall goal is to make available to the church and for her service the fruits of the labors of scholars who are committed to their Christian faith.

The *New International Version* (NIV) is the reference version of the Bible used in this series; however, the focus of exegetical study and comments is the biblical text in its original language. When the commentary uses the NIV, it is printed in bold. The text printed in bold italics is the translation of the author. Commentators also refer to other translations where the text may be difficult or ambiguous.

The structure and organization of the commentaries in this series seeks to facilitate the study of the biblical text in a systematic and methodical way. Study of each biblical book begins with an **Introduction** section that gives an overview of authorship, date, provenance, audience, occasion, purpose, sociological/cultural issues, textual history, literary features, hermeneutical issues, and theological themes necessary to understand the book. This section also includes a brief outline of the book and a list of general works and standard commentaries.

The commentary section for each biblical book follows the outline of the book presented in the introduction. In some volumes, readers will find section *overviews* of large portions of scripture with general comments on their overall literary structure and other literary features. A consistent feature of the commentary is the paragraph-by-paragraph study of biblical texts. This section has three parts: **Behind the Text**, **In the Text**, and **From the Text**.

The goal of the **Behind the Text** section is to provide the reader with all the relevant information necessary to understand the text. This includes specific historical situations reflected in the text, the literary context of the text, sociological and cultural issues, and literary features of the text.

In the Text explores what the text says, following its verse-by-verse structure. This section includes a discussion of grammatical details, word studies, and the connectedness of the text to other biblical books/passages or other parts of the book being studied (the canonical relationship). This section provides transliterations of key words in Hebrew and Greek and their literal meanings. The goal here is to explain what the author would have meant and/or what the audience would have understood as the meaning of the text. This is the largest section of the commentary.

The **From the Text** section examines the text in relation to the following areas: theological significance, intertextuality, the history of interpretation, use of the Old Testament scriptures in the New Testament, interpretation in later church history, actualization, and application.

The commentary provides **sidebars** on topics of interest that are important but not necessarily part of an explanation of the biblical text. These topics are informational items and may cover archaeological, historical, literary, cultural, and theological matters that have relevance to the biblical text. Occasionally, longer detailed discussions of special topics are included as **excurses.**

We offer this series with our hope and prayer that readers will find it a valuable resource for their understanding of God's Word and an indispensable tool for their critical engagement with the biblical texts.

Roger Hahn, Centennial Initiative General Editor
Alex Varughese, General Editor (Old Testament)
George Lyons, General Editor (New Testament)

AUTHOR'S PREFACE

Many stories from the Gospel of Luke have entered our shared imagination. Only Luke tells us about Zechariah and Elizabeth and the birth of John the Baptist. Likewise, it is Luke who tells us about Mary's visit from Gabriel and the joyous encounter some months later with Elizabeth. Luke writes of Mary's song of joy, the shepherds at the manger, and the adoration of Anna and Simeon in the temple.

Other well-known stories are found only in Luke: the boy Jesus in the temple, the Good Samaritan, the prodigal son, the Pharisee and the tax collector praying in the temple, and the diminutive Zacchaeus high up in a tree. In his postresurrection narrative, Luke alone portrays the disciples walking along the road to Emmaus after the resurrection, heads bent in conversation with the risen Jesus. And alone among the Evangelists, Luke describes the ascension of Jesus in detail in ch 24 of the Gospel, and then further in Acts 1.

All of these stories are a rich part of the Christian heritage contributed by the Gospel of Luke. But it is not just his special material that makes Luke such a gratifying study. Writing under a sense of divine compunction, he took these stories and combined them with various existing bodies of material at his disposal to create a unique theological and historical document. Beginning in the Gospel, and continuing in Acts, Luke sets out a new paradigm for the story of salvation. In Luke's gospel world, the good news bursts the confines of its original Jewish context to spread throughout the Roman world, inviting all people, both Jew and Gentile, into a new community of faith based on repentance and forgiveness in the name of Jesus.

All these images make his Gospel unique. But an emphasis on the freedom of the human spirit is his hallmark. It is the freedom to choose an old life or a new life. The seeds of what can be interpreted as a universally accessible salvation are present in all of the Gospels. But Luke's Gospel codifies this access in a new theological paradigm. He offers readers, whatever their identity, the chance to start life anew each time there is repentance. It is this human freedom to choose redemption that marks out Luke's distinctive theological emphasis. His is a gospel of second chances. Many of the stories only he has preserved have this overriding theme.

A literary work becomes a classic because it has a timeless quality, touching readers across cultures, generations, and centuries. All Scripture belongs in this category, as does certainly the Gospel of Luke. From Augustine, Tertullian, Origen, and Ambrose early in the Christian era (see Kealy 2005, 12-13, 28), to the painting of the *Return of the Prodigal* by Rembrandt, Luke has captured the hearts of past generations.

In the modern imagination, at least among the biblically literate, Lazarus still reclines in the bosom of Abraham and the images of the parable of the Good Samaritan continue to resonate. All these stories demonstrate the appeal of Luke's Gospel across the boundaries of culture and time.

The Gospel of Luke remains particularly relevant among the Gospels because of its optimism for the healing of the human condition. It is here that his Gospel connects most poignantly with the openness and optimism of Wesleyan theology. Luke guides us not just by his literary genius but by his understanding of the human experience of sin and suffering. He refers to this in the traditional language of Scripture: sin, disease, and impurity. Along the way in his narrative these human burdens are relieved as sin gives way to righteousness, impurity gives way to purity, and disease gives way to healing. The means by which this redemption arises is through repentance, forgiveness, and salvation through the Son of a gracious God. Most importantly, this is available to all in Luke's story: lepers, sinful women, a Gentile king, tax collectors, Pharisees, Jews, and Roman centurions.

The story Luke tells seems to argue that, as a human family, we have never been able to set aside our shared experience of sin, impurity, and disease, nor our need for salvation. Luke's Gospel remains relevant because its solution to the problem of human suffering remains relevant. And even though our world has changed since he penned his Gospel, it seems apparent that human nature has remained the same.

Luke offers solace to the modern heart in the same way he did to the ancient heart. We are alienated from a sense of the divine by our willful selfishness and we find our way back to the divine by means of humble repentance. We are plagued by guilt and regret for the failures of our lives, and Luke gives us a path back to holiness through forgiveness and the empowering presence of the Spirit. And so, by revisiting this story with a modern perspective, we refresh its meaning for the modern reader. A rereading of Luke is always valuable, and the powerful ideas found here will bring a rediscovered sense of hope, a second chance to all.

ABBREVIATIONS

With a few exceptions, these abbreviations follow those in *The SBL Handbook of Style* (Alexander 1999).

General

ad loc.	*ad locum*, at the place discussed
A.D.	anno Domini (precedes date) (equivalent to C.E.)
B.C.	before Christ (follows date) (equivalent to B.C.E.)
B.C.E.	before the Common Era
C.E.	Common Era
ca.	circa, approximate time
cf.	confer, compare
ch	chapter
chs	chapters
e.g.	*exempli gratia*, for example
esp.	especially
etc.	*et cetera*, and the rest
f(f).	and the following one(s)
i.e.	*id est*, that is
ktl.	etc. (in Greek transliteration)
lit.	literally
LXX	Septuagint (Greek translation of the OT)
MS	manuscript
MSS	manuscripts
MT	Masoretic Text (of the OT)
n.	note
n.d.	no date
nn.	notes
n.p.	no place; no publisher; no page
NT	New Testament
OT	Old Testament
s.v.	*sub verbo*, under the word
v (vv)	verse (verses)
vs.	versus
‖	Synoptic Gospel parallel

Frequently Cited Reference Works

ABD	*Anchor Bible Dictionary.* See Freedman.
BDF	*Greek Grammar of the New Testament and Other Early Christian Literature.* See Blass and Debrunner.
TDNT	*Theological Dictionary of the New Testament.* See Kittel.

Modern English Versions

ASV	American Standard Version
KJV	King James Version
NASB	New American Standard Bible
NIV	New International Version
NKJV	New King James Version
NLT	New Living Translation
NRSV	New Revised Standard Version

Print Conventions for Translations

Bold font	NIV (bold without quotation marks in the text under study; elsewhere in the regular font, with quotation marks and no further identification)
Bold italic font	Author's translation (without quotation marks)

Behind the Text:	Literary or historical background information average readers might not know from reading the biblical text alone
In the Text:	Comments on the biblical text, words, phrases, grammar, and so forth
From the Text:	The use of the text by later interpreters, contemporary relevance, theological and ethical implications of the text, with particular emphasis on Wesleyan concerns

Old Testament

Gen	Genesis
Exod	Exodus
Lev	Leviticus
Num	Numbers
Deut	Deuteronomy
Josh	Joshua
Judg	Judges
Ruth	Ruth
1—2 Sam	1—2 Samuel
1—2 Kgs	1—2 Kings
1—2 Chr	1—2 Chronicles
Ezra	Ezra
Neh	Nehemiah
Esth	Esther
Job	Job
Ps/Pss	Psalm/Psalms
Prov	Proverbs
Eccl	Ecclesiastes
Song	Song of Songs / Song of Solomon
Isa	Isaiah
Jer	Jeremiah
Lam	Lamentations
Ezek	Ezekiel
Dan	Daniel
Hos	Hosea
Joel	Joel
Amos	Amos
Obad	Obadiah
Jonah	Jonah
Mic	Micah
Nah	Nahum
Hab	Habakkuk
Zeph	Zephaniah
Hag	Haggai
Zech	Zechariah
Mal	Malachi

(Note: Chapter and verse numbering in the MT and LXX often differ compared to those in English Bibles. To avoid confusion, all biblical references follow the chapter and verse numbering in English translations, even when the text in the MT and LXX is under discussion.)

New Testament

Matt	Matthew
Mark	Mark
Luke	Luke
John	John
Acts	Acts
Rom	Romans
1—2 Cor	1—2 Corinthians
Gal	Galatians
Eph	Ephesians
Phil	Philippians
Col	Colossians
1—2 Thess	1—2 Thessalonians
1—2 Tim	1—2 Timothy
Titus	Titus
Phlm	Philemon
Heb	Hebrews
Jas	James
1—2 Pet	1—2 Peter
1—2—3 John	1—2—3 John
Jude	Jude
Rev	Revelation

Apocrypha

Bar	Baruch
1—2 Macc	1—2 Maccabees
3—4 Macc	3—4 Maccabees
Pr Man	Prayer of Manasseh
Tob	Tobit
Wis	Wisdom of Solomon

Church Fathers

Irenaeus *Haer.*	*Against Heresies*
Eusebius *Hist. eccl.*	*Ecclesiastical History*
Tertullian *Marc.*	*Against Marcion*

OT Pseudepigrapha

1 En.	*1 Enoch* (Ethiopic Apocalypse)
As. Mos.	*Assumption of Moses*
Jos. Asen.	*Joseph and Aseneth*
Jub.	*Jubilees*
Pss. Sol.	*Psalms of Solomon*
T. Ab.	*Testament of Abraham*
T. Jac.	*Testament of Jacob*

Dead Sea Scrolls and Related Texts

Q	Qumran
1QH[a]	*Hodayot*[a] or *Thanksgiving Hymns*[a]
1QM	*Milhamah* or *War Scroll*
1QS	*Serek Hayaḥad* or *Rule of the Community*

Josephus

Ant.	*Jewish Antiquities*

Rabbinic Texts

Avot	Aboth
b.	Babylonian Talmud
Ḥag.	*Ḥagigah*
m.	Mishnah
Sabb.	*Sabbat*
Sanh.	*Sanhedrin*
Tamid	*Tamid*
Yoma	*Yoma*

Greek Transliteration

Greek	Letter	English
α	*alpha*	*a*
β	*bēta*	*b*
γ	*gamma*	*g*
γ	*gamma nasal*	*n* (before γ, κ, ξ, χ)
δ	*delta*	*d*
ε	*epsilon*	*e*
ζ	*zēta*	*z*
η	*ēta*	*ē*
θ	*thēta*	*th*
ι	*iōta*	*i*
κ	*kappa*	*k*
λ	*lambda*	*l*
μ	*mu*	*m*
ν	*nu*	*n*
ξ	*xi*	*x*
ο	*omicron*	*o*
π	*pi*	*p*
ρ	*rhō*	*r*
ρ	initial *rhō*	*rh*
σ/ς	*sigma*	*s*
τ	*tau*	*t*
υ	*upsilon*	*y*
υ	*upsilon*	*u* (in diphthongs: *au, eu, ēu, ou, ui*)
φ	*phi*	*ph*
χ	*chi*	*ch*
ψ	*psi*	*ps*
ω	*ōmega*	*ō*
‛	rough breathing	*h* (before initial vowels or diphthongs)

Hebrew Consonant Transliteration

Hebrew/ Aramaic	Letter	English
א	*alef*	*'*
ב	*bet*	*b; v* (spirant)
ג	*gimel*	*g; gh* (spirant)
ד	*dalet*	*d; dh* (spirant)
ה	*he*	*h*
ו	*vav*	*v* or *w*
ז	*zayin*	*z*
ח	*khet*	*ḥ* or *kh*
ט	*tet*	*ṭ*
י	*yod*	*y*
ך/כ	*kaf*	*k; kh* (spirant)
ל	*lamed*	*l*
ם/מ	*mem*	*m*
ן/נ	*nun*	*n*
ס	*samek*	*s*
ע	*ayin*	*ʻ*
ף/פ	*pe*	*p; f* (spirant)
ץ/צ	*tsade*	*ṣ*
ק	*qof*	*q*
ר	*resh*	*r*
שׂ	*sin*	*ś*
שׁ	*shin*	*š*
ת	*tav*	*t; th* (spirant)

BIBLIOGRAPHY

Abrahams, Israel. 1967. *Studies in Pharisaism and the Gospels.* New York: KTAV Publishing House. Originally published 1917.

Adams, Dwayne. 2008. *The Sinner in Luke.* Eugene, Ore.: Pickwick Publications.

Aland, Kurt. 1964. *Synopsis Quattuor Evangeliorum.* Stuttgart: Württembergische Bibelanstalt.

Barnstone, Willis, ed. 1984. *The Other Bible.* San Francisco: Harper and Row.

Bauckham, Richard. 2002. *Gospel Women: Studies of the Named Women in the Gospels.* Grand Rapids: Eerdmans.

_____. 2006. *Jesus and the Eyewitnesses: The Gospels as Eyewitness Testimony.* Grand Rapids: Eerdmans.

Bauer, Walter, W. F. Arndt, and F. Wilbur Gingrich. 1957. *A Greek-English Lexicon of the New Testament and Other Early Christian Literature.* Chicago: University of Chicago Press.

Beale, G. K., and D. A. Carson. 2007. *Commentary on the New Testament Use of the Old Testament.* Grand Rapids: Baker Academic.

Blass, F., and A. Debrunner. 1961. *A Greek Grammar of the New Testament and Other Early Christian Literature.* Translated and edited by Robert W. Funk. Chicago: University of Chicago Press.

Blomberg, Craig L. 2005. *Contagious Holiness: Jesus' Meals with Sinners.* Downers Grove, Ill.: InterVarsity Press.

Bock, Darrell L. 1994. *Luke 1:1—9:50,* vol. 1. Baker Exegetical Commentary on the New Testament. Grand Rapids: Baker Books.

Borg, Marcus J. 1984. *Conflict, Holiness, and Politics in the Teaching of Jesus.* Lewiston, N.Y.: Edwin Mellen.

_____. 1991. *Jesus: A New Vision.* New York: HarperSanFrancisco.

_____. 1994. *Jesus in Contemporary Scholarship.* Valley Forge, Pa.: Trinity Press International.

Bornkamm, Günther. 1960. *Jesus of Nazareth.* Translated by Frances and Irene McLuskey and James M. Robinson. London: Hodder and Stoughton.

Brower, Kent. 2005. *Holiness in the Gospels.* Kansas City: Beacon Hill Press of Kansas City.

Brower, Kent, and Andy Johnson, eds. 2007. *Holiness and Ecclesiology in the New Testament.* Grand Rapids: Eerdmans.

Brown, Raymond E. 1970. *The Gospel According to John: XIII-XXI.* Anchor Bible 29a. Garden City: Doubleday.

_____. 1979. *The Birth of the Messiah: A Commentary on the Infancy Narratives in the Gospels of Matthew and Luke.* New York: Doubleday.

Bultmann, Rudolf. 1958. *Jesus Christ and Mythology.* New York: Charles Scribner's Sons.

Capps, Donald. 2000. *Jesus: A Psychological Biography.* St. Louis: Challis Press.

Carey, Greg. 2009. *Sinners: Jesus and His Earliest Followers.* Waco, Tex.: Baylor University Press.

Carlson, Stephen C. 2010. The Accommodations of Joseph and Mary in Bethlehem: *Katalma* in Luke 2.7. *New Testament Studies* 56:326-42.

Chance, J. Bradley, and Milton P. Horne. 2000. *Rereading the Bible: An Introduction to the Biblical Story.* Upper Saddle River, N.J.: Prentice Hall.

Charlesworth, James H., ed. 1983. *The Old Testament Pseudepigrapha, Vol. 1: Apocalyptic Literature and Testaments.* Garden City, N.Y.: Doubleday.

_____. 1985. *The Old Testament Pseudepigrapha, Vol. 2: Expansions of the "Old Testament" and Legends, Wisdom and Philosophical Literature, Prayers, Psalms, and Odes, Fragments of Lost Judeo-Hellenistic Works.* Garden City, N.Y.: Doubleday.

Chilton, Bruce, and J. I. H. McDonald. 1987. *Jesus and the Ethics of the Kingdom.* Grand Rapids: Eerdmans.

Clines, David J. A. 1989. *Job 1-20.* Word Biblical Commentary 17. Dallas: Word.

Conzelmann, Hans. 1982. *The Theology of St. Luke.* Translated by Geoffrey Buswell. Philadelphia: Fortress. Original, *Die Mitte der Zeit.* New York: Harper, 1961.

Corley, Kathleen. 1989. Women in the Context of Greco-Roman Meals. *Society of Biblical Literature: 1989 Seminar Papers.* Atlanta: Scholars Press.

Craddock, Fred B. 1990. *Luke.* Interpretation: A Bible Commentary for Teaching and Preaching. Louisville, Ky.: John Knox Press.

Crossan, John Dominic. 1991. *The Historical Jesus: The Life of a Mediterranean Jewish Peasant.* New York: HarperCollins Publishers.

Danby, Herbert. 1938. *The Mishnah*. London: Oxford University Press.

Darr, John A. 1992. *On Character Building: The Reader and the Rhetoric of Characterization in Luke-Acts*. Louisville, Ky.: Westminster/John Knox Press.

Delling, Gerhard. 1964. *katartizō*. Pages 475-76 in vol. 1 of *TDNT.*

Derrett, J. D. M. 1970. *Law in the New Testament*. London: Darton, Longman & Todd.

Dodd, C. H. 1958. *The Parables of the Kingdom*. London: James Nisbet, 1935. Repr. New York: Charles Schribner's Sons.

Douglas, Mary. 1970. *Purity and Danger: An Analysis of Concepts of Pollution and Taboo*. London: Routledge & Kegan Paul, 1966. Repr. London: Pelican Books.

Dunn, James D. G. 1970. *Baptism in the Holy Spirit*. Studies in Biblical Theology Second Series 15. London: SCM Press.

_____. 1975. *Jesus and the Spirit*. Philadelphia: Westminster Press.

Eichrodt, Walther. 1961. *Theology of the Old Testament*. Vol. 1. Translated by J. A. Baker. Philadelphia: Westminster Press.

Ervin, Howard M. 1984. *Conversion-Initiation and the Baptism in the Holy Spirit: A Critique of James D. G. Dunn's* Baptism in the Holy Spirit. Peabody, Mass.: Hendrickson.

Evans, C. F. 1990. *Saint Luke*. London: SCM Press.

Evans, Craig A., and James A. Sanders. 1993. *Luke and Scripture: The Function of Sacred Tradition in Luke-Acts*. Eugene, Ore.: Wipf and Stock.

Fitzmyer, Joseph A. 1981. *The Gospel According to Luke I—IX: Introduction, Translation, and Notes*. Anchor Bible 28. New York: Doubleday.

_____. 1985. *The Gospel According to Luke X—XXIV: Introduction, Translation, and Notes*. Anchor Bible 29. New York: Doubleday.

_____. 1997. *The Semitic Background of the New Testament*. Grand Rapids: Eerdmans, 1971. Repr. 2 vols. in 1: *The Semitic Background of the New Testament* and *A Wandering Aramean*, in notes as volumes 1 and 2.

Freedman, David Noel, ed. 1992. *The Anchor Bible Dictionary*. 6 vols. New York: Doubleday.

Funk, Robert, and Roy W. Hoover. 1993. *The Five Gospels: The Search for the Authentic Words of Jesus*. New York: Macmillan.

Garrett, Susan R. 1989. *The Demise of the Devil: Magic and the Demonic in Luke's Writings*. Minneapolis: Fortress.

Gaventa, Beverly Roberts. 1999. *Mary: Glimpses of the Mother of Jesus*. Minneapolis: Fortress Press.

Gerhardsson, Birger. 2001. *The Reliability of the Gospel Tradition*. Peabody, Mass.: Hendrickson.

Gibson, Shimon. 2004. *The Cave of John the Baptist*. New York: Doubleday.

Goodacre, Mark. 2002. *The Case Against Q: Studies in Markan Priority and the Synoptic Problem*. Harrisburg, Pa.: Trinity Press International.

Green, Joel. B. 1997. *The Gospel According to Luke*. The New International Commentary on the New Testament. Grand Rapids: Eerdmans.

Grundmann, Walter. 1964. *daimōn*. Pages 1-25 in vol. 2 of *TDNT*.

Hadas-Lebel, Mireille. 1993. *Flavius Josephus: Eyewitness to Rome's First-Century Conquest of Judea*. New York: Macmillan.

Hall, Robert G. 1992. Circumcision. Pages 1025-31 in vol. 1 of *AB*.

Hamilton, Victor P. 1992. Satan. Pages 985-89 in vol. 5 of *AB*.

Hengel, Martin. 1977. *Crucifixion*. Translated by John Bowden. Philadelphia: Fortress Press.

Herr, M. D. 1971. Midrash. Pages 354-66 of vol. 2 of the *Encyclopedia Judaica*. New York: Macmillan.

Hock, Ronald F. 1992. Cynics. Pages 1221-26 of vol. 1 of *AB*.

Horsley, Richard A. 1992. Messianic Movements in Judaism. Pages 791-97 in vol. 4 of *AB*.

Hurtado, Larry. 2003. *Lord Jesus Christ: Devotion to Jesus in Earliest Christianity*. Grand Rapids: Eerdmans.

Jeal, Roy. 2011. *A Sociorhetorical Commentary on Colossians and Philemon*. Rhetoric of Religious Antiquity Series. Blandford Forum, Dorset, United Kingdom: Deo Publishing, forthcoming.

Jeremias, Joachim. 1962. *Jerusalem in the Time of Jesus*. Translated by F. H. Cave and C. H. Cave. Philadelphia: Fortress.

_____. 1972. *The Parables of Jesus*. 2d ed. Translated by S. H. Hooke. Upper Saddle River, N.J.: Prentice Hall.

Johnson, Luke Timothy. 1991. *The Gospel of Luke*. Sacra Pagina 3. Edited by Daniel J. Harrington. Collegeville, Minn.: Liturgical Press.

Just, Arthur A., Jr., ed. 2003. *Luke*. Ancient Christian Commentary on Scripture: New Testament 3. Edited by Thomas C. Oden. Downers Grove, Ill.: InterVarsity.

Kealy, Seán A. 2005. *The Interpretation of the Gospel of Luke: From Apostolic Times Through the Nineteenth Century*. Lampeter, Wales: Edwin Mellen.

Kimball, Charles A. 1994. *Jesus' Exposition of the Old Testament in Luke's Gospel*. Sheffield: JSOT Press.

Kingsbury, Jack Dean. 1991. *Conflict in Luke: Jesus, Authorities, Disciples*. Minneapolis: Augsburg Fortress.

Kittel, Gerhard, and Gerhard Friedrich, eds. 1964-76. *Theological Dictionary of the New Testament*. 10 vols. Translated and edited by Geoffrey William Bromiley. Grand Rapids: Eerdmans.

Kjärgaard, Mogens Stiller. 1986. *Metaphor and Parable: A Systematic Analysis of the Specific Structure and Cognitive Function of the Synoptic Similies and Parables Qua Metaphors*. Leiden: E. J. Brill.

Klawans, Jonathan. 2000. *Impurity and Sin in Ancient Judaism*. New York: Oxford University Press.

Kraft, Robert. 1992. Didache. Pages 197-98 in vol. 2 of *AB*.

Lane, Anthony S., ed. 1996. *The Unseen World: Christian Reflections on Angels, Demons, and the Heavenly Realm*. Grand Rapids: Baker.

Lewis, Theodore J. 1992. Beelzebub. Pages 638-40 in vol. 1 of *AB*.

Longenecker, Richard, ed. 2000. *The Challenge of Jesus' Parables*. Grand Rapids: Eerdmans.

Maccoby, Hyam. 1988. *Early Rabbinic Writings*. Cambridge: Cambridge University Press.

Mackay, Christopher S. 2004. *Ancient Rome: A Political and Military History*. Cambridge: Cambridge University Press.

Maddox, Randy L. 1994. *Responsible Grace*. Nashville: Kingswood Books.

Marshall, I. Howard. 1978. *Commentary on Luke*. Grand Rapids: Eerdmans.

Martitz, Peter Wülfing von. 1972. huios, huiothesia. Pages 334-40 in vol. 8 of *TDNT*.

McArthur, Harvey K., and Robert M. Johnston. 1990. *They Also Taught in Parables: Rabbinic Parables from the First Centuries of the Christian Era*. Grand Rapids: Zondervan.

McGehee, Michael David. 1992. Hasmonean Dynasty. Pages 67-76 in vol. 3 of *AB*.

Metzger, Bruce. 1975. *A Textual Commentary on the Greek New Testament*. New York: United Bible Societies.

Michel, A. 1972. telōnēs. Pages 88-105 in vol. 8 of *TDNT*.

Miller, John W. 1997. *Jesus at Thirty*. Minneapolis: Augsburg Fortress.

Moule, C. F. D. 1982. ". . . As We Forgive . . .": A Note on the Distinction Between Deserts and Capacity in the Understanding of Forgiveness. Pages 278-86 in *Essays in New Testament Interpretation*. Cambridge: Cambridge University Press.

Mullen, Patrick J. 2004. *Dining with Pharisees*. Collegeville, Minn.: Liturgical Press.

Nave, Guy D., Jr. 2002. *The Role and Function of Repentance in Luke-Acts*. Atlanta: Society of Biblical Literature.

Neale, David. 1991. *None but the Sinners: Religious Categories in the Gospel of Luke*. Sheffield: Sheffield Academic Press.

————. 1993. *Was Jesus a Mesith?* Tyndale Bulletin 44.1:89-101.

Neusner, Jacob. 1971. *The Rabbinic Traditions about the Pharisees Before 70*. Vol. 3. Leiden: Brill.

————. 1973. *The Idea of Purity in Ancient Judaism*. Leiden: Brill.

Newman, Luis E. 2010. *Repentance: The Meaning and Practice of Teshuvah*. Woodstock: Jewish Lights Publishing.

Neyrey, Jerome. 1985. *The Passion According to Luke: A Redaction Study of Luke's Soteriology*. New York: Paulist Press.

Nolland, John. 1989. *Luke 1—9:20*. Word Biblical Commentary 35a. Dallas: Word Books.

Oden, Thomas C. 1994. *John Wesley's Scriptural Christianity: A Plain Exposition of His Teaching on Christian Doctrine*. Grand Rapids: Zondervan.

O'Toole, Robert F. 1992. Theophilus. Pages 511-12 in vol. 6 of *AB*.

Pagels, Elaine. 1995. *The Origin of Satan*. New York: Random House.

Perry, Tim. 2006. *Mary for Evangelicals: Toward an Understanding of the Mother of Our Lord*. Downers Grove, Ill.: InterVarsity.

Phipps, William E. 1993. *The Wisdom and Wit of Rabbi Jesus*. Louisville, Ky.: Westminster/John Knox Press.

Price, S. R. F. 1984. *Rituals and Powers: The Roman Imperial Cult in Asia Minor*. Cambridge: Cambridge University Press.

Reed, Jonathan L. 2000. *Archaeology and the Galilean Jesus*. Harrisburg, Pa.: Trinity Press International.

Robinson, James M., gen. ed. 1977. *The Nag Hammadi Library*. San Francisco: Harper and Row.

Rogerson, John. 1989. *Atlas of the Bible*. Oxford: Phaidon Press Limited.

Ryken, Leland, James C. Wilhoit, and Tremper Longman III, eds. 1998. *The Dictionary of Biblical Imagery*. Downers Grove, Ill.: InterVarsity.

Safrai, S., and M. Stern, eds. 1974. *The Jewish People in the First Century. Compendium Rerum Iudaicarum ad Novum Testamentum*. 2 vols. Philadelphia: Fortress.

Sanders, E. P. 1992. *Judaism: Practice and Belief 63 BCE-66 CE*. London: SCM Press.

———. 1995. *The Historical Figure of Jesus*. London: Penguin Press.

Schmitz, Philip C. 1992. Census. Pages 882-84 in vol. 1 of *AB*.

Schrenck, Gottlob. 1964. *dikaios*. Pages 182-225 in vol. 2 of *TDNT*.

Schürer, Emil. 1979. *The History of the Jewish People in the Age of Jesus Christ*. Rev. ed. 3 vols. Edited by G. Vermes, F. Millar, and M. Black. Edinburgh: T & T Clark.

Scott, Bernard Brandon. 1989. *Hear Then the Parable: A Commentary on the Parables of Jesus*. Minneapolis: Augsburg Fortress.

Shillington, George V. 1997. *Jesus and His Parables: Interpreting the Parables of Jesus for Today*. Edinburgh: T & T Clark.

Snodgrass, Klyne R. 2008. *Stories with Intent: A Comprehensive Guide to the Parables of Jesus*. Grand Rapids: Eerdmans.

Stein, Robert. 2000. *The Genre of the Parables*, in Longnecker, Richard, ed. *The Challenge of Jesus' Parables*. Grand Rapids: Eerdmans.

Stronstad, Roger. 1984. *The Charismatic Theology of St. Luke*. Peabody, Mass.: Hendrickson.

Sussman, Max. 1992. Sickness and Disease. Pages 6-15 in vol. 6 of *AB*.

Tannehill, Robert C. 1986. *The Narrative Unity of Luke-Acts: A Literary Interpretation*. Philadelphia: Fortress.

———. 1996. *Luke*. Abingdon New Testament Commentaries. Nashville: Abingdon Press.

———. 2005. *The Shape of Luke's Story*. Eugene, Ore.: Cascade Books.

Taylor, Joan E. 1997. *The Immerser: John the Baptist Within the Second Temple Judaism*. Grand Rapids: Eerdmans.

Taylor, Vincent. 1952. *The Gospel According to St. Mark: The Greek Text with Introduction, Notes, and Indexes*. New York: Macmillan.

Theissen, Gerd, and Annette Merz. 1996. *The Historical Jesus: A Comprehensive Guide*. Translated by John Bowden. Minneapolis: Fortress Press.

Thompson, Richard. 2007. Gathered at the Table: Holiness and Ecclesiology in the Gospel of Luke. Pages 76-94 in *Holiness and Ecclesiology in the New Testament*. Edited by Kent E. Brower and Andy Johnson. Grand Rapids: Eerdmans.

Tuckett, Christopher M. 1996. *Q and the History of Early Christianity*. Peabody, Mass.: Hendrickson.

Tyson, Joseph B. 1992. *Images of Judaism in Luke-Acts*. Columbia: University of South Carolina Press.

Urbach, Ephraim E. 1987. *The Sages: Their Concepts and Beliefs*. Cambridge: Harvard University Press.

Vermes, Geza. 1973. *Jesus the Jew*. London: William Collins Sons.

Watts, John D. W. 1985. *Isaiah 1—33*. Word Biblical Commentary 24. Waco, Tex.: Word.

Webb, Robert L. 1991. *John the Baptizer and Prophet: A Socio-Historical Study*. Sheffield: Sheffield Academic Press.

Wesley, John. 1981. *Explanatory Notes on the New Testament*. Vol. 1. Grand Rapids: Baker Book House. Reprinted from an undated edition published by the Wesleyan-Methodist Book-Room in London.

Wigoder, Geoffrey, ed. 1989. Conversion to Judaism. Pages 184-85 in *The New Encyclopedia of Judaism*. New York: New York University Press.

Wilson, Robert. 1980. *Prophecy and Society in Ancient Israel*. Philadelphia: Fortress.

Wright, C. J. H. 1992. Family. Pages 761-69 in vol. 2 of *AB*.

Wright, David P., and H. Hübner, 1992. Unclean and Clean (OT). Pages 729-45 in vol. 6 of *AB*.

Wright, David P., and Richard N. Jones. 1992. Leprosy. Pages 277-82 in vol. 4 of *AB*.

Wright, N. T. 1996. *Jesus and the Victory of God*. Minneapolis: Fortress.

Yoder, John Howard. 1972. *The Politics of Jesus: Behold the Man! Our Victorious Lamb*. Grand Rapids: Eerdmans.

Young, Brad. 1989. *Jesus and His Jewish Parables: Rediscovering the Roots of Jesus' Teaching*. New York: Paulist Press.

Zeisler, J. A. 1979. Luke and the Pharisees. *New Testament Studies* 25:146-57.

INTRODUCTION

A. Luke and His Community

I. Authorship and Date

Since the author's name appears nowhere in its narrative, the Gospel is an anonymous work. The attribution to someone named Luke is a matter of tradition for which the external evidence is sparse. The title found on the last page of the oldest manuscript is *euangelion kata Loukan—The Gospel According to Luke* (the papyrus codex P[75] dating from A.D. 175-225; Fitzmyer 1981, 1:35). In addition to this, several early manuscripts indicate that the attribution of this Gospel to Luke was already common in the late second century and early third century.

The earliest reference to Luke's authorship is found in the Muratorian Canon (A.D. 170-180). "The third book of the Gospel: According to Luke. This Luke was a physician. After the ascension of Christ, when Paul had taken him along with him as one devoted to letters, he wrote it under his own name from hearsay. For he himself had not seen the Lord in person, but, insofar as he was able to follow (it all), he thus began his account with the birth of John" (quoted from Fitzmyer 1981, 1:37).

In a passage dated at the end of the second century, Irenaeus refers to the authorship of this Gospel (*Haer.* 3.1.1): "Luke, too, the companion of Paul, set forth in a book the gospel as preached by him." A late second century document known as the Prologue to the Gospel reported: "Luke was a Syrian of Antioch, by profession a physician, the disciple of the apostles, and later a follower of Paul until his martyrdom. He served the Lord without distraction, without a wife, and without children. He died at the age of eighty-four in Boeotia, full of the holy Spirit" (Fitzmyer's translation [1981, 1:38]; for Greek, see Aland 1964, 533). In Tertullian's *Against Marcion* 4.2.2 (early third century), we find: "Luke, however, was not an apostle, but only a man of apostolic times; not a master, but a disciple, inferior indeed to a master—and at least as much later (than they) as the Apostle whom he followed, undoubtedly Paul (was later than the others)" (Fitzmyer 1981, 1:40).

Other early references are made to Luke as the author of the Gospel by Tertullian (A.D. 207-208), Origen (A.D. 254), Eusebius (A.D. 303), and Jerome (A.D. 398; see Fitzmyer 1981, 1:39-40). These texts establish that Luke was considered the author of the third Gospel. But they give only indirect data about his identity and when he lived.

Evidence internal to the NT for the identity of Luke is of two kinds. The first refers to Luke outside the Luke/Acts tradition. Here we have three references. In Col 4:14 Paul offers greeting to the Colossians from his "dear friend Luke, the doctor." In Paul's greetings to Philemon in vv 23-24, he wrote: "Epaphras, my fellow prisoner in Christ Jesus, sends you greetings. And so do Mark, Aristarchus, Demas and Luke, my fellow workers." In 2 Tim 4:11 Paul confides that "only Luke is with me." These passages, written prior to A.D. 60, name Luke as an intimate companion of Paul. But they cannot connect him directly to the Gospel that bears this name, since it had not yet been written.

The second type of evidence for the authorship of the third Gospel is inductive in nature—internal evidence from within the Gospel and Acts. First, we know the author was not an eyewitness of the Jesus events, because he tells us so (1:2). However, the "we" sections of Acts (16:10-17; 20:5-15; 21:1-18; 27:1—28:16) suggest that the author was a companion of Paul.

If the man who wrote the third Gospel was the Luke of Paul's letters, it is interesting to consider what connection existed between the communities of Paul and the Synoptic tradition, even if this is not apparent from Paul's writings. There must have been a pervasive presence of the Synoptic tradition in the first century, from the Judaism of Palestine, which gave birth to the tradition, to the form in which it spread across the Mediterranean basin through itinerant evangelists like Paul.

From the internal evidence of the Gospel other observations can be made about the mind-set of the author. Maps were not generally available in this period, and he has a vague grasp of the geography of Palestine, particularly Samaria (17:11-19). Thus, he is not a Palestinian and has perhaps never even been there. And yet, he is an ardent admirer of temple Judaism, as is evident throughout the infancy narratives of John and Jesus. He holds the priesthood in high regard (1:5), and considers obedience to the Law desirable (1:6-7). For Luke, John the Baptist is a Palestinian Jewish prophet. These traits mark out Luke's temple- and Torah-based perspective on the Jesus story.

More specifically, Luke addresses his work in both the Gospel and Acts to a man within his community named Theophilus. The Greek name means "friend of God," so the identity of this individual is debated (see O'Toole 1992, 6:511-12). Some believe he was an actual person, the benefactor who sponsored Luke's literary project. Others suggest the name represents the type of reader to whom Luke/Acts was written. Or, it may have been a clever pseudonym to protect the recipient from political persecution by concealing his identity. Luke's is the only Gospel addressed to an individual.

Luke's writing probably dates to the late first century (the 80s). This can be seen indirectly in another aspect of his narrative. His Gospel, most notably ch 21, seems to interpret the eschatological narrative (apparently derived from Mark 13) in a nonapocalyptic way. In particular, Jerusalem's destruction (A.D. 70), already a historical fact by the time Luke writes, is not a sign of the end of the age, but a signpost along a longer path to the culmination of history (see the commentary on 21:20-24). The destruction of Jerusalem exists within the drama of the church; it is not the culmination of that drama. This significant difference in Luke's view of the world has sometimes been called his view of "salvation history"—the long drama of the life of the church, yet to be concluded. This is another reason Luke seems so relevant to the modern church. For him the drama of human life is ongoing, and he shapes his presentation of the gospel to this perspective.

2. Synoptic Sources

The so-called Synoptic Problem is an ongoing debate about the inter-dependency of Matthew, Mark, and Luke as literary sources. Although not universally accepted, the "primacy of Mark" is the idea that his Gospel was written first and then used by Matthew and Luke. It is reasonable to say that this has been the majority view in Gospel studies for two centuries.

The position assumed in this commentary is that Luke freely shapes the Gospel of Mark to his own literary purposes. He includes almost the whole of Mark's text in one form or another. Yet, it is so skillfully interwoven that even an attentive reader can barely discern the seams. Even so, Luke did not write a commentary on Mark, but a new narrative about Jesus (Evans and Sanders 1993, 4). He presumably thought his was either better than had yet been produced or supplied essential material lacking in Mark.

Luke also expands the story of Mark by the addition of other source materials. These include some 230 sayings of Jesus, which both Matthew and Luke contain. Some scholars believe a single Q-source existed (from *Quelle*, meaning "source"). Others dispute it (on the debate, see Tuckett 1996, 1-39; Goodacre 2002). In any case, Matthew and Luke have a significant body of material in common, which Mark likely did not have or chose not to include. Gospel studies have not resolved whether Luke used the supposed Q-source or had Matthew's Gospel to consult.

3. The Old Testament as a Source

The relationship of the text of Luke to the canon of the OT is central to the literary study of the Gospel. As is obvious from the Synoptic tradition in general, Jesus was intimately acquainted with the biblical story of Judaism—Torah, Prophets, and Writings. He often drew upon the OT to provide the context of his message to his contemporaries. One author has identified 590 direct or indirect references to Isaiah alone in the NT. These allusions cover the full breadth of Isaiah and many of these citations occur in the Gospels (Evans and Sanders 1993, 14). The sacred texts of the OT were the shared lexicon of meaning among first-century Palestinian and Diaspora Jews and Gentile god-fearers. It is not surprising then, that the NT is full of references to the OT.

Various terms have been used in recent scholarship to describe the use of the OT in the NT. New Testament authors are said to have "reread" the text of the OT and reinterpreted it for their time. This phenomenon is sometimes called the "Bible rewritten" or "intertextuality." Others use the term "comparative midrash" to highlight how the NT treatment of OT texts has some affinity with the Jewish habit of commenting on sacred texts in a commentary-like form. Other terms such as the "haggadah within Scripture," "inner-biblical exegesis," and "parabiblical rewriting" have also been used to describe the habit of NT writers to reshape the meaning of OT texts within NT literary contexts (Evans and Sanders 1993, 3).

As a matter of historical and literary fact, Jesus used the OT as the foundation of his gospel message. And this is how all the Evangelists portray Jesus' message. Yet, in the Gospel of Luke, Jesus' teachings are reread through the lens of Luke's *own* understanding of the OT.

This is part of the human process of preserving sacred tradition. As the decades go by, that tradition is reappropriated to keep it relevant to a new generation of readers. This is done incrementally so as not to break the chain of tradition in any substantial way, lest the reinterpretation be rejected by the keepers of the tradition. The reinterpretation of the text always travels *through* the minds and hearts of its most recent interpreters, not around them, as though the story was an entity with an independent existence. A rhetorical and literary reading suggests the text's meaning resides ultimately in the heart and mind of the next reader. Luke is a reader of the OT, who interprets it for a new generation, who then in turn bring their own hearts and minds to the task of interpretation.

This is a process in which divine inspiration is understood to require human participation. The Gospel-author occupies the foundational role in the process of inspiration. But the inspiration of the Holy Spirit continues in every new generation of readers who access the meaning of the text. This is not a rote or verbal conception of divine inspiration, but an understanding rooted in the belief that God's engagement with human beings is real—even to the point of human participation in the creation of the sacred text of Scripture.

Thus, the interpretation of the OT presented in Luke can tell us a great deal about how his gospel message was contemporized for a new audience. He uses the text of the OT to show the first reader how the events of Jesus' life are to be understood in his or her own contemporary community and life situation. That is, Luke's presentation of the OT not only reflects the underpinnings of Jesus' historical message but also explains the present moment to his readers.

This dependence on the OT is not just top dressing for his story of Jesus, an obligatory nod to the Jewish scriptural tradition. It is, in fact, the deep structure upon which the gospel story rests. "Luke uses biblical prototypes to construct entire scenes. In both volumes [Luke and Acts], uniquely Lukan stories appear to depend on the imitation of biblical models, either for details of language or for the entire structure of the story" (Johnson 1991, 409). Luke's story-world is not a new world at all; it is an extension of an existing world of meaning already known to the readers. In this sense "parabiblical rewriting" accurately described Luke's literary activity. The key point is that he uses the OT story to explain the world in which his audience lives—a living story constantly unfolds new levels of meaning for Luke and his readers.

All of the Gospel writers used the OT as the bedrock of their story-world, but Luke used this approach far more extensively. It can be seen in two important ways. The first is in the way the structure of Luke's infancy narratives of John and Jesus refer to the OT. Among the many examples that will be noted in the commentary, note the barrenness of Elizabeth (1:6-7—Genesis; Exodus; Deuteronomy), the Nazirite tradition behind John's abstinence (1:15—Numbers; Leviticus), the semblance of John's ministry to that of Elijah (1:17—Malachi), the succession to Davidic power (1:32-33—2 Samuel; Isaiah; Psalms), the intertextual dependence of Mary's song on that of Hannah (1:46-56—1 Samuel; Psalms; Micah), and even references of Jesus' physical stature, which reflect the Samuel, Saul, and David stories (1:80—1 Samuel). These are but a few of the ways in which the first chapter depends on OT themes for the deep structure of the story-world. Every page of the Gospel contains some connection to the OT.

Second, Luke's Jesus rereads the OT extensively in his postresurrection appearances. In the last chapter of the Gospel, Luke's Jesus engages in an extended Bible study, which rereads and reapplies numerous OT texts, now to be understood in the light of the resurrection event. Jesus upbraids the two disciples on the road to Emmaus: "'How foolish you are, and how slow of heart to believe all that the prophets have spoken! Did not the Christ have to suffer these things and then enter his glory?' And beginning with Moses and all the Prophets, he explained to them what was said in all the Scriptures concerning himself" (24:25-27).

The disciples are, in effect, given a new hermeneutical lens with which to reread their Bibles and reinterpret the meaning of the crucifixion and resurrection. The answers are there in Moses and the Prophets, Jesus contends. But it is only through the resurrection that the disciples are given the key to understand what had lain hidden in those texts.

This observation has significance for the self-understanding of Luke's community. They were not merely conduits for the OT tradition but were clarifiers of that tradition. Through the risen Jesus they possessed a new and deeper understanding, hidden from previous generations and now revealed by the resurrection.

4. The First Readers

To whom did Luke write his Gospel? Since nothing is known about the community in which he lived, attempts to describe it are a matter of surmise. But information about the community of first readers can be deduced by his theological approach.

First, the message has a fundamental appeal to those outside of ethnic Judaism. It is an invitation for the previously excluded to join the salvation of Israel's God. Numerous stories in the Gospel make this point evident (the widow of Zarephath in Sidon, Naaman the Syrian [both L material], the centurion, the Gerasene demoniac [both Synoptic material], the messianic banquet where the sons of Israel are excluded and other included [Q material]). When this emphasis is combined with Acts' message of the gospel to the Gentiles, it suggests that Luke's audience was at least partly non-Jewish.

But this is not the full story, since Luke, as do all the Gospels, also appeals to ethnic Jews experiencing exclusion within Israel (lepers, tax collectors and sinners, the woman with the flow of blood [all Synoptics], the sinful woman, Samaritans, the prodigal son, Lazarus, Zacchaeus [all L], the great banquet ignored [Q]). Thus, it is difficult to categorize the Gospel's audience as either Jewish or Gentile, since it appeals to all who are experiencing exclusion based on religious orthodoxy. Luke's first audience almost certainly included both Jews and Gentiles.

If this Luke is the companion of Paul and he lived and traveled widely in the Mediterranean basin, we can assume that his audience was largely non-Palestinian. His poor grasp of the geography of Palestine suggests that Luke's Gospel was a Diaspora creation; and its main appeal would have been to audiences in that world.

B. Theological Themes in Luke

I. Sinners Find Repentance

In Luke's theological world, sinners repent and find their way to salvation through their encounter with Jesus. This is the governing theological paradigm of his Gospel. In his recent treatment of the role and function of repentance in Luke—Acts, Guy Nave describes Luke's emphasis:

> The principal Greek words for "repent" and "repentance" occur 25 times in Luke-Acts. That is more than 45 percent of all the occurrences in the entire New Testament. Only Luke presents John the Baptist defining what the "fruits worthy of repentance" look like. Only Luke tells stories of Jesus calling on people to repent. Only Luke depicts Jesus persuading the wicked to repent and pay back their ill-gotten gains. Only Luke-Acts gives explicit accounts of people responding to the calls for repentance issued by John the Baptist, Jesus and the apostles. Only Acts portrays Peter echoing John the Baptist by urging the people to "Repent and be baptized . . . so that your sins may be forgiven" (Acts 2:38). It is Acts, rather than the Pauline epistles, that records Paul declaring (on two occasions) that his ministry included proclaiming a message of repentance. Repentance is without question a fundamental aspect of Luke-Acts. (2002, 3)

The theology of repentance in Luke is based on a dichotomy in which people are separated into groups, those who understand and accept Jesus' divine status and those who deny and reject it. The characters in the story are, on the one hand, sinners, tax collectors, the disciples, and the crowds, who accept Jesus as a man of God. On the other hand, the religious elite, the priests, Pharisees, scribes, and their associates are unwilling to accept Jesus as a prophet. The irony, of course, and an overriding one for all of the Gospels, is that the sinners have spiritual sight and the religious elite are spiritually blind.

The initial proclamation of the call to repentance is made by John the Baptist in 3:3, 8. The repentance theme is next fleshed out in the lives of six individuals who encounter Jesus (see Tannehill 2005, 84-101). The confession from Simon Peter introduces the theme: "Go away from me, Lord; I am a sinful man!" (5:8). It appears next in the story of the call of Levi (5:27-32) and the controversy between Jesus and the Pharisees about fellowship with sinners. At the end of that story Jesus announces, "I have not come to call the righteous, but sinners, to repentance."

Repentance is also the paradigmatic proclamation of the central section of Luke. Next comes the repentance of the sinful woman in 7:36-50, the prodigal son in 15:11-32, the tax collector in 18:1-8, and finally, the repentant tax collector Zacchaeus in 19:1-10.

In the final passage about Zacchaeus on this theme, the concluding announcement on the repentance of sinners is found: "Today salvation has come to this house, because this man, too, is a son of Abraham. For the Son of Man came to seek and to save what was lost" (19:9-10). This statement brings the Galilean ministry to a close, as Jesus enters Jerusalem at the end of ch 19. Perhaps it is Luke's aim that those who read carefully will find the opportunity for their own redemption in the stories of these penitents. If these arch sinners can be saved, readers may well conclude that they too can be saved. If this is so, Luke's rhetorical purpose is not just the telling of Jesus' story, but the wooing of readers to repentance.

The causes for their repentance are various: a miracle (Peter), a call (Levi), being in Jesus' presence (the sinful woman), the experience of extreme need (the prodigal), the holiness of the temple (the tax collector), and a visit from Jesus (Zacchaeus). The results of the experience are also different: Peter falls to his knees, Levi leaves his tax table, the sinful woman is overtaken by grief and gratitude, the prodigal humbles himself by his return home, the tax collector beats his chest, Zacchaeus pledges his money. But all are changed somehow.

There is a narrative thread that holds these sinner vignettes together—a shared sense of the holy. They all experience fear and awe in their encounters with Jesus. And there is a resulting sense of personal (and corporate) guilt that leads to repentance and transformation. These experiences of Luke's characters fuel his paradigm of repentance and forgiveness throughout the Gospel.

From the perspective of practical theology, does this salvation by repentance and forgiveness express itself in the ultimate transformation of individuals? We do not see in this Gospel the result of disciples transformed into Spirit-filled believers. In the sinner vignettes we see the front end of the operation of repentance and forgiveness, not the back end. Peter remains a broken figure at the end of the Gospel. We do not know the fate of the sinful woman of ch 7 or the future of the prodigal in ch 15 or the fate of the repentant tax collector in ch 18.

The Spirit-filled life of the believer, the culmination of this theme, will be sketched out in the story of Pentecost and beyond in the book of Acts. There, we will find many examples of how the penitent will be empowered to live a new life in the Spirit. But here in the Gospel the "fruits worthy of repentance," as John described them, remain out of view.

It is through Jesus' encounters with these individuals and the conflict this generates with his religious contemporaries that Luke defines what Jesus came to accomplish. Sinners repent and the religious leaders evince only scorn for the outcasts. This is the engine of conflict that drives the Gospel narrative forward.

2. Election Redefined

In Luke, the terms used to describe humanity's relationship to God are changed from the elect (Israel) and non-elect (the nations or Gentiles) of the OT, to the lost and found of the Gospel. Put another way, Israel as the people of God at the center of salvation history is replaced by a new people—those who repent and are forgiven, regardless of their ethnic identity. The new elect are the repentant. The category of the "nations," characteristic of OT theology, is supplanted by a new category, the lost—all who refuse to accept Israel's Messiah.

In this new concept of salvation Israel is neither privileged nor excluded, condemned nor saved; she simply loses her status as being alone among the chosen. As with all peoples, she must repent and humble herself before God. To use the imagery of Luke 13:22-30, those who do not repent, be they Jewish or Gentile, will find themselves excluded from the messianic banquet. They are left outside in the dark and dangerous streets. "In Luke-Acts the extension of salvation to and the inclusion of all people within the family of God represents the plan of God. Furthermore, the human response of repentance to the offer of salvation comprises a vital part of that plan" (Nave 2002, 29).

In Luke, then, the covenant between God and his vineyard Israel (Isa 5) has been subsumed by a broader message of salvation. This is a theological innovation so radical within the narrative that Jesus' disciples respond, "May this never be!" (20:16; see 20:9-19). In Luke's paradigm, Israel has full access to salvation, but no longer on the basis of election. Rather, its access is on the basis of repentance and forgiveness, as for all the nations.

While this is demonstrated in each of the sinner vignettes above, it reaches its fullest expression in the story of the prodigal son, at the heart of Luke's Gospel. In ch 15, Luke shows what we must feel (humility) and what we must do (repent) to make our way into the gracious will of God. As such, Luke's Gospel provides the anthropology of the new salvation experience. The existential essence of the appropriate response to the gospel is the experience of humility and repentance—two very human emotions.

At the center of this new paradigm of salvation is the ability of the lost to find their way back to God. It is not only by means of his will that they should be saved but also by what they feel and do to respond to that grace. It is made possible by God's grace, and even caused by prevenient grace (as Wesleyans might say). But what is new here from the perspective of the Synoptic Gospels is the profound role of the human will and its ability to seek and find God's salvation. In fact, in Luke's understanding of the gospel, God's salvation cannot be found *without* the movement of the human heart toward God. In this sense, Luke's theology operates with the view that Wesleyans have adopted as a theological premise: What we do and even what we feel has significance for our salvation. Actions and the attitude of the heart do not *cause* salvation. They are not even salvation's central operative mechanism (which is God's grace). But salvation can never be experienced without right action and a heart of humility. This is fully in accord with the teachings of Jesus, as Luke presents him.

The examples of sinners from Luke's special material demonstrate the point. The sinful woman of 7:36-50 weeps in penitence at Jesus' feet. And her sins are declared "forgiven" (v 48). The prodigal son, humbled and full of grief at his monumental misdeeds, finds a father's embrace and restoration to his family (15:11-32). The Pharisee and the tax collector stand side-by-side at the altar in the temple. But it is the man who beats his breast and evinces a humble heart of repentance that goes "down to his house justified" (18:14 KJV). Jesus declared Zacchaeus to be one of the lost he "came to seek and to save" (19:10) because he zealously promised to be just and make recompense for any sins in his past. These sinners all demonstrate how salvation now operates. Their conduct as repentant sinners exemplifies the life of holiness and wholeness Jesus comes to spread.

Gentiles do find their way to Jesus in the Gospel and, in fact, demonstrate great faith (7:1-10; 23:7). The seed of Gentile inclusion is contained within Jesus' inaugural sermon at Nazareth. In it he extols God's gracious inclusion of Gentiles through Elijah and Elisha (4:25-30). But the significance of this new paradigm is not fully actualized in Luke's theology until his second volume, Acts. There, the first non-Jews to be included in the Christian movement do so on the basis of repentance and forgiveness, demonstrating that it is not ethnic identity or the historic terms of reference of God and his elect nation by which the new salvation operates (Acts 10:43).

The new mechanism of salvation is the attitude of the heart—regardless whether one is a Jew or a Gentile. It is here, in the movement of the gospel from Jerusalem to Rome in Acts, that Luke's new vision of universal access to salvation emerges—the stage of salvation is vastly expanded for the new era of the church (see further, Behind the Text, Luke 15:1-10).

3. Other Themes

Jerusalem. Luke is an author whose gaze rests on the geographic center of temple Judaism—Jerusalem. The narrative travels in a circuit, beginning in and about Jerusalem with the birth narratives of John and Jesus, and then moving from Galilee back to Jerusalem in chs 5—19, where the final drama takes place in chs 20—24. As the city of his destiny (9:31, 44, 51), Jesus cannot perish elsewhere (13:33). He *departs* from Jerusalem after his resurrection, indicating the outward trajectory the gospel will now travel (24:15, 46-47). From this orbit around Judaism's holiest city, this center of gravity, the message will be flung into the Gentile world.

Hope Deferred. There is also a strong sense of Davidic messianic expectation throughout the Gospel (1:32; 18:35-43). The community of Luke had grown discouraged in its anticipation of deliverance. Many decades had passed since Jesus walked the hills of Galilee, and Paul was long dead. It was a community that wanted to give up. Luke deals with this theme in his special material at 18:1-8 (see also the comment on 21:19). Hostility to the Christian movement had become the dominant reality by the time this Gospel was written. The perseverance of the community of faith is one of the primary lenses through which the narrative of Luke should be read. It is to this sense of hope deferred that Luke's material on messianic expectation speaks.

C. Literary Themes and Methods

All commentaries have methodological bases on which they approach the text, and the tools of NT study have been richly varied in the history of scholarship. In the premodern period interpretive methods read Scripture through the lenses of personal piety, church authority, allegory, and even philosophical inquiry. This period was characterized by the absence of the historical skepticism so characteristic of the modern period.

As questions about the historical accuracy of the Gospels began to arise in the middle of the nineteenth century, other more scientific methods began to be applied to the study of Scripture. These methods often sought to establish "what really happened" and to remove what was believed to be a veneer of pious myth that had accrued to the literature in its earliest stages of preservation.

In the past century, many types of interpretive methods have produced new insights into the meaning of Scripture. The names are familiar to students of biblical literature: form criticism, source criticism, textual and linguistic criticism, to name a few. More recent interpreters have used methods of historical, sociological, feminist, postmodern, and literary theory to mine the ancient texts of the NT for additional dimensions of meaning.

The overriding concern in this volume is to read Luke as a literary unit. That is to say, the purpose here is more "interpretive" than "documentary" (as in Green 1997, 15). The methods employed focus on Luke's distinctive themes, messages, and methods. A significant amount of material found in Luke is neither in Mark nor Matthew. Thus, the "special" Lukan material is especially important for the purposes of this literary reading. The analysis of this material provides the richest source for understanding Luke's unique perspectives and receives particular attention.

We will also emphasize throughout the persuasive, rhetorical forces Luke brings to bear on his readers. He is an evangelist in the sense that he seeks to persuade his readers to adopt a life of repentance and redemption. There is a strong current of reader response at work in the narrative as Luke seeks to influence his readers to make redemptive decisions about his message. On occasion, we will pause to consider the response Luke's Gospel seeks to elicit from his readers.

This commentary does not presume to present a highly technical literary analysis. Rather, it deals with the simple realities of the story as literature in order to mine Luke's meaning and intent. Some of the elements that will be commonly referred to are the narrative's OT intertextuality, its plot development, the structure of the narrative, and especially the way the author develops his characters (characterization). The frequent use of the term "narrative," for example, indicates the Gospel is to be understood as a unitary literary creation. This simple literary frame of reference intends to elucidate meaning that sometimes goes undetected by historical inquiry alone.

On occasion the term "story-world" is used. This refers to the general ideas that comprise the author's thought world. In Luke's story-world, for example, supernatural interventions are real, God has foreseen the advent of the Messiah, demons exist, voices from heaven are heard, the dead are raised, and the sick are miraculously healed. These realities constitute the basis of Luke's story-world, his ideological frame of reference. We may share belief in these realities with Luke; or we may find such events fantastic, even unbelievable. But they are realities for Luke, and none of the Gospels can profitably be read without an appreciation for this first-century view of the world and its rich tapestry of spiritual powers.

Literary analysis does not concern itself overly with historical inquiry. It emphasizes the role of the author in conveying meaning rather than assessing his historical accuracy or seeking to discover "what really happened." This use of literary method is not meant to devalue historical inquiry, or even supplant it. It is intended to supplement the historical method, which is interested in other kinds of questions. While historical inquiry is also present in this commentary, literary analysis brings alternate tools to bear on uncovering other levels of meaning in the text.

D. Structure and Plot

Some general observations can be made about the plot of the Gospel of Luke. In Mark and Matthew, Jesus' adult ministry springs to life fully formed in ch 1. Luke, following a formal prologue, sets out a complex chronological and religious context for the origins of Jesus. His story begins with an extensive birth narrative of Jesus' precursor, John the Baptist. Having created this context, Luke moves to the birth of Jesus and two events in the temple that confirm his identity as God's chosen one (Simeon and Anna). Jumping a dozen years forward, Luke has a vignette of the boy Jesus in the temple, bringing further affirmation and complexity to the young man's portrayal. With another chronological leap of eighteen years, the story begins to converge with the Synoptic portrayal of the beginning of John's ministry as a fully grown man.

Following the inaugural test of his loyalty to God in the desert, the center section of Luke's Gospel begins by recounting Jesus' ministry in his hometown and surrounding environs. The Galilean portion of his ministry extends to 9:50. In a series of healings, exorcisms, and teaching events, the ministry of Jesus is presented with approbation by his followers and the general public. Dark edges begin to emerge, however, as the religious leaders begin to take exception to his conduct. Ranging from legal issues, to the company he keeps, to the increasingly overt references to his identity as God's Son, an ethos of conflict begins to build around Jesus as a controversial figure. The culmination of this section is the transfiguration, in which his identity is fully revealed and his opponents clearly revealed to be unrighteous. The stage is now set for the remainder of the story.

At the end of ch 9, numerous references to martyrdom begin to arise in the text, and his course for Jerusalem, the city of his destiny, is set. There, he will meet his preordained death. From chs 10 to 19, Jesus ministers on the road to Jerusalem in a loosely presented geographic and chronological narrative context. As the narrative builds toward the climactic entrance to Jerusalem, much of Luke's unique material is found: his parables about the lost, the clever manager, the Pharisee and the tax collector, and the story of Zacchaeus. These features are the most striking Lukan influence on the Gospel tradition.

Once Jesus enters the holy city the story of his suffering parallels the Synoptic tradition closely. Following his death, Luke again brings unique material to bear in the postresurrection narrative on the road to Emmaus. Here, the resurrected Jesus becomes the Jesus of the church—a teacher, interpreting the Scriptures to his discouraged disciples, who will now be commissioned to teach his gospel to the nations. Here ends the gospel story, to be continued in Luke's "second volume," the book of Acts.

E. Conflict

The plot has an engine of conflict driving the story forward. In Luke, five conflict stories provide the fuel for controversy surrounding Jesus: the healing of the paralytic (5:17-26); the calling of Levi (5:27-32); the question on fasting (5:33-39); the plucking of grain on the Sabbath (6:1-5); and the Sabbath healing of the man with a withered hand (6:6-11). Luke follows Mark in this material (Mark 2:1—3:6).

All five have a common format.
- A healing or provocative event occurs in the ministry.
- Jesus' opponents take exception and challenge him verbally.
- Jesus responds with a saying that brings resolution to the passage.
- Furthermore, they all identify the Pharisees as his primary opponents.
- They all report an incident that engenders opposition.
- All conclude with a saying or action that vindicates Jesus.

These are partisan conflict stories, of course, and have limited value in reconstructing historical Judaism in the time period. Still, we do get a sense of how Jesus likely differed from some of his contemporaries.

From a reader's perspective, the stories appeal to an innate sense of what is right and proper in religious practice. Jesus and his followers see common sense; and the Pharisees are characterized as staid religionists who cannot see the obvious truth. This portrayal of the Pharisees is contrasted starkly with that of the sinners and sick who accept Jesus' self-identification as the Son of Man and rejoice at his words and deeds. These are "healthy" sinners, ones who, in fact, have already responded to the physician of 5:31.

These two paradigmatic groups each represent the extreme margin of the unrighteous (that is, the sinners, who are really the saints!) and the righteous (that is, Pharisees and others, who are really the sinners!). They are set in conflict, with Jesus mediating in the middle.

The roots of this idea are in the rhetoric of "the lost sheep of Israel," first seen in Ezek 34 (see From the Text on Luke 5:29-32; Behind the Text on Luke 15:1-10 and the commentary; and the Zacchaeus story in 19:1-10). This idea is reiterated by Jesus; and so it enters the Gospel tradition. That some members of Israel are "lost sheep" draws on the OT prophetic critique of temple Judaism (see the sections noted above), and places the core conflict of the Gospel story on the bedrock of that criticism.

F. Characterization

Authors construct characters to populate their story-worlds. At points in the commentary, reference will be made to how Luke constructs his characters. He assigns the characters of his story, among other things, opinions, motivation, patterns of behavior and speech, emotions, ambition, flaws, and shortcomings. Characters develop in relation to one another. Some are protagonists, others antagonists, and yet others bystanders. Through the relationships between these characters, the author constructs a story-world of meaning.

In Luke's telling of the Gospel, we have the devil, God, the prophets, Jesus, Joseph, Mary, Zechariah and Elizabeth, John the Baptist, Simeon and Anna, disciples, crowds, sinners and tax collectors, Herod, Zacchaeus, the prodigal son, the good Samaritan, the Pharisees and lawyers, and many others. These are the players in the story, and what we know about them comes entirely from the author's characterization of them. A brief look at Jesus and the Pharisees can demonstrate the point.

In all four Gospels, Jesus is a complex figure, one who bridges the world of the divine and the human. In Luke, Jesus is able to overcome all manner of opposition and is confident in the fulfillment of his role as God's Son. He astonishes those around him, speaking and acting in ways that transform those he encounters. Throughout the narrative, he overcomes the devil and the Pharisees on the one hand, and physical illness, insanity, and death (son of the widow of Nain) on the other. Demons, centurions, and crowds heed his words and do his bidding. His divinity is attested to by all these deeds, by the voice of God himself, and by the prophets of old, who stand beside him on the Mount of Transfiguration.

When he enters Jerusalem, however, he yields to the gathering powers of death and submits willingly to the Jerusalem authorities, even to death on the cross. He "must suffer" and "be killed" (9:22), the narrative tells us. It is a matter of cosmic compulsion and he ultimately, even readily, submits to the authority of the priests as a matter of choice. As Jesus dies, he does so because he chooses ("not my will, but yours" [22:42]). And this is where the moral and spiritual force of the death reside. He is a complex and mystical figure, but one with whom the reader quickly becomes fully sympathetic.

The choice he makes to submit to the cross is central to the meaning of his death. It might even be said that, from the perspective of Luke, Jesus acquiesces to death on the cross as the ultimate act of humility. This is the same trait that saves all in the Gospel of Luke (see further the commentary on 23:32-43).

This characterization is all part of Luke's theological frame of reference. While evil has its day in the crucifixion of Jesus, it occurs with divine permission. At the same time, Jesus has a human responsibility that arises from his incarnate existence. The dual dramas of providence and human agency intermingle in Luke's presentation of the passion. The human aspect of Jesus' nature is free to act (as Wesleyan theology asserts). Yet all this occurs within God's sovereign agency. This is the ultimate mystery of the incarnation—God and humans as coactors in one world. Wesleyan theology's strength is its willingness to embrace the mystery of the human role in divine action and attempt to understand life in the ambiguity of that mystery. In this sense, the characterization of Jesus carries the heart of Luke's theological message.

The characterization of the Pharisees, on the other hand, is almost entirely negative in the third Gospel. They serve as the perfect foil for the wisdom and power of Jesus, neither of which can they comprehend. They are the reader's negative example, instructing us in how we ought not to think and act in relation to Jesus' claims of sonship.

Contemporary readers should not, however, adopt Luke's characterization as a historical portrait of the Jewish leaders in general or the sect of the Pharisees in particular. While some of his contemporaries did oppose Jesus, this characterization of Jewish leaders in opposition to Jesus should be recognized as a literary device. The typecasting of "the Pharisees" as Jesus' opponents originated in Mark and was taken up by Matthew and Luke. Each writer gave the characterization of the Pharisees a unique patina, sometimes sympathetic but usually a thoroughly negative one.

In John's Gospel this typology reached its most vitriolic form as Jesus' opponents are referred to simply as "the Jews." This usage reflects the growing rift between Christianity and Judaism in the later years of the first century. Too often in Christianity's past, the negative characterization of the Gospels was taken at face value as a historical description, turning Judaism into the implacable foe of truth.

Scholarship since the mid-twentieth century has shown that Judaism was diverse in the first century A.D. A negative characterization of all Jews in Palestine in the period is no more appropriate than it would be of any religious group at any time. Jesus was a Jew, after all, as were all of the disciples and first Christians. Still, the historical reality was that some, perhaps many within the religious leaders of Judaism, felt that the teacher from Galilee was a threat to the practice of traditional Judaism as they understood it. This was particularly true with regard to the Law and ritual holiness. All teachers in the period debated these issues. But Jesus was a wonder worker *and* someone who had controversial positions on the Law, the Messiah, and other issues. With large crowds following him, he attracted the attention of powerful people. This set him apart for violent controversy (Luke 11:53; 19:47).

G. Luke and the Christian Life

I. The Apocalypse

The passing of the present age and the coming of the future one was a central feature in the ideology of primitive Christianity. The earliest writings of Paul are evidence that the end of history was thought to be imminent, especially 1 and 2 Thessalonians. The Synoptic tradition also contains material that deals with the end of history and the introduction of the heavenly world to come. Taken together, the witness of the Gospels and the writings of Paul indicate that there was a strong sense among Jesus' earliest followers that the present age was quickly passing away and the kingdom of God would soon be established.

The concept of a cosmic age to come, which would supplant the historical world, did not begin within Christianity. Its original roots probably lie somewhere in the distant origins of Persian religion. The idea of a culmination to history was likely brought into Judaism through the sojourn of the Jews in exile in Babylon in the fifth century B.C. It began to make its way into the Judaism of the first century before Jesus. In the two centuries prior to Jesus, the Pharisees adopted the idea of an afterlife and an end to history, and incorporated it into their theology. Traditional Judaism of the OT had little to say about heaven and the afterlife, concepts fully formed in the teachings of both Paul and Jesus.

The seventh- and eighth-century prophets of the OT looked into the future to discern God's path for the nation. But they did not look far into the future. Hebrew prophecy tended to concern itself with the near-term social and historical realities of the nation of Israel, not with the far distant future and the end of the world, which was characteristic of first-century apocalyptic literature. This near-term prophecy was anchored in a particular sociohistorical setting and was based on the hope that reform of the current order would come. In this kind of prophecy God was to work *through* his people to effect reform; the prophet interpreted "his vision of God's presence into real socio-historical reality" (Chance and Horne 2000, 122).

Israel's national status was eroded by foreign powers in the middle of the millennium before Christ. Concurrent with this, the rise of the apocalyptic ideal gave rise to a change in prophetic impetus. Its focus changed from the near to the distant future. In its new focus, the present world order would end and the oppression and injustice of the enemies of Yahweh would be swept away by God's final intervention in history.

As hope for the earthly preeminence of Israel declined, the reliance on a worldview in which history would be swallowed up by a new cosmic reality gained popularity. This worldview was characterized by a loss of hope that the world, as it existed, could be redeemed. That is, the current age was so corrupt that its reform was impossible. It must be swept away, replaced by a new heavenly reality in which God reigns without the constraint of evil. In this more apocalyptic form of eschatology God works *for* his people to effect the introduction of *his* kingdom.

Thus, we have these two competing views of the future in the biblical record. Was Jesus more like a Hebrew prophet, concerned with reforming the present? Or, did he conceive of a soon to be kingdom on earth? In Gospel studies Mark appears to many to be the most apocalyptic in tone (Mark 13; see, however, the views expressed by Brower, *Mark* forthcoming in this series, who sees Mark 13 as primarily related to the destruction of the temple). The redaction of Mark by Matthew is also thought to lean more toward the apocalyptic. Luke, however, seems to have dampened down the apocalyptic nature of that material (see Fitzmyer 1981, 1:18-22), as we shall see.

The community of each Evangelist had its own perspective on the shift of the ages. The more desperate the communal situation with respect to the powers of the region, the more likely a community was to engage in apocalyptic speculation to alleviate the seeming hopelessness of their plight. Luke appears to have further softened the apocalyptic tone of Mark and Matthew.

A number of features give rise to this observation: The most obvious one is that Luke wrote a two-volume work, which told not only the story of Jesus but also the story of the early church. That is, Luke saw the drama of history unfolding in three stages: the age of the Law and the Prophets, the age of Jesus on earth, and the age of the church (to which Acts is dedicated; Conzelmann 1982, 95). The last stage was understood by Luke as a long period of time, the epoch of the church. This emphasis gave the young church encouragement to live in the world as it was, endure its persecutions, and to engage in the missionary enterprise in an effort to reform it.

The inclination to soften the apocalyptic feeling of the Gospel material can be seen in other ways. Luke is known, as abundant evidence will demonstrate in the commentary, for his concern for the present suffering of the poor, sick, and marginalized. The evidence of the kingdom is the healing of the sick and the casting out of demons in the present. That is, in the alleviation of suffering in *this* world.

In Luke 6:20 the beatitude says, "blessed are you who are poor," not the "poor in spirit," as in Matthew (5:63). In Luke, the theology of repentance and forgiveness seem to overshadow the theology of redemption through the work of the cross. His followers are exhorted to pick up and carry that cross "daily" (9:23). Luke's community had accepted Christian living as a lifelong commitment, with no expectation of premature death brought on by the eschaton.

Whether Mark 13 should be considered an apocalyptic text is a matter of debate. But Luke specifically casts the so-called Little Apocalypse in the context of the destruction of Jerusalem. For Luke, the events of 17:22-37 and 21:5-38 are an exhortation to endure the conquest of Jerusalem by the Roman army in A.D. 70. Thus, Luke chose to cast the apocalyptic material of Mark in the sociohistorical setting of the period of the destruction of Jerusalem.

2. Discipleship

The next observation on Luke's distinctive theology comes from the new view of discipleship that emerges in the postresurrection narrative. It has long been observed that Luke has a "salvation history" perspective in his two-volume work. That is, he sets the Christian experience in a context in which a lengthy church age is expected. Thus, the second volume of his work (Acts) deals with the early days of the church and its transformation from a Jerusalem sect to a religious movement in Rome. Luke's Gospel develops a theology to take the church into that extended life on earth after Jesus' departure at the ascension.

The foundation for this transition in Luke/Acts is the enlightenment of the disciples in the postresurrection period. As we will note in the commentary on 24:13-27, the encounter with the risen Jesus on the road to Emmaus is an indication that discipleship will entail a lifelong commitment, not just a brief interlude before the arrival of the kingdom. There, and in subsequent resurrection appearances to the disciples, Jesus becomes the resurrected teacher. He reinterprets the Hebrew Scriptures for his grieving followers. He chides them, "Don't you remember I told you I must suffer, and on the third day rise?"

He then brings a new exegesis to bear on Hebrew Scripture in light of the resurrection, "And beginning with Moses and all the Prophets, he explained to them what was said in all the Scriptures concerning himself" (24:27). To the assembled disciples he says, "This is what I told you while I was still with you: Everything must be fulfilled that is written about me in the Law of Moses, the Prophets and the Psalms" (v 44).

This is of importance to the affective aspect of Christian life in Luke and its illumination in the postresurrection period. The disciples will not receive the hoped for public vindication of Jesus' messianic identity in the Parousia. Rather, they will be called to live out the duration of their lives in faith, study, and reflection. The postresurrection disciples will have to seek a new understanding of Scripture. Then, they must live in witness to a truth that remains veiled to all but believers.

The understanding of the Christian life as a long journey of service to God lies at the foundation of the Wesleyan commitment to holy living. It is a Spirit-empowered life, but also a strenuous life involving witness, study, prayer, and persistence. According to the risen Jesus of Luke, these were the new realities of the postresurrection Christian experience. A life of striving to be holy in faith and word is bequeathed to the church on the road to Emmaus that day. It is from this new paradigm of discipleship that Christians derive their calling, and the holy life derives its necessity.

Another important aspect of the new discipleship in Luke is the observance of the Lord's Supper. It is an experience that connects believers in a sacred ritual of unity (see the commentary on 24:28-35, From the Text). Since it represents the presence of Jesus within the church, the theological symbol of communion resides near the center of a theology of sanctification. Prior to his passion, Jesus met with his disciples at table to institute the Eucharist. The wine and the bread represented his presence in memoriam.

After the resurrection, the risen Jesus appears at table with the two from the Emmaus road. "When he was at the table with them, he took bread, gave thanks, broke it and began to give it to them. Then their eyes were opened and they recognized him, and he disappeared from their sight" (24:30-31). The idea of Jesus' presence within the meal appears again as he eats in the presence of his disciples in 24:41-44. During this meal their minds are "opened" by Jesus.

In Luke's story-world, the preresurrection church is united with the postresurrection church by a shared table with Jesus. The table of communion unites and sanctifies believers across time, preresurrection and postresurrection. And likewise, it unites all believers in the presence of Christ, regardless of denomination, doctrine, or nationality. Sanctification is mediated to the church by the presence of Jesus at the table. It is Luke who shows how the table spans the gulf between his earthly ministry and his resurrected presence in the church.

Further to the life of the believer, there is a Wesleyan emphasis in the topic of persistence in prayer from 18:1-8 (see From the Text). Here we encounter the story of the unjust judge who relents to the entreaty for justice of the poor widow. In this story, God is represented by the figure of the judge who responds to a human entreaty (11:1-4). In a similar vein, in vv 5-8 God is analogous to the importuned neighbor, or the compassionate heavenly Father who is no less loving than a human father in vv 9-13. In other words, human will and action can move God when they come by way of an ardent and holy heart.

This is Luke's theology of the necessity of prayer. It is a distinctly relational theology, which highlights the dynamism between God and the believer. Choice has moral importance and the responsibilities of discipleship determine one's relationship to God. Human responsibility is relevant to life. This emphasis is highlighted in Wesleyan theology's emphasis upon responsible grace.

Finally, Luke stirs our hearts to think about moral questions. He challenges us to accept a radical call to holiness. It is, in fact, the moral confusion of our rapidly changing world that calls for renewed interpretation of Luke and the other Gospels. In times of rapid change, a longing for the permanent and true brings us back to the story of Jesus.

Any reader who seriously engages the text of a Gospel will find it a morally productive experience. But those who do so with a heart of faith will also find it spiritually enlivening, opening up new vistas of possibility for the life of holiness. Luke's gift to Gospel theology is the freedom of the human spirit to choose redemption. The responsibility of choosing holiness comes along with that freedom. By embracing the good news of the freedom and grace to choose redemption, the Gospel also calls its readers to the imperative of holy living.

Excursus: The Parables in Luke

A central feature of Jesus' teaching in the Gospels is the use of the genre of the parable. Luke first uses the term "parable," *parabolē*, in 4:23, 5:36, and 6:39. But these sayings are more like proverbs than fully developed examples of the genre (Evans 1990, 369). In 4:23, the NIV translates the word as "proverb." In 8:4 Luke uses the word in the first substantial example of a parable in the narrative (‖ Matt 13:1-23 and Mark 4:1-20).

Luke contains many unique parables. Jeremias identifies thirty-seven Synoptic parables, fourteen appearing only in Luke (1972, 247-48). With such a heavy concentration of unique material, Jesus is, as one author expressed it, the author of these parts of the third Gospel (Shillington 1997, xiii).

Parables Unique to Luke

The Two Debtors	7:41-43
The Good Samaritan	10:25-37
The Importunate Friend	11:5-8
The Rich Fool	12:16-21
The Barren Fig Tree	13:6-9
Places at the Banquet	14:7-11
The Tower-Builder and the King Going to Battle	14:28-32
The Lost Drachma	15:8-10
The Prodigal Son	15:11-32
The Unjust Steward	16:1-8
The Rich Man and Lazarus	16:19-31
The Servant's Reward	17:7-10
The Unjust Judge	18:1-8
The Pharisee and the Publican	18:9-14

(titles following Jeremias 1972)

The issues that arise in parable interpretation in Luke are, of course, common to all three Synoptic Gospels. First, the definition: What is a parable? It is a brief illustrative story with a moral to tell. Yet, complex issues of interpretation arise in reading parables. Are parables riddles meant to hide meaning? Or, are they self-explanatory stories whose lessons are intended to be apparent to all? Do they convey only low-level objective meaning, as provided in allegorical interpretations? Or, are they complex metaphors, the experience of which is different for readers in different times and places?

These are some of the questions that parable research has posed. At the end of the nineteenth century, Adolf Jülicher (*Die Gleichnisreden Jesu*, 1886) was the first to challenge the age-old method of allegorical interpretation for parables, a method of which both the NT Evangelists and early church fathers were particularly fond. Jülicher, following Aristotle, thought parables had a single moral—free from allegorical preoccupation with details (Young 1989, 23). He further distinguished "direct" and "indirect" (literal and nonliteral) use of language in parables. The former convey the conventional sense of language. The latter communicate the more complex world of metaphor (Kjärgaard 1986, 136). This distinction becomes important when enquiring whether Jesus intended to veil his meaning through parables or reveal it.

In the twentieth century, C. H. Dodd (*Parables of the Kingdom*, first published in 1958) and Joachim Jeremias (*The Parables of Jesus*, first published in 1954) spoke of the eschatological significance of Jesus' parables and elucidated their Jewish background. They believed the key to the interpretation of parables lay in understanding their *Sitz im Leben*, or historically and socially conditioned "situation-in-life" (see Young 1989, 20-54).

Their work supported the view that modern readers should understand parables as metaphors, not allegories. This has the effect of releasing the meaning of the parable from the constraints of allegorical interpretations—ones imposed on it by either the biblical text or subsequent interpreters. Once interpreters depart from the allegorical method, multiple meanings of parables emerge and the complexity of the interpretive task compounds.

As parable research progressed through the twentieth century, other more technical definitions of parable emerged. These emphasized the sophisticated nature of the genre. Bernard Brandon Scott described the parable as a "short narrative fiction which makes reference to a transcendent symbol" (1989, 8). Evans referred to parables as "oracular utterances in story form urging attention to some aspect of the rule of God or the divine purpose" (1990, 372). Shillington calls them "encrypted images of a new reality," which explain the transcendent symbol of the kingdom of God (e.g., 8:1, 10; 19:11; 21:29-31; also Matt 13:24, 31, 33; 1997, 1).

These definitions highlight the power of parables to communicate complex metaphysical ideas, not just simple life lessons. On balance, the modern consensus is that parables are far more than homespun folk stories with a single, simple moral.

One of the more controversial issues in modern parable research is whether the interpretations provided in the Gospels are original to Jesus or supplied by the church. In eighteen of Luke's parables, he supplies an interpretation for their meaning (Stein 2000, 33). Most modern scholars think these interpretations arose in the communities that preserved the parables (see the sidebar Jesus and Allegory in the Parables). These interpretations reflect, scholars argue, the situation of the author's community rather than Jesus' setting. In this view, the interpretations are considered applications of Jesus' original (and often ambiguous) parables in the later context of the various communities that preserved them. If this conclusion is accepted (i.e., if the application is a secondary expansion of the original parable), studying the unadorned parable can yield other levels of meaning beyond those supplied by the Evangelists.

Perhaps the ambiguities that arise in interpreting parables are the richest source of meaning. When embraced in their ambiguity, parables can be, as Dodd suggested, both historical and modern, both literal and nonliteral, both direct and metaphorical in fascinating combinations. They "interpret life to us" and thus are "historical and contemporary in the deepest possible sense" (1958, vii).

The ambiguities and unresolved moral dilemmas of the parables cause reflection. They force hearers to grapple with their meaning, projecting their teaching power further into the mind. They are not simply "bearers of meaning" in an objective sense, as in similitude and allegory, but they "create meaning by forcing the reader to participate in the parabolic event" (Stein 2000, 35).

A scholar on the parables once wrote, "We stand right before Jesus when reading his parables" (Jeremias 1972, 12). They are a window into the thought world of Jesus. The language of parables seems to reveal how his mind worked—moving from common, daily symbols to deeper levels of spiritual meaning. His use of parables indicates the liveliness of his mind. He expressed himself colorfully, humanly, not speaking of doctrine or legal pronouncements.

Parables are not a shortcut to wisdom. They foster wisdom through reflection, meditation, and emotional engagement. They challenge accepted norms and subvert attempts to assign simplistic meaning (e.g., see comments on 5:36-39). In interpreting parables one must work for the reward, and then own the result. Ironically, attempts to explain parables risk ruining their beauty. That Jesus' parables continue to stimulate, even centuries after they were spoken, proves that he was a master of the genre.

COMMENTARY

I. THE BIRTH AND EARLY LIFE OF JESUS: LUKE 1:1—2:52

A. The Prologue (1:1-4)

BEHIND THE TEXT

The first four sentences of Luke are a literary prologue. This technical opening has precedent in the literature of that day. The purpose of the prologue is to shape the expectations of readers and apprise them of the nature of the document. Luke's introduction invites readers to consider the history of his narrative, the authenticity of his sources, and the purpose of his writing.

In their introductions, all the Gospel writers shape their readers' expectations in various ways. Mark uses a single simple sentence to introduce his Gospel: "The beginning of the gospel about Jesus Christ, the Son of God" (Mark 1:1). Matthew opens his account with a genealogy of Jesus, emphasizing the importance of Jewish lineage and history for the coming story. John's famous prologue opens with a sophisticated theological statement about the nature of Christ's being.

Luke opens by appealing to seekers of historical truth. In this sense, Luke's avowed method is particularly "modern." Many readers today will resonate with his historical frame of reference, even if they are not entirely convinced of his historical accuracy.

The generally objective tone of vv 1-4, however, is quickly replaced beginning with v 5 by a more Jewish style of history, one characterized by epiphanies and numerous allusions to the OT. This is especially the case throughout the birth narratives (chs 1—3). Although these chapters have historical information about rulers and dates, this concern gives way in ch 4 to the more imprecise chronological style characteristic of the Bible in general and synoptic material in particular.

"The body of the Gospel itself abandons any pretense of secularity and is as much proclamation as any of the others" (Nolland 1989, 11). More like Josephus than Thucydides in this regard, Luke sees God's hand in everything that transpires and is never reticent to invoke divine involvement in human affairs.

IN THE TEXT

■ I The first words in a book are important; and Luke has chosen his carefully. In his first sentence he identifies three issues about how his narrative is to be understood. First, he acknowledges that others have already written on this subject and that their work informs his. Second, he appeals to eyewitnesses instrumental in the process of preservation. Third, his own historically considered account is for Theophilus, either his patron or his broader audience symbolized as "friends of God" (see Luke and His Community in the Introduction).

First among these issues is the recognition of others who have written on Jesus' life. **Many have already written a narrative about the things that have been fulfilled among us** (v 1). In saying this he indicates that, as a narrative (*diēgēsin*), his story has substantial textual and oral precursors. We cannot be sure whether he intends to supplant these others or simply recast and enhance their story for his audience. Regardless, his motivation drives him to undertake the task of writing a Gospel.

The subject of Luke's narrative is **the things that have been fulfilled among us** (v 1). The Greek phrase emphasizes the divine origin of these **fulfilled** (*peplē ˉrophorēmenōn*, passive voice) events. That is, they were brought to pass by God, not just by human action. Luke sees these events through the lens of his reading of the OT, the deep structure on which his story rests. This fulfillment language does not so much indicate a promise/fulfillment motif as an intertextual exegesis. The OT story is central to all *these things* that have occurred.

Luke the historian has already tipped his hand on his views about divine causation. Unlike the historical style of Thucydides, he readily finds a divine cause at work in these events. Thus, Luke continually refers to the OT as a way to explain *why* these events occurred. As subsequent chapters reveal, the

OT is the foundation of Luke's theology; and the God who acts in history is its center.

■ **2** Luke's second concern is that the accounts created by his predecessors are attested by eyewitnesses. He hands on these sacred traditions—**just as they were handed down to us by those who from the first were eyewitnesses and servants of the word** (v 2). To "hand down" a tradition (*paredosan*), in biblical parlance, is to convey it faithfully to others (see 10:22). In Acts, Luke refers to the traditions "handed down" by Moses (6:14), and the apostles as they "delivered" the decrees of the Jerusalem Council (16:4). *Paradidōmi* in the Pauline letters refers to the faithful transmission of sacred tradition, especially in 1 Cor 11:2, 23; and 15:3. Luke uses this idea more than the other Synoptic Evangelist (see only Matt 11:27), perhaps under the influence of Paul (assuming with tradition that Luke was Paul's unnamed traveling companion in the "we" sections of Acts; see Acts 16:11 and Col 4:14).

It is particularly important for Luke that those who attested to the tradition were **eyewitnesses and servants of the word** (v 2). The term "eyewitness" (*autoptai*) occurs only here in the Bible. It refers to a beginning point for ancient historiography, which anchors an event in time and space (Green 1997, 41; Evans 1990, 126-27; see 2 Pet 1:16). Josephus and Thucydides also use the term for this very reason. The proximity of these eyewitnesses to the events of Jesus' life, in Luke's view, gives their testimony particular weight. He is eager to preserve it, perhaps aware that these original members of the community are passing away. For Luke, they are more than sterile witnesses, as in a courtroom. They are **servants of the word** (v 2) who gave their lives in service to this testimony.

Ironically, the witnesses in the Lukan narrative are hardly above reproach. They are terrified by what they see (1:12; 9:34), disbelieve what they are told (1:18; 8:53), and misunderstand apparently plain talk (9:45). In this sense, Luke's eyewitnesses are an unreliable lot. But from a postresurrection perspective, a true witness is someone who has "been with us the whole time the Lord Jesus went in and out among us, beginning from John's baptism to the time when Jesus was taken up from us" (Acts 1:21-22). These witnesses are to be heard not because they are a reliable source of historical information, but because they exemplify faithful endurance. Luke views the *autoptēs* as both a witness to history and one who has proven loyal to Jesus. This makes Luke more an evangelist than a dispassionate historian. His soulful bond to this band of witnesses is essential to his understanding of his narrative.

■ **3-4** Verse 3 begins with *edoxe*, **it seemed good . . . to me.** This is one of the most "familiar idioms of the Greek language" (Evans 1990, 128). Early commentators on Luke, such as Origen, criticized him for the intellectual presumption inherent in this phrase. His was "the Greek humanist confidence in human reason and judgment" (Evans 1990, 128). Luke differs from the other Evangelists in this respect: he boldly projects his presence into the narrative from these first lines. He is present not only as narrator but also as an investigator who announces his dependence on reason and historical enquiry as adjudicating factors within the narrative.

The boldness of Luke's authorial presence moderates in subsequent chapters as he relies more heavily on synoptic sources to structure his narrative. Throughout most of his Gospel, in fact, his presence as narrator is subdued. He subtly shapes his sources and quietly supplements existing traditional material with his own additions and themes. Ultimately, Luke shows himself to be a traditional evangelist, one whose presence is hidden behind the message, rather than the confident rationalist of vv 1-4.

Luke describes his method as having **carefully investigated everything from the beginning** (v 3). The adverb *akribōs* (**carefully**) is best taken as a modifier of the participle *parēkolouthēkoti* (investigating). That is, he performed his research "accurately."

His research starts at the historical **beginning** (v 3, *anōthen*) of the Jesus story, the birth narratives, not the cosmic inception of the Word, as in John. He writes an **orderly** (v 3, *kathexēs*) account, "in consecutive order" (NASB). This is similar to Peter's "step by step" (NRSV) explanation of his activities in Caesarea (Acts 11:4, *kathexēs*). These phrases indicate a bold and engaged narrator.

The **most excellent Theophilus** (v 3) was Luke's patron, friend, or simply a "catechumen or neophyte" (Fitzmyer 1981, 1:301). Theophilus was under instruction: **the things you have been taught** (v 4). The name Theophilus means literally "friend of God." It was a common name of the time, so most commentators assume this was a real individual, not a symbolic reference to an implied reader (Evans 1990, 132; Marshall 1978, 43; contra Nolland 1989, 10). Perhaps he was an important figure in a Christian community who commissioned the work to advance the cause of the gospel for a broader audience. Or, he may have been a person Luke was attempting to win to the faith. We cannot be sure.

The purpose of Luke's narrative is stated in v 4. He writes so that Theophilus can **know the certainty of the things you have been taught** (v 4). The verb *asphaleian*, **certainty**, has a connotation of "reliability, assurance, guarantee" in a cognitive sense (Fitzmyer 1981, 1:300). This is the "language of history" and "part of the studied secularity of the preface" (Nolland 1989, 11). Despite the historicist nature of the prologue, Luke's purpose is ultimately that of a Christian partisan: to create confidence in "the truth of everything you were taught" (NLT).

FROM THE TEXT

For Luke, the gospel is a living tradition, passed on from witness to witness. Through his story, these "eyewitnesses and servants of the word" (1:1) enter the present to testify to a new audience. In spite of his confessed interest in historical certainty, Luke is not so much a judge of this sacred history as a participant in it. Still, the desire to know "what actually happened" is as old as the act of remembering. For Luke, factual information is important in seeking the truth. We must, he argues, be able to rely on our information. Thus, Luke begins his Gospel with the premise that a community cannot function without a shared understanding of reality.

In *A Hundred Years of Solitude*, Gabriel Garcia Marquez tells the story of a village that contracts communal amnesia due to a strange virus. Eventually, as the shared basis of language is lost, the community members resort to putting signs on things to remind themselves of their names. In time they forget the alphabet itself. This collective amnesia leads to a complete breakdown of community and culture in the village.

Similarly, Christian communities cannot function without a shared alphabet of meaning. Luke believes that the historical trustworthiness of his account is foundational to shared community. This tells us something significant about the nature of biblical inspiration. Luke's account is informed by those who had previously researched and compiled the story. It then is reformulated through his mind, fueled by intellectual curiosity and the desire to know the real story. The inspiration of the text derives from the Spirit but arrives on the written page through an intellect on a human quest for meaning. This marriage of human mind and the experience of the divine Spirit creates a text that binds the community together.

When a set of shared truths in the text are held in common in the Spirit, the possibility of profound community is created. Conversely, when a shared sense of truth breaks down it is inevitable that community will break down—an important warning for the modern church. If we surrender the idea of shared truth to modern or postmodern relativism, the church will surely lose its way in the world, as did Marquez's fictional Latin village.

B. The Birth of John the Baptist (1:5-80)

1. Zechariah and Elizabeth (1:5-7)

BEHIND THE TEXT

Luke is unique among the Gospel writers in his careful citation of political events and rulers, here in the birth narratives of John and Jesus. For him, political realities are historical signposts within his story, especially in the first three chapters of the Gospel (see 2:1-2; 3:1-2; see Acts 26:26: "it was not done in a corner").

The Herod of v 5 is Herod the Great, who ruled in Judea from 37 to 4 B.C. His reign came at the end of the Hasmonean dynasty. The Maccabean era the Hasmoneans ruled began in 165 B.C., when Mattathias and his son Judas Maccabeus revolted against the Seleucid ruler Antiochus IV Epiphanes. This introduced a period of national resurgence in which an independent Jewish nation grew to a size equal to the kingdom of Solomon centuries earlier. In time, the political and religious tensions of the period brought about the decline of the Hasmoneans as Rome began to exert a dominating influence in the regions (see McGehee 1992). As a result of this influence, Herod, declared king of Judea by the Romans in 40 B.C., took the country by force in 37 B.C.

This Herod expanded the temple and was generally a supporter of the Jewish people. Even so, as an Idumean, he was disliked by the Jews of Judea and Galilee. Idumeans were a mixed population of Edomites, Jews, and Arabs that inhabited the southern end of Palestine from Hebron to Beersheba. The ancient Edomites would not allow Moses and the Israelites to pass through their land after the Exodus—Edom was located southeast of the Dead Sea (Num 20:14-21; 1 Chr 18:12-13). The Idumeans were forcefully converted to Judaism by the Maccabee John Hyrcanus in 129 B.C. His Idumean ancestry as a "half-Jew" was only a pretext for the real reason for Jewish animosity toward Herod. He was a compromising client king installed by Rome.

Herod was a cruel sovereign who clung to power at any cost. In his lust to retain power he murdered his wife Mariamne I and eventually three of his own sons—Alexander, Aristobulus, and Antipater. In his campaign of 37 B.C., he callously drowned the last living heir to the Hasmonean high priesthood, a seventeen-year-old named Aristobulus. He then had every relative of the boy killed. In place of the Hasmonean high priests, he appointed ordinary priests selected for their loyalty to him. His corruption of the high priesthood was an unforgivable sin to many Jews.

The high priest at the time of Zechariah's service was one of the sons of the non-Zadokite Boethus, either Joezer or Eleazar. Luke does not mention the illegitimacy of his claim to the office and avoids the political problems of the priesthood in describing the heritage of Zechariah and Elizabeth. Even so, the profanation of the priestly lineage by Herod was one of the principal sources of sectarian strife among Jews in this tumultuous period.

Some groups, such as the sectarians of Qumran, broke completely with Jerusalem. Scholars surmise that their removal to an isolated encampment on the shores of the Dead Sea was a response to the corruption of the Jerusalem priesthood. Tensions over the purity of Jewish observance always carried political overtones in Palestine, and eventually these tensions led to the Jewish rebellion against Rome in A.D. 66. Disputes such as these culminated in the destruction of the temple in A.D. 70.

The Priestly Sons of Levi

The priesthood in Israel traditionally consisted of the descendants of Jacob's son Levi (Gen 35:23). Both Moses and Aaron were descended from Levi (Exod 6:16-20), but Aaron and his sons were designated to perform the holiest services in the tabernacle (Exod 28:1-5; 2 Chr 26:18). Priests in the line of Zadok, a descendant of Aaron (1 Chr 6:8), served as high priests from the time of David to the Maccabean Revolt (see Jeremias 1962, 181-82). Thereafter, the high priests were of Maccabean, or Hasmonean, descent. By the time of our narrative, as we have noted, the position was a political appointment.

The second tier of priestly status after the Zadokites was the remaining sons of Aaron. Zechariah was a member of this group. The third tier was the Levites, the non-Aaronic descendants of Levi. The Levites were a *"clerus minor,"* who performed lesser duties such as handling livestock, collecting of the temple tax, cleaning, and crowd management. They took no part in the sacrifices. The total number of priests and Levites in Palestine at the time of Jesus would have been in the range of 18,000 to 20,000 (see Jeremias 1962, 204; Sanders 1992, 77; compare the much larger number in 1 Chr 23:3).

The sons of Aaron and the Levites were ordinary citizens who worked as laborers, craftsmen, and shopkeepers throughout the villages and towns of Judea and Galilee. Twice yearly a priest such as Zechariah would travel to Jerusalem to fulfill a one week rotation of service in the precincts. As heirs of the priestly tradition initiated by David, these men served the temple just as generations of their forefathers had before them.

IN THE TEXT

■ **5** After the prologue, the narrative immediately shifts to a new tone. Luke abandons technical language and adopts a style more like Jewish storytelling than Thucydidean objectivity. He introduces the main character of the chapter: **there was a priest named Zechariah.** Zechariah is an ordinary village priest serving one of his semiannual rotations of service in the temple. He is a member of the **division of Abijah,** one of twenty-four divisions of priests that served in rotation (1 Chr 24:10). It is worth noting that the division of Abijah immediately precedes the ninth rotation of Yeshua (the Hebrew name of Jesus), just as John precedes Jesus in this drama.

Luke is careful to point out that even John's mother has a flawless priestly pedigree. **Elizabeth** is herself *one of the daughters of Aaron* (*ek tōn thugaterōn Aarōn*). The marriage of priests to the daughters of priests was highly valued in Jewish custom. The care taken in these matters was such that the lineage of a prospective bride had to be confirmed for many past generations. This priestly pedigree of John's family, both father and mother, elevates the status of the Baptist in the narrative. Ultimately, it is lineage that determines status among the common people in ancient Palestine, not wealth or position. While Jesus himself is not from a priestly line (see Heb 7:14), his birth is fully affirmed by the priestly tradition in Luke.

■ **6** Not only do Zechariah and Elizabeth have the proper priestly lineage, but their lives are **upright in the sight of God** (v 6). Upright (*dikaioi*) is the language of the OT for those who observe the laws of God with a pure heart. "At least in narrative passages which describe Jewish relationships, the word *dikaios* always refers here to fidelity to the Law" (Schrenk 1964, 189; see also Marshall 1978, 52-53; see 1:17; 2:25; and 12:57).

This is echoed in the rest of the phrase, **observing all the Lord's commandments and regulations blamelessly** (v 6). **Commandments** (*entolais*; see 18:20; 23:56) mean legal decrees. The word **regulations** (*dikaiōmasin*) is frequently found in the LXX as a legal statute or law (e.g., Gen 26:5; Deut 4:40). The LXX is an early Greek rendering of the OT used in Greek-speaking synagogues in this era.

The word *dikaiōma* should also be understood as referring to the keeping of "the tradition of the elders" (a term alluded to in 11:37-41; ‖ Mark 7:3; Matt 15:2). These are the Jewish *halakahot*, or legal prescriptions, both written and oral, which were a prominent part of Jewish life and piety (see the sidebar at 6:6-11).

In Luke's narrative, Zechariah and Elizabeth represent all that is noble in the practice of first-century Judaism: personal devotion, respect for God and his temple, and moral uprightness in observance of the Law. They held, in Luke's telling, the observance of law in perfect balance with devotion to Yahweh. By emphasizing their righteousness and their priestly lineage, Luke shows that he does not share the view of other Jewish sects, such the Qumran community, that the temple is hopelessly corrupt. Although perhaps a romantic ideal, this is the religious environment from which John arose in Luke's story-world.

■ **7 They had no children, because Elizabeth was barren; and they were both well along in years.** This is ironic given the ideal of Judaism the couple represents. Childlessness and infertility in the Bible are considered a sign of God's disfavor, even an indication of sin (Exod 23:26; Deut 7:14; Prov 30:16). Yet, this is the situation in which Elizabeth and Zechariah find themselves. As with other biblical couples whose childlessness became a source of blessing to Israel, their barrenness has a particular purpose and role to play in the covenant story.

The story resembles that of Abraham and Sarah (Gen 18:9-15). Green sees extensive interdependence between the Abraham story in Gen 11—21 and Luke 1:5—2:52 (1997, 52-58). Noting the reference to Abraham in Luke 1:55 and 73, he regards Luke's opening as a continuation of a story "rooted in the Abrahamic covenant" (1997, 57). Both couples are advanced in years, childless, and receive a special visitation from an angelic being. As an active priest, Zechariah must have been under fifty (see Num 8:25), young by contemporary Western standards.

Although Elizabeth was not nearly as old as Sarah (Gen 17:17), she was **barren** and **well along in years** (v 7). Both couples disbelieve God's promise to make them parents. Yet, ultimately, Sarah bears the son who establishes the nation of Israel, Isaac. Elizabeth, after a life of childlessness, bears the herald of Israel's Messiah.

By aligning the birth narrative of John to that of Isaac, Luke highlights the momentous implications of John's birth. Just as the narrative of Isaac stands at the inauguration of the nation of Israel, the narrative of John stands at the inauguration of the messianic Davidic kingdom. Both figures proceed from a barren womb as sign of the blessing of fertility, which attends God's presence in the turning points of history.

FROM THE TEXT

Holiness theology emphasizes that the obligations of ethical living are to be held in balance with a genuine inner fidelity to God. This view finds support in the balance of law and devotion found in the Zechariah narrative. The rules and regulations of the religious life are mere legalism unless infused with genuine devotion to God. Conversely, religious enthusiasm ungoverned by the moral and ethical imperatives of the gospel is mere emotionalism. The art of the holy life is found in the integration of these two imperatives: heartfelt devotion and faithfulness to the moral demands of an upright life.

Zechariah and Elizabeth are presented as an idealized couple. They are faithful in heart and practice, priestly in heritage, and yet ordinary village people. This must be something like a Jewish ideal for the period. Yet, their life has its disappointments; her barrenness is the antithesis of the command of the Abrahamic covenant to multiply. This irony seemed cruel to Elizabeth, who refers to "the disgrace I have endured among my people" (1:25 NRSV).

Even as God intervenes in their lives with a pregnancy, their pain is not at an end. Their joy is mixed with the shame of Zechariah's disbelief. Later, John's life as an ascetic prophet may have engendered alienation from family and home, as it seems to have done in the experience of Jesus. The visitation from God to Zechariah and Elizabeth is joyous, but it is also the beginning of a life of turmoil and uncertainty. When God's angelic messenger appears, all sense of normalcy and order disappear.

These biblical stories resonate with modern believers. An encounter with the holy sometimes replaces peace with chaos and the familiar with the unknown. The life of faith is not the cessation of the travails of life or a disengagement from its harsh realities. It is a bold undertaking to create good in a fallen world, a life with its own travail to be patiently born by the faithful.

2. Zechariah's Epiphany (1:8-25)

IN THE TEXT

■ **8-10** Zechariah is **serving as priest before God** (v 8). The opportunity to bear the incense offering fell to a man once in a lifetime (see *m. Tamid* 5:2—6:3), and then only to those **chosen by lot** (v 9). This singular moment for Zechariah must be seen as a matter of providence and blessing. Zechariah enters the ***sanctuary*** (v 9, *ton naon*, not simply the **temple**, *ieron*). There the appointed priest is to **burn incense** on the altar of sacrifice, a vestibule within the structure that housed the holy of holies. A curtain covering a door separated the vestibule from the inner sanctum. Zechariah's offering in this text is the *tamid*, or daily whole offering (Exod 30:7-8).

Five individuals enter the sanctuary to prepare the offering: "one having the ash-bin, another the oil-jug, another the firepan, another the [incense] dish, and another the ladle and its cover" (Mishnah *Tamid* 7:2). After all the preparations are made, the priest with the incense is left alone in the sanctuary to burn the offering and fall prostrate in reverence. It was probably the afternoon offering rather than the dawn offering, since a crowd was present: "the whole assembly of the people was praying outside" (v 10 NRSV; see Ezra's moving *Tamid* prayer in Ezra 9:6-15). This assembly would include priests, Levites, and male Jews, but no women. The altar was within the Court of the Israelites, thus off limits to women and Gentiles.

■ **11-15a** An angel **appeared** (*ōphthē*) to Zechariah **standing at the right side of the altar of incense**, the place of honor (v 11; see Dan 9:21). He is identified as Gabriel in 1:19 (see Behind the Text on 1:26-38). The angel's position means he brings good, not bad news (see Matt 22:44). He tells Zechariah: **do not be afraid** (v 13, *mē phobou*), a stock phrase in Luke on the occasion of miracles, epiphanies, and prophetic messages (1:30; 2:10; 5:10; 8:35, 50; 9:34; otherwise, only in Mark 5:36 in the Synoptics). Fear is the normal human response in the Bible to the manifestation of the divine (*mē phobou* appears thirty-six times in the LXX). An epiphany is an aberration, a deviation from the natural order. That is, it cannot be predicted. A sudden appearance of the divine is, by its nature, a spontaneous event—God takes the initiative. Fear seems a natural response when God or his agents appear.

The angel also says: **your prayer has been heard** (v 13; see Dan 9:22-23). Readers assume he refers to the couple's prayer for a son; but they may also have prayed for the deliverance of the nation (see 2:25). Perhaps this is the prayer to which the angel refers. One such prayer from the period expressed the messianic yearning of all Jews: "See, Lord, and raise up for them their king, the son of David, to rule over your servant Israel in the time known to you, O God" (*Pss. Sol.* 17:21, first century A.D.). The angel's statement refers to more than the birth of a son to a barren couple. It refers to the joy that comes with national deliverance: that **many will rejoice because of his birth, for he will be great in the sight of the Lord** (vv 14b-15a; also 1:32, 69, 76; 2:10-11, 28-32).

■ **15b-17** The direct discourse of the angel continues through v 17. The promised child **is never to take wine or other fermented drink** (v 15b). This phrase alludes to the Nazirite vow in Num 6:1-21. Three prominent biblical figures are called lifelong Nazirites: Samuel (1 Sam 1:11); Samson (Judg 13:3-5); and John the Baptist. All three stories have birth narratives with divine interventions.

Thus, the phrase **and he will be filled with the Holy Spirit even from birth** (v 15c) emphasizes the divine ordination of John's ministry as an intervention of God in history. It also evokes John's connection to Samuel as a fellow Nazirite. Samuel was the inaugural Nazirite/prophet of original Davidic monarchy and John is the inaugural Nazirite/prophet of the new Davidic age.

The Nazirite Vow

The term *nzr* in Hebrew means "consecrated one." The Nazirite vow called for a period of abstinence from any product of the grapevine, the use of razors, and uncleanness from contacting a corpse. In Num 6, the vow is voluntary and temporary, as with Paul in Acts 21:23-24. This makes the lifelong vows of John and his predecessors, Samuel and Samson, unique acts of devotion to God. That priests abstain from wine while serving in the temple gives the Nazirite vow a priestly feel (Lev 10:9). Jesus' brother James, the head of the Jerusalem church, was called a Nazirite by Hegesippus (ca. A.D. 180, Eusebius *Hist. eccl.* 2:23.4).

The idea that John will bring **the people of Israel . . . back to the Lord their God** (v 16) identifies his ministry as a renewal movement of Judaism. Given Luke's early emphasis on Zechariah's connection to the priesthood, at least part of the summons is back to faithfulness to that tradition. But he quickly broadens that context by mentioning the prophetic power of Elijah in the angel's discourse; John will come **in the spirit and power of Elijah** (v 17). This alludes to the prediction of Mal 4:4-6 that **Elijah** will appear before the Day of the Lord. The NT expands on the idea of Elijah's reappearance in Matt 17:10-13 ‖ Mark 9:11-13 (see also Matt 11:10 and Luke 7:27). There, John is identified as Elijah *redivivus*, or **come alive again**.

Elijah will **make ready a people prepared for the Lord** and **turn the hearts** of the sons of Israel to the Lord their God, and the **fathers to their children** (v 17; quoting Mal 4:6; on sons and fathers here see Marshall 1978, 59-60). Alienation between parents and children seems to be a malaise in the covenant community Luke wishes to address.

This malaise parallels another: those who are **disobedient to the wisdom of the righteous** (v 17). These two conditions, familial alienation and rebellion, will somehow be righted by this Elijah-like figure. The text does not suggest how this will be accomplished. But it characterizes John's reform movement as concerned with healing families (see the comments on 12:49-53) and restoring the authority of the "righteous" within the community.

The connection to Elijah again emphasizes that John leads a renewal movement as a precursor to the Day of the Lord (see Fitzmyer 1981, 1:327). John is more prophet than reformer, announcing the fulfillment of OT prophecy (Webb 1991, 62-63). Nevertheless, John's commitment to change foreshadows Jesus' similar attempts to reform corrupt practices within Judaism.

Proper Jewish practice for Luke's Jesus includes the pillars of temple and Law (e.g., 5:14; 11:42; 18:18-22), but these practices are to be enlivened with humility, repentance, forgiveness, and concern for one's neighbor (e.g., 1:52; 5:32; 10:25-37; 13:3; 17:4; 24:47).

■ **18-25** Zechariah is unable to understand how the angel's message could occur. **How can I be sure of this?** (v 18). His doubt elicits a rebuke and judgment from Gabriel: **And now you will be silent and not able to speak until the day this happens, because you did not believe my words, which will come true at their proper time** (v 20). Zechariah fails to believe the angel's words. Consequently, he **could not speak** (v 22). Thus, he is unable to join in the recitation of the traditional blessing (*m. Tamid* 7:2) when he emerges from the sanctuary.

The loss of speech sometimes comes at God's command in the Bible (Exod 4:11). Being mute is a biblical symbol for lack of understanding (Isa 56:10). The silencing of Zechariah is an early indication in the Gospel of the consequence of rejecting its message. Zechariah's doubt is contrasted to the faithfulness of Elizabeth who, **five months** pregnant (v 24), rejoices: **The Lord has done this for me. . . . In these days he has shown his favor and taken away my disgrace among the people** (v 25). Elizabeth is not blessed as a reward for believing the "right things." But unlike Zechariah, when confronted with evidence for divine intervention, she responds with faithfulness, not doubt (Green 1997, 89). In this regard Elizabeth and Mary both evince a positive response to Gabriel (see 1:38 and Mary's hymn to God in 1:46-55).

3. The Visit of Gabriel to the Virgin Mary (1:26-38)

BEHIND THE TEXT

Mary's hometown is "Nazareth, a town in Galilee" (v 26) with a population of no more than a few hundred people. It is so obscure that it is never mentioned in the OT, or in Josephus' list of fifty-six towns in the Galilee. Neither is Nazareth mentioned in the Talmud, which lists sixty-three towns there. "From Jewish literary texts, then, across almost one thousand five hundred years, nothing" (Crossan 1991, 15). This utter obscurity is in itself a literary motif; Jesus, a "nobody" from a town no one notices, rises to prominence on the center stage with Jerusalem, albeit tragically so.

Yet the village was not isolated. It was near Sepphoris, seven kilometers (four miles) distant. Sepphoris was the administrative center of Lower Galilee, a city with a mixed Jewish and Gentile population of thirty thousand. Josephus called it the "ornament of all Galilee." Surprisingly, none of the Gospels mention Sepphoris. Nor do they mention the second most prominent city of the Galilee, Tiberius (see Theissen and Merz 1996, 170-71).

Jesus probably visited these cities, but the silence of the Gospels may have political undertones. Local Sanhedrins of the larger cities practiced a form of civic expulsion for renegade preachers based on Deut 13 (see Neale 1993, 87-101; see the commentary on 9:1-6 and 10:8-16). Certainly, Jesus would have been exposed to Roman culture and the bustle of a major trade route as he grew up in Nazareth. He may, in fact, have worked as an artisan in Sepphoris (but direct evidence for this is lacking).

Mary's epiphany opens with an appearance of the angel Gabriel (v 26). Little is said about Gabriel in the Bible. He appears in Scripture only here and in Daniel (8:16; 9:21). But he is often mentioned in the nonbiblical literature of the intertestamental period. There Gabriel is identified as one of seven archangels of Jewish tradition: Uriel, Gabriel, Raphael, Raguel, Michael, Sariel, and Jeremiel. According to the extrabiblical *Testament of Jacob* (*T. Jac.* 5:10-15; about A.D. 100), Gabriel is the archangel of Paradise who escorted Jacob to heaven. These Pseudepigrapha stories were a common part of the Jewish story-world of the first century and probably informed readers' understanding of this colorful character. Even "God-fearing" Gentiles may have been generally familiar with this Jewish literature (see Tyson's profile of this implied reader [1992, 35-37]).

This appearance to Mary is the second "annunciation type scene" in Luke (Green 1997, 83, 51-58). The similarities of Jesus' birth to John's are immediately apparent (see Fitzmyer 1981, 1:313-16; Green 1997, 82-85). Luke's treatment of the two narratives in ch 1 share the following features:

	Zechariah	Mary
Circumstances	5-9	27
They are "troubled"	11	28
Angel reassures	12	29
Pregnancy details	13	31
Naming	13	31
Ode to John/Jesus	14-18	32-33
Doubt	18	34
Angel's riposte	19-20	35-37

The broader intertextual background of these narratives is found in the stories of barrenness that occur at pivotal points in the story of Israel. Repeatedly in the OT, God demonstrates his ability to shape history by overcoming infertility, the primary threat to his promise of nationhood to Abraham.

The examples are well-known stories of the Bible. Sarah, wife of Abraham, mother of Isaac, was barren for a period in her life (Gen 15:1-6; 17:1-22; 18:9-15). So also was Rebekah, wife of Isaac, the mother of the patriarchs of two nations, Jacob and Esau (Gen 25:21). Rachel, the wife of Jacob, was also barren until late in life (Gen 29:31-35; 30:22-24), yet, her son Joseph delivered Israel from the Egyptian famine. The nameless mother of Samson was barren until she bore the one who delivered Israel from the Philistines (Judg 13:2-24). Barrenness repeatedly threatens the promise of fertility in Israel's story, and God's intervention repeatedly preserves the lineage.

Luke has a similar device at work—the key individuals in the birth narratives are also childless. Elizabeth is old and barren and Mary is young and a virgin. Two very different "problems," but still, both are barriers to the fulfillment of the story of salvation. Thus, a long line of barren biblical women who bore pivotal figures is evoked by Luke.

The biblical drama is evolving dramatically. Whereas the plan of salvation has repeatedly dangled by a thin thread of infertility in generations past, the pattern is now radically altered. Elizabeth, like all her predecessors in this biblical theme, is typically barren, but conceives naturally. But now a *virgin* will conceive and bring the drama of infertility to its conclusion. Finally, in the birth of Mary's child, Abraham's promise of nationhood will be fully realized (1:55 and 73) and the threat of infertility removed permanently.

Of particular importance to the Mary narrative is the barrenness of Hannah (1 Sam 1—2), the mother of the first prophet of the Israelite monarchy (ca. 1000 B.C.). Mary's song of praise in Luke 1 depends heavily on the form and content of Hannah's. Luke believes the allusion to an eternal heir to the throne of David in 2 Sam 7:13 is fulfilled in Luke 1:32-33. Mary is not barren; but her childlessness is similar to Hannah's. In both cases, it is an obstacle to the fulfillment of the story of salvation. In each case, God intervenes to reverse the childlessness of these women and preserve the plan of God for the salvation of humanity.

Verses 26-38 also introduce into the narrative the idea that Jesus is the "Son." Matthew's birth narrative refers to "Jesus Christ the son of David, the son of Abraham" (1:1, 18) and to "the Christ" (2:4). But for Luke, Jesus is the "Son" in the infancy narrative.

A number of social and linguistic contexts may have influenced the adoption of this language in reference to Jesus' identity. The OT, Greek philosophy, Qumran, and the imperial Roman cult all used son-language to refer to the divinity of unique individuals.

The Roman imperial cult, for example, sought to locate the ontology of emperor somewhere between the human and the divine. This concept has been cited as a cultural intertext for the use of divine sonship language in the NT. Terms familiar to us from the Gospels had also been applied to Caesar: *sōtēr*, "savior" (see 1:47; 2:11) and *huios tou theou*, "son of god" (see 4:3, 9, 41; 8:28; 22:70). The Roman practice was especially prevalent from the time of Caesar Augustus and later, 27 B.C.-A.D. 14 (for Greek and Roman texts with these terms see Price 1984, 54-57; also Jeal 2011, 5-10). In the Priene inscription, dating from 9 B.C., Augustus is referred to as the "savior" (*sōtēr*), the one "of God" (*tou theou*) whose "appearance" (*epiphaneia*) brings "good news" (*euangelion*). This is important for understanding the linguistic contexts that inform the emerging NT literature.

Religion and politics were not separate spheres in the ancient Near East, as demonstrated by the imperial divinity cult. This conflation of political power and religion has been called the "web of power" that existed in the Mediterranean basin in the first two centuries of the Christian era (Price 1984, xi; 56-59). The Roman practice of the period provides valuable background for the early Christian community's use of this language in connection with Jesus. Early Christians refused to hail the divinity of the emperor in public ceremonies, a significant source of conflict with Roman authorities (Mackay 2004, 259). In their view, Jesus alone was entitled to the language of divinity.

IN THE TEXT

■ **26-28** The prose account of the epiphany to Mary contains both intimate personal details and great theological themes. Note the similarity of style and content with the story of Samson's birth. Both are very human, even charming stories. Both deal with a childless woman, the appearance of an angel, the message of a deliverer, and a miraculous birth (see Judg 13:2-24, and the commentary on Luke 1:15b-17).

Luke's report of Gabriel's appearance to Mary (vv 26-38) follows the same pattern as the appearance to Zechariah (vv 5-20). This repetition of the pattern ties the two incidents together and builds dramatic energy in the story. A divine promise first brings a baby to an aged barren wife, and then a baby to a young virgin, women at opposite ends of the experience of life and fertility. This creates a poignant, all-inclusive contrast of the female experience, all mediated by the same angelic messenger.

Mary is **a virgin pledged to be married to a man named Joseph, a descendant of David** (v 27). Engagement was a process in which the young betrothed woman (aged twelve or thirteen) continued to live in her father's house for a period of time after the engagement. It was during this period that Gabriel appeared to Mary. The Davidic theme is introduced here for the first time in Luke; but it will be referred to twelve times in Luke's Gospel (see the comment on 1:32-33; see Tannehill 1996, 47-49).

In Luke's Greek rendering of Gabriel's greeting to Mary there is an alliterative rhythm: *chaire, kecharitōmenē,* **Greetings, you who are highly favored!** (v 28). The phrase **highly favored** conveys the sense of a divine blessing (the cognate *charin* appears in v 30: "you have found favor with God"). The greeting *chaire,* "rejoice," is exuberant, similar to the joy of restored people of God in Zeph 3:14: "Sing [*chaire*], O Daughter of Zion." The greeting "fills in further the picture of rejoicing that will pervade the Third Gospel" (Green 1997, 87). The perfect passive *kecharitōmenē* indicates one favored by God. The visitation of **Gabriel** (v 26) shifts the narrative to the realm of the supernatural and confirms the birth (see 1:11).

■ **29-31** Mary is **greatly troubled** by the appearance of Gabriel (see 1:12, 29: *tarassō/diatarassō,* "deeply confused or upset"). The exhortation *fear not* is frequent in OT epiphanies, and also in Luke (1:30; 2:10; 5:10; 8:35, 50; 9:34). Gabriel gently tells Mary: **Do not be afraid, Mary, you have found favor with God** (v 30; see v 13).

Since Gabriel appears only in Daniel in the OT, this epiphany reminds readers of Daniel's central event, the desecration of the temple under Antiochus

IV Epiphanes (167 B.C., Dan 8:16; 9:21-27). In echoing the image of the victory over Antiochus, the text implies that history has again come to a turning point and that God will restore the dignity of Israel. Readers may well expect this will take place as it did in the days of the Maccabeans—through a peasant revolt. Since that victory over Antiochus was political and military in nature, it would not be surprising if some understood this epiphany as pointing to events that were destined to free Israel from the bonds of Roman oppression.

The narrative deconstructs this militant view of Jesus' mission. But it is not until 6:27-38 that we begin to learn that enemies are to be loved and retribution forsaken. Until then, the characterization of Jesus in Luke retains the potential for revolutionary change in Maccabean style. This builds a dramatic tension that eventually places the way of nonviolence and love adopted by Jesus in high relief.

The angel tells Mary, **You will be with child and give birth to a son, and you are to give him the name Jesus** (v 31). The name of the child is a common one. But, in this case, it has particular symbolic significance. The Hebrew for Jesus is *Yeshua*, meaning "Yahweh is salvation." Verse 31 is similar in construction to Isa 7:14 and may be meant to echo the sense of messianic expectation there (despite Fitzmyer 1981, 1:336). Knowledgeable readers may have caught an allusion to a translation of this passage in the LXX: "Therefore the Lord himself will give you a sign: The virgin will be with child and will give birth to a son, and will call him Immanuel."

The term for "virgin" in the Greek of Isa 7:14 is *parthenos* (see Brown 1979, 143-49). The Hebrew text uses the word *almah*, normally "young woman," not necessarily precluding a "virgin" (see Watts 1985, 98-99). A case can be made for either meaning. Some Greek translations used *neanis*, "young woman," rather than *parthenos*. This translation probably makes better sense of the original Hebrew text in Isaiah. There the statement was directed to wicked King Ahaz in a prophecy about Judah's future (Brown 1979, 147; Watts 1985, 98). But the LXX retains the more particular *parthenos*. The translation of *parthenos*, **virgin**, by early Jewish and Gentile Christians was part of the debate with traditional Jews of the first century. When some Christians reread the Greek translation of Isa 7:14 looking for prophetic evidence foretelling Jesus' birth, they naturally preferred the translation "virgin" to "young woman," since Mary has declared herself as such (Luke 1:34). While Luke's account could be understood as a pregnancy by natural means (as Fitzmyer argued [1981, 1:338; see Brown 1979, 517-33; see Watts 1985, 100-104], Matt 1:18-25 unequivocally presents the birth of Jesus as virginal.

■ **32-33** Gabriel tells Mary that Jesus would be **the Son of the Most High. The Lord God will give him the throne of his father David, and he will reign over the house of Jacob forever; his kingdom will never end** (vv 32-33). These words give the essence of Luke's understanding of the identity of Jesus as the "Son." His various expressions of Jesus' sonship are different ways of expressing his unique relationship to God. He is the Son of God (1:35; 3:22; 4:3, 41; 9:35), Son of the Most High (1:32; 8:28), and Son of Man (5:24; 6:5; 7:34; 9:22; etc.).

Luke's unique representation of Jesus' birth in this language was likely informed by a variety of linguistic contexts, including the OT. The Davidic Messiah as Son of God originates in 2 Sam 7:14; Pss 2:7; 89:26; Wis 18:13. There may also be some influence from the Greek idea of the *theios anēr,* "divine man" (Martitz 1972, 338-40). In the Qumran literature, the phrases "Son of God" and "Son of the Most High" appear for the first time in a Pseudo-Danielic text (from the last third of the first century B.C.; see Fitzmyer 1997, 2:90-93 and 102-7, citing Milik). The terms may originally have applied to one of the Seleucid rulers of Syria.

These various bodies of literature point to a complex social and linguistic environment for the language of the human and the divine in the first century. Early Christians adopted that language of divinity for their Lord and argued for his exclusive right to its use.

Jesus will also ascend to the throne of **David** according to Luke (v 32; also 1:27, 69; 2:4, 11; 18:38; 20:41). Here Jesus as the "Son" is first linked to a concept of Davidic messianism. Furthermore, the eternality of the Davidic dynasty, the **house of Jacob,** is implied in v 33: **His kingdom will never end.** This is an intertextual reference to 2 Sam 7:12-16. Here God first promises to establish a Davidic dynasty that will continue forever (see Pss 89:3-4; 132:11-12; Isa 9:7; Dan 7:14; Mic 4:7). That Jesus' reign as the Son of David will endure forever transforms Nathan's prophecy in 2 Samuel. It expected an everlasting earthly dynasty; Luke, however, expected an eschatological "endless reign of the Messiah"—a subtle but significant shift (Tannehill 1996, 49).

The expectation of a Davidic heir to the throne was current among Jews in the first century, not just as a religious concept, but also as a political one (Wright 1996, 491; Horsley 1992, 792). *Psalms of Solomon* 17:21-22 raises the specter of a Jerusalem reclaimed from the Gentiles by "the Son of David." Readers would be inclined to see a militant potential for Jesus' advent.

Are the references to Jesus as the "Son," the "Savior," the "Messiah," and the "Lord" (2:11, 26; 9:20) intended by Luke to indicate his divinity? While many make this case, others are more circumspect. Divine sonship was part of "the royal-messianic rhetoric of pre-Christian Judaism." While son language points to a "special status" before God, it does not necessarily signal a divine status in the sense that emerged in classical Christology (Hurtado 2003, 103).

■ **34-38** Mary, being only betrothed, is astonished at the angel's announcement. Here a true Greek continuous present tense is used by Luke: ***How can this be, since I am not currently with*** [ginōskō] ***a man*** (v 34)? Gabriel responds to Mary's question: **The Holy Spirit will come upon you, and the power of the Most High will overshadow you** (v 35). This is clearly poetic parallelism, not a euphemism for intercourse (Marshall 1978, 70). The language is "highly figurative" (Fitzmyer 1981, 1:337). The visual images of descent and covering refer to being subsumed by the divine presence. In Luke, the spiritual powers often "come over" people on momentous occasions (9:34; 11:22; 21:26; at Pentecost, Acts 1:8; 8:24). The language is symbolic of the totality of God's presence in these events.

Similarly, the Greek word *episkiadzō* normally means "to overshadow" or "cover" in a physical sense. Its use here in reference to conception is unique from a linguistic point of view (Fitzmyer 1981, 1:337-38). In Exod 40:35 the word connotes the presence of God over the tabernacle in the wilderness (see Exod 25:20; 40:34-38; Num 9:22; Deut 33:12; 1 Sam 16:13; Ps 91:4; 1 Chr 28:18; Isa 11:1-2; 32:15; and in the NT: Matt 17:5; Acts 5:15). Similarly, at creation (Gen 1:2), the *ruah*, the spirit of God, hovered figuratively over the waters. Thus, Mary's visitation by the Spirit is described so as to suggest that the Spirit of God hovers over Mary in a new act of creation (see Brown 1979, 290).

Luke now applies the most exalted of titles to Jesus. **So the holy one to be born will be called the Son of God** (v 35b). The significance of this title arises from its obvious importance in the vocabulary of Luke's Trinitarian theology (Father, Son, and Holy Spirit; e.g., 9:26; 10:21-22; 1:35b; and esp. 3:21-22). But its importance comes from Luke's particular care to locate the birth of Jesus in a political context (1:5; 2:1-7; 3:1-3). By placing the birth in a larger geopolitical story-world, he asserts that Caesar, in spite of his claims to divine status and vaunted power as emperor, is not in control of history. The Son of God has a precreation relationship with God that trumps all human power. God, not Caesar, rules.

Then, in obvious contrast to the response of Zechariah to Gabriel's announcement, Mary simply says, **May it be to me as you have said** (v 38). This expression of faith befits the mother of the Son of God. And Luke holds it up as exemplary.

4. Mary Visits Elizabeth (1:39-45)

BEHIND THE TEXT

The traditional location of the home of Zechariah is Ain Karem in the hill country a few kilometers west of Jerusalem and approximately seventy miles from Nazareth (one hundred kilometers). It is the city of Beth Hakkerem of Jer 6:1, modern Ramat Raziel (see Gibson 2004, 25-31), accessible only along the ridges of the hills to the west of Jerusalem. To get there required an arduous and dangerous journey for any traveler, especially for a young woman. Mary could not have undertaken such a journey alone. Bandits and brigands were a constant threat to travelers there, and some sort of entourage must have accompanied her. Luke either did not know the name of the village to which Mary traveled or chose to not mention it.

■ **39-45** **Mary got ready and hurried to a town in the hill country of Judea** (v 39). When Mary arrives, Elizabeth has an ecstatic experience in which she is **filled with the Holy Spirit** (v 41). This infilling accomplishes the prophecy of Gabriel in 1:15 that John, as a lifelong Nazirite, would be filled with the Holy Spirit "even before his birth" (NRSV; see the commentary on 1:15b-17).

The theme of the presence and the infilling of the Holy Spirit is prominent in the infancy and boyhood narratives, occurring nine times in chs 1—3 (1:15, 35, 41, 67; 2:25, 26, 27; 3:16, 22). That theme culminates in the descent of the Spirit on Jesus at his baptism (3:22). Thereafter, the Holy Spirit is mentioned seven times in Luke, the last appearance in ch 12 (4:1, 14, 18; 10:21; 11:13; 12:10, 12). Certainly, the Holy Spirit is one of the dominant characters in the early stages of the story of Luke's Gospel. He appears always in connection with proclamations about the identity of Jesus as the Christ.

Elizabeth is the first to recognize the advent of the holy child, referring to Mary as **Blessed . . . among women** (v 42; the so-called "Hail Mary," Latin: *Ave Maria*) and **the mother of my Lord** (v 43). The physical presence of Mary causes the unborn infant Baptist-to-be to leap in Elizabeth's womb (see Gen 25:22 LXX; *skiptaō* as in Luke 1:42).

This shows Jesus' primacy in the drama. He causes rejoicing in Elizabeth's womb. Both women experience this advent with an intense physical and spiritual intimacy that Zechariah and Joseph cannot know. Elizabeth's experience of the Spirit is physically invasive, penetrating even **her womb** (v 41; see 1:15b). There the Spirit physically (in "bodily form" [*sōmatikō*]) invades Jesus at his baptism (see 3:21-22 and the sidebar at 3:16). Likewise, John is invaded even in his mother's womb. As a prenatal prophet, his leap declares the advent of the Son (Green 1997, 95).

From a narrative perspective, the men are secondary figures who stand to the side as disbelieving (Zechariah) or unnecessary (Joseph). The women are at the center of Luke's drama as holy vessels through whom God fulfills his purpose, people of faith who live out the prophetic power of the angel's proclamation.

This reversal of male/female roles in a key biblical drama prefigures the redefinition of social relationships in Luke. In a number of ways, the Gospel will reverse social categories. The lowly will be elevated and the powerful brought low. The sinners and the "righteous," the poor and the rich, the powerful and the powerless, and now the man and the woman—all these will find their places reversed in the new kingdom.

A maiden in a backwater village receives a messenger from God, far from Jerusalem and its temple. Her story could not be more different from that of Zechariah and Elizabeth. They have a priestly pedigree and are faithful servants of the Jerusalem temple. As a relative of Elizabeth, Mary must share this heritage, but she is burdened by the suspicion of infidelity to her betrothed. Only through Joseph does she have any connection to the tribe of Judah and the house of David, the Root of Jesse from which the Messiah will arise (Isa 11:10; Luke 3:23 ‖ Matt 1:16; Rom 15:12; see 1 Sam 17:12; Heb 7:14-19; Rev 5:5). She is an unlikely candidate for her role as the mother of the Lord (v 43).

Luke's story derives dramatic energy from the irony of this reversal of expectation. Mary's location on the physical, social, and religious spectrum is at the extreme margins. The priestly lineage and status of Zechariah and Elizabeth ought to trump Mary's lowly position; but the social order is being upended. Jerusalem, the exalted center of Jewish worship, ought to trump humble Nazareth of Galilee; but the order of sacred geography is being redefined. John has priestly credentials; but the commoner Mary will beget the new king, the Son of David who rules over the priesthood. John is the "prophet of the Most High" (v 76), but Jesus is more exalted as **great and . . . Son of the Most High** (v 32). Outward appearances and inward reality are juxtaposed in the story, just as the extremes of the social world are juxtaposed in the chapters to come.

This redefinition of social reality has a special focus in Luke's Gospel. As we will see, the new community that arises in response to Jesus' life and message includes those at the extreme margins of society. Their place in society is transformed by the emergence of a new community shaped by its experience of the Spirit. Holiness will no longer be defined by position, office, and exclusion from fellowship, but by the infilling of the Spirit, humility, grace, and inclusion for all. This is indeed good news (see Brower 2005, 59-60, 122-29).

5. Mary's Hymn (1:46-56)

BEHIND THE TEXT

Mary's hymn, the Magnificat (Latin), is special Lukan material and the first of four canticles in the Gospel. We have also the Benedictus by Zechariah (1:67-79), the Gloria in Exclesis by the heavenly host (2:13-14), and the Nunc Dimittis by Simeon (2:28-32; on Luke's canticles, see Brown 1979, 346-50). Mary's hymn is structured like hymns of praise in the Psalter with an introduction (vv 46-47), body (vv 48-53), and conclusion (vv 49-53). The hymn is Luke's first use of an extended speech by a main character to elucidate his theological themes (see the comments on Thucydides in 1:1-4; other extended speeches occur in 1:67-79; Acts 2:14-36; 7:2-53; 17:22-31).

Mary's hymn is modeled on the Song of Hannah in 1 Sam 2:1-11. The sidebar highlights the relationship of Mary's song to Hannah's. It also calls attention to Hannah's reliance on ideas from elsewhere in the OT (esp. the Minor Prophets and the Psalms).

The songs of both women juxtapose the humble with the proud, the poor with the rich, the weak with the strong, and the righteous with the wicked. Both are hymns of rejoicing by a woman who finds herself with child as a blessing from God. The Song of Mary is deeply rooted in the biblical story.

A Comparison of the Hymns of Mary and Hannah

Theme	Mary in Luke	Hannah in 1 Samuel	Related OT Texts
Rejoicing	1:46-47	2:1	Zeph 3:14; Zech 2:10
Humility	1:48	1:11	
Lord Holy	1:49	2:2	Ps 111:9
Generations	1:50	—	Ps 103:13, 17
Proud	1:51	2:3	Ps 89:10; 2 Sam 22:28
Weak/Strong	1:52	2:4	Job 12:19; 5:11
Hungry	1:53	2:5, 8	Ps 107:9
Israel	1:54	—	Ps 98:3; Isa 41:8
Abraham	1:55	—	Mic 7:20; Gen 17:7

Hannah's song questions the established powers and calls for a return to biblical justice for the oppressed. By modeling Mary's song on Hannah's and other OT texts, Luke (like the other Evangelists) portrays the message of Jesus as similar to that of an OT prophet (Matt 21:11; Mark 6:4; Luke 13:33; John 6:14). This is a theme that will permeate the story of Luke (Evans and Sanders 1993, 8).

Additionally, the idea of an ideal future king creates the expectation of an answer to the problems of society articulated in the hymns (Luke 1:32-33; see 2 Sam 7:12-13). These problems, especially the oppression of the weak by the strong, are the same as those identified in the Samuel story (Luke 1:51-53; see 1 Sam 2:11; 2 Sam 7:14). A new king in the line of David will introduce a new society in which justice reigns and society's problems are addressed.

IN THE TEXT

■ **46-50** Mary rejoices at the birth of her child and the prophecies about him. Her words, **My spirit rejoices in God my Savior** (v 47), are from Habakkuk's prayer for help in the midst of trouble (Hab 3:18; see 1 Sam 2:1; Mic 7:7). This is fitting considering Mary's situation. **Savior**, *sōtēr*, is infrequent in the Gospels, occurring only here and in 2:11 and John 4:42 (see Acts 5:31 and 13:23). It evokes a common phrase from the OT (Pss 24:5; 25:5; Hab 3:18). Like the barren Hannah, Mary characterizes her status as that of God's **humble . . . servant** (v 48; see 1 Sam 1:11).

Mary is a woman at the lowest levels of village culture, and one now under suspicion of immorality. Her humility is born of shame and gratitude: **for the Mighty One has done great things for me—holy is his name** (v 49). The "Mighty One" is the warrior God (Zeph 3:17). Mary's response to the situation is to declare God's holiness, as Hannah did (1 Sam 2:2).

Mary describes God's mercy as extending to those who fear him **from generation to generation** (v 50). This shows continuity with the OT tradition and its past heroes and heroines and identifies the present characters as living links in this pan-generational story (see 1:1-2). And it also implies that the drama reaches into the future with the promised children yet to be born.

■ **51-53** Verses 51-53 are a diatribe against the proud (see again, 1 Sam 2:3-8). All the verbs are in the prophetic aorist tense. That is, the birth introduces an accomplished present reality rather than a future promise. This emphasizes the "perfective" force of the aorist, rather than its temporal force (Beale and Carson 2007, 262). Mary's pregnancy means that **those who are proud in their inmost thoughts** are already **scattered** (v 51). Rulers are already **brought down . . . from their thrones** (v 52), and the **humble** already **lifted up** (v 52). Those who experience hunger now (present active participle) are already **filled** (v 53). Those who are **rich** are already **sent . . . away empty** (v 53). These aorist verbs suggest that the oppression of the poor and humble is already overcome by God's action toward Mary.

The concept of a present social order already being reformed by the presence of God's Spirit is typical of the Hebrew prophets. It is a prophecy anchored in a particular sociohistorical setting. Yet, it expresses hope for the reform of the current order through the presence of God's people in the world. The world will not be swept away and replaced by an eschatological kingdom; it will be reformed from within.

This idea has long informed the Wesleyan approach to social justice. Believers are called to bring the prophetic vision into reality by their labors, spirituality, and moral purity. This new order is the reality that our Christian hope tells us is meant to be. As such, Mary's hymn is a call to engagement in social action to right the wrongs brought on by pride and oppression, to right the wrongs visited on the downtrodden.

■ **54-56** Verses 54 and 55 echo Isa 41:8-9, in which Israel is described as God's "servant" and "descendants of Abraham [God's] friend." In v 54 God **has helped his servant Israel**. The deeper background of the Abrahamic covenant is invoked for the first time in Luke. The promise to **Abraham and his descendants forever** (v 55) refers to God's assurance to give land and progeny to Abraham in Genesis (12:1-4; 17:7; 18:18; see Luke 1:73).

The repetition of "forever" in v 55 calls to mind again the messianic covenant with David through the house of Jacob from 1:33. In the distant past, this promise resulted in the creation of a powerful nation-state under Solomon. That state had centuries before declined under foreign domination. But God is already bringing about the reconstitution of his nation in radically different terms than expected. The new Davidic kingdom (v 32) will be unlike its predecessor socially and politically. But it will survive "forever."

6. The Birth, Circumcision, and Naming of John (1:57-66)

BEHIND THE TEXT

Luke employs a common structure for the birth, circumcision, and naming of John and Jesus. John's is the shorter of the two:

- The setting of the scene (1:57-58 || 2:1-7)
- A birth (1:57 || 2:8-20)
- A circumcision and naming (1:59-64 || 2:21)
- The public reaction (1:65-66 || 2:22-38)
- A conclusion indicating the baby's maturation (1:80 || 2:39-40; see Brown 1979, 408-12)

Following a brief description of John's birth, the neighbors and family gather. **On the eighth day they came to circumcise the child** (v 59). John is circumcised according to the command of Gen 17:9-14.

Circumcision was practiced in various forms around the ancient Near East from an early period, mostly by priests and warriors in Syrian and Egyptian cultures (Hall 1992, 1025-31). The Israelites adopted the practice as a sign of inclusion in the covenant of Abraham, which promised him descendants as a "multitude of nations" and the land of the Canaanites in perpetuity. Circumcision is also a biblical metaphor for a heart fully obedient to God's will or recommitted to God (Josh 5:2-9; Jer 4:4).

Greco-Roman culture in the first century A.D. considered circumcision a degenerate practice. This led to mockery and exclusion of Jews from broader society, especially in the gymnasium, an important institution of Hellenized culture in Jerusalem at the time of John's birth.

IN THE TEXT

■ **57-66** Luke narrates the circumstances of John's naming in a straightforward style. The **Lord** elevated Elizabeth from "disgrace" to **great mercy** (1:25 and 58). **Lord,** *kyrios,* is found frequently in the Gospels as a reference to God. In ch 1, *kyrios* is used several times referring to God (1:25, 28, 32, 45, 58, 66). But *kyrios* also serves as a respectful form of address (comparable to **Sir**) when people speak to Jesus and others.

Luke characterizes God directly, as personally involved in the unfolding events. Thus, in v 58, that **the Lord has shown** Elizabeth **great mercy** indicates that this is more than good fortune or general providence. Both women are recipients of God's personal attention, as in the OT stories in which God intervenes in the lives of barren women.

Newborn male children were traditionally named on the day of circumcision, and the naming ritual was crucial to perpetuating and verifying the genealogy of a family. This was especially important in priestly families such as Zechariah's. Thus, the **neighbors** are surprised and protest when Elizabeth chooses the name **John** (vv 65, 60; see 1:13), not part of the family tree. Elizabeth spontaneously picks the name the angel gave to Zechariah, part of the miracle of the birth (Brown 1979, 369, 375).

The crowd is not prepared to take a woman's word on such an important matter. So they **made signs** to the father (v 62, *eneneuon*, "to nod or make signs"). In v 22, Zechariah is "making signs" (*dianeuōn*). We have been told that Zechariah is "mute" (*kōphos*; v 22). But since the relatives and family gesture to him, he must be deaf as well (see 1:20; see 7:22: "the deaf hear"). Zechariah confirms Elizabeth's choice by writing **his name is John** on a tablet (v 63).

Gabriel had prophesied that Zechariah's silence would be broken when these events "come true at their proper time" (1:20). And, thus, his **mouth was opened and his tongue was loosed, and he began to speak, praising God** (v 64). Zechariah is healed from his deafness and dumbness as the divine timetable unfolds in Luke. Luke will later report that Jesus appeals to his healing of the deaf as proof to John that the time of the Messiah has come (7:22).

With Gabriel's first prophecy fulfilled, the narrator summarizes events in vv 65-66. The neighbors experience *fear* (*phobos*, rather than **awe**) and were **talking about** and **wondered about** all these things (v 65). The community is gripped by the unfolding drama of John's birth and its implications for their lives.

7. Zechariah's Prophecy (1:67-80)

IN THE TEXT

■ **67** As with the hymn of Mary, the hymn of Zechariah has an introduction (v 68), a body (vv 69-79), and a conclusion (v 80). It has another twofold structure: vv 68-75 refer to the coming Messiah; vv 76-79 refer to John the Baptist.

Now Zechariah too is **filled with the Holy Spirit and prophesied** (v 67) just as Elizabeth and the baby John had been filled with the Spirit at Mary's visit (vv 15, 41). The verbs of filling are passive voice (*plēsthēsetai/eplēsthē*), indicating that Elizabeth, Zechariah, and John are recipients, not initiators of the divine action. In the narrative about Mary, the Holy Spirit will "overshadow" her (v 35). In an almost contagious fashion, the presence of the Holy Spirit is spreading in the narrative, engulfing all those involved in the drama.

This intrusion of the Spirit into personal lives is the defining aspect of the new community. As people enter the community, they share a common experience in the Spirit. The Spirit's work is both personal and collective. This anticipates a Lukan theme, especially evident in Acts. There the infilling of the Spirit always attends entrance into the Christian community (Acts 2:1-4; 8:14-25; 9:17-19; 19:1-6).

This contagious Spirit is reminiscent of early Israelite prophecy in which the invading divine presence had a physicality to it, affecting those in proximity to the event (see 1 Sam 10:9-13). Like a prophet overcome by a divine compulsion (Jer 4:19), Zechariah experiences a spreading, ecstatic holiness that sweeps everything up in its path.

Luke defines Zechariah's speech as **prophecy** (Luke 1:67), rather than a prayer or hymn of thanksgiving. As a *priest* who prophesies, he is a rarity in Israelite tradition (Wilson 1980, 26-27). Here, Zechariah brings to bear on the drama his status as a priest with the authority of the temple and the prophetic power of the Spirit. The contagious presence of the Holy Spirit acquires a cultic, temple-related aspect. The Spirit operates through the institution of the temple in addition to directly invading the lives of our characters.

■**68-70** Luke uses the aorist tense for his verbs in v 68, again indicating the redemption is already accomplished in a prophetic sense (as in vv 51-53). God **has come** and he **has redeemed his people** (v 68b). The Greek *epeskepsato*, "has come" or "visited," occurs at the beginning and end of the song (vv 68b, 78b), creating literary bookends around the hymn.

Luke quotes the stock phrase from the LXX identifying God: "Blessed be the Lord God of Israel" (v 68a NRSV; see Pss 41:13; 106:48; 1 Kgs 8:15). The announcement that **he has redeemed his people** (Luke 1:68b) is a remarkable statement of faith and messianic hope, given the dire political circumstances of Israel at this time.

This is Luke's first use of the word *lytrōsis*, **redemption** or **ransom**, which occurs only here and in 2:38 ("redemption of Jerusalem"), and otherwise in the NT only in Heb 9:12. The word occurs in the LXX referring to a life (Ps 49:8), his people (Pss 111:9; 130:7), and the work of Yahweh (Isa 63:4). Its use here is a significant theological statement on the importance of the birth of John and Jesus.

He has raised up a horn of salvation for us (Luke 1:69; see 2 Sam 22:3; Ps 18:2). The animal horn is a symbol of power in biblical literature. Its size denotes its relative power (see Dan 7:8; 8:21). When it is cut off, it signifies the loss of power (Jer 48:25). The Messiah is to be "a mighty savior" (Luke 1:69 NRSV), that is, he will "bring a powerful rescue." **The house of his servant David** (v 69) reiterates vv 27 and 32. Zechariah does not have his own son John in view (since he is of the house of Abijah), but a new Davidic king to follow John (see Jesus' genealogy in 3:23-37).

■**71** **Salvation from our enemies** and **the hand of all who hate us** is biblical language. It would have resonated with Jews living under Roman occupation in Zechariah's time (see 2:38 and Ps 106:10). It would also have been welcomed by Luke's community, living in a post-temple world of Roman hegemony. The reiteration of this theme in Luke 1:74 reinforces the political significance of the prophecy as a near-term event. Zechariah is not speaking of spiritual enemies in ages to come, but of temporal ones in the present age.

Jews in First-Century Roman Society

Jews suffered persecution within the Roman Empire in the first century for many reasons (see Hadas-Lebel 1993, 200-206).

- In antiquity there was no such thing as a day without work. The Jews were considered lazy and disloyal to the empire because they rested one day in seven in honor of the Lord's Sabbath.
- We already noted that circumcision was a practice for which they suffered derision (see on 1:59).
- Jews were also considered atheists for their refusal to worship Roman gods or the emperor. Political turmoil arising from Rome's imposition of the client kingship of Herod the Great and subsequently direct political rule in Judea after A.D. 6 compounded these difficulties.

The Great Revolt of A.D. 66-70 was an expression of the national anguish, already part of Jewish life in Zechariah's day. This anguish increased to a crisis in the seventh decade of the first century. Thus, the destruction of Jerusalem and the temple seven decades after John's birth shows that Zechariah's words had real meaning. His hope for salvation was as political as religious in nature. Living in the postdestruction era, Luke's community continued to hope for political redemption, a hope that only receded as time passed.

■ **72-75** Reference is made for the second time in the chapter to the **oath** God **swore to our father Abraham** (v 73; see v 55). In birth narratives, the promise of fertility is the main idea in view. The miraculous birth of a son to Zechariah and Elizabeth is a renewed affirmation of the ancient promise of fertility to the people of Israel (Gen 12:1-4; 22:16-17). John's birth affirms the fulfillment of the promise of procreation. God will show mercy to Israel and **remember his holy covenant** (v 72).

The theme of rescue in v 71 is reiterated in v 74 in the context of this promise of fertility. Compare "from the hand of all who hate us" in v 71 and to **rescue us from the hand of our enemies** in v 74. Fertility and national safety are the two axes of Israel's existence. Without both the nation cannot survive; without both the concept of a "horn of salvation" is impossible to Zechariah.

■ **76-77** Here the emphasis moves from the coming Messiah (vv 69-75) back to the forerunner John (vv 76-77). **And you, my child, will be called a prophet of the Most High; for you will go on before the Lord to prepare the way for him** (v 76). The text amplifies the words of Gabriel in 1:17: "in the spirit and power of Elijah . . . to make ready a people prepared for the Lord." It also foreshadows the prophetic themes that will emerge in John's ministry in 3:1-6 and 7:26-27 (Tannehill 1986, 33).

There are certainly echoes here of Mal 3:1: "See, I will send my messenger, who will prepare the way before me. Then suddenly the Lord you are seeking will come to his temple" (see also Mal 4:5; Luke 1:17; Matt 11:14). Luke 1:76 also anticipates John's quotation of Isa 40:3-5 at the beginning of his ministry (Luke 3:4-6): "Prepare the way for the Lord!" Luke intends John's proclamation, no doubt, to be understood as the fulfillment of this prophecy of Isaiah.

The text in v 77 continues with this phrase: **to give his people the knowledge of salvation through the forgiveness of their sins.** The theme of forgiveness of sins was central to John's public ministry. (As indicated in Josephus in *Ant.* 18.5.2, §§116-119—John "exhorted the Jews to lead righteous lives." See Luke 3:1-21; 7:18-36 for more on John's ministry.) The language in v 77 foreshadows the importance forgiveness will assume in Luke's larger story-world as his narrative progresses. The theme of repentance and forgiveness of sinners is Luke's guiding paradigm of salvation (see the Introduction, Theological Themes).

■ **78-79** Verse 78a shows the means through which the forgiveness of sins will become available: **because of the tender mercy of our God** (v 78). The **mercy of God** is not simply the cause of the forgiveness of sins (as in the NIV). It is the agency through which forgiveness is found (NKJV: "through the tender mercy of our God"). Forgiveness is a journey undertaken through the exercise of repentance, as Luke's many stories of sinners will illustrate.

Notice again the parenthesis created by the use of *episkepsetai*, **visited**, in vv 68b and 78b. In Luke's telling we are **visited** by an overshadowing presence of God in these events. The visitation comes to us like a sunrise: **by which the rising sun will come to us from heaven** (v 78b). We have not caused it nor sought it; it is simply the time for its coming—its appointed hour. As in all epiphanies (vv 11-15a), this sunrise is about God acting first, entering the human drama unbidden.

For Luke the advent of the Messiah means the light of God will **shine on those living in darkness** (v 79). This imagery is dependent on Isaiah's prophecy about Galilee in Isa 9:1-2 (see Matt 4:15-16). It is a continuation of the metaphor of the sunrise in Luke 1:78b. In Ps 107:10 and Isa 42:7 the prisoners God rescues "sit in darkness." The *hodon eirēnēs*, "way of peace" (Luke 1:79 NRSV), is the one promised by the "Prince of Peace" in Isa 9:6-7 (Luke 1:32; see Isa 59:8; Rom 3:17).

■ **80** In a standard stylistic feature, Luke concludes the John birth narrative with a summary statement: **And the child grew and became strong in spirit; and he lived in the desert until he appeared publicly to Israel.** The same formula will appear at the end of Jesus' birth narrative and also at the end of the youth narrative (Luke 2:40, 52). These summary statements owe their form to 1 Sam 2:26: "And the boy Samuel continued to grow in stature and in favor with the LORD and with men." (See the comment on Luke 2:52 for parallels. Notice the lesser known instance of Ishmael in Gen 21:20-21.)

John lived an ascetic life **in the desert** (see 3:2, 4; 7:24) until he entered public ministry. This evokes comparisons with other major figures in the OT, such as Abraham, Moses, and Elijah. Each also wandered in the wilderness as they followed God (see Behind the Text, 9:1-6). John seems to have been an ascetic of a different type, however, since he appears to have been a permanent resident of the wilderness (3:2-3; 7:24). People came to him there; he did not go to their cities.

The Gospel of John places the activities of John at this time somewhere southeast of Jericho (see John 1:28 and further the comments on Luke 3:1-6). There is an affinity between John's mode of life and the Qumran believers, an ascetic community also located southeast of Jericho on the shores of the Dead Sea. Like John, this group separated themselves from what they believed to be the corruption of Jerusalem and her temple priesthood.

John the Baptist and the Qumran community were both representative of protest movements within Judaism at the time of Jesus. They had similar ascetic and antiestablishment views and used similar mystical language.

Religious movements, however, do not arise in a social vacuum. They emerge in the context of complex social and religious conflicts. The motivations that drove John into the desert may have had similar origins to those that drove the Qumran protestors to the shores of the Dead Sea.

Physical Stature as a Sign of Kingliness

The corollary of the promise of fertility to Abraham is that his children grow and become strong. In 1 Samuel, the biblical book that deals with the establishment of Israel's monarchy, physical stature and beauty were the marks of a natural-born leader. Saul, the nation's first king, was lauded for his stature and beauty: "There was not a man among the people of Israel more handsome than he; he stood head and shoulders above everyone else" (1 Sam 9:2 NRSV).

Likewise, when searching for a replacement for Saul among the sons of Jesse, Eliab, David's oldest brother, was lauded by Samuel for his height and beauty. "When they arrived, Samuel saw Eliab and thought, 'Surely the LORD's anointed stands here before the LORD.' But the LORD said to Samuel, 'Do not consider his appearance or his height, for I have rejected him. The LORD does not look at the things man looks at. Man looks at the outward appearance, but the LORD looks at the heart'" (1 Sam 16:6-7). Even David, though short, "was ruddy, and had beautiful eyes, and was handsome" (1 Sam 16:12 NRSV). David compensated for his lack of physical stature with a brave and faithful heart, a central theme of the Davidic narratives.

FROM THE TEXT

The ministry of John is theologically important to Luke because John emphasizes that repentance and forgiveness of sins are required of the community for the coming of the Messiah (1:77; 3:8). In this theology, the very thought of a messiah inspires contrition because his advent is to be the consummation of the human quest for the forgiveness of sins. More broadly in the NT, this consummation is the resolution of the entire history of human rebellion, from Adam to Christ (see Rom 4:15; 1 Cor 15:22, 45).

If John's ministry seems harsh in its insistence on penance in the chapters to come (see 3:1-21), it is because anything less than penance is arrogance in the presence of the Messiah. From this theological perspective, the message of John is not so much harsh as bluntly realistic.

A community, be it Zechariah's, Luke's, or our own, cannot present itself before a coming messiah with a glib attitude about sin and rebellion. That very glibness was an affront to all the prophets before John. Luke, through John, renews this prophetic call to Israel for personal and national repentance. At the national level, John's hearers were called to present themselves to the Messiah as a holy people—a nation of penitents, prepared for his advent.

C. The Birth and Early Years of Jesus (2:1-52)

I. The Second Prologue (2:1-5)

BEHIND THE TEXT

There are five stages in the overall structure of the Gospel:

1. The infancy narratives of John and Jesus (1:1—2:40)
2. The brief report of Jesus' boyhood experience in the temple (2:41-52)
3. Jesus' life in Galilee (3:1—9:50)
4. Jesus' journey south to Jerusalem (9:51—19:44)
5. Jesus' final week in Jerusalem (19:45—24:53)

With ch 2 we enter the main body of the Gospel, the section that deals with the life of Jesus, chs 2—24. As to the unity of the structure, almost all scholars believe Luke composed the whole of the Gospel. There is no evidence that Luke ever circulated without the first chapters. But some scholars observe that the Gospel could start at 2:1 or even 3:1 without undermining the main features of this story (Fitzmyer 1981, 1:3, 11, 392; Brown 1979, 240). Some even suggest that Luke composed 3—24 first and appended the infancy narratives (Fitzmyer 1981, 1:310-11; Green [1997, 48] calls 1:5—2:52 a "self-contained unit within the Third Gospel").

Luke 2:1-5 is, in fact, a "second prologue." A reader might note that ch 2 begins with the decree of a census and v 5 that Joseph's wife is with child, although we are already well aware of this from ch 1. Later (3:2), Luke again identifies John as the son of Zechariah, not presupposing the reader's familiarity with ch 1. Material from the naming scene is also repeated (see 1:31; 2:21; also 1:27, 32; 2:11). Still, the first chapter provides crucial background to the story-world. No literary reading of Luke can or should decouple the initial chapters from the rest of the book.

The representation of the passage of time in this fivefold structure is complex. The material in the infancy narratives covers a period of about fifteen months. The story then skips a dozen years to Jesus' boyhood visit to the temple, covering less than a week. The central section picks up about fifteen years after the boyhood scene and is an indeterminate period of time in his adult life. The final week of his life in Jerusalem occupies more than twenty percent of the text.

Luke alternately jumps in time, slows down time, or speeds up time, according to his literary purposes. This can be seen, for example, when comparing Luke's infancy narrative about Jesus with Matthew's account. Matthew's wise men visit a "house" (*oikos*; 2:11) not the "manger" (*phantē*) visited by Luke's shepherds (2:16). Matthew emphasizes Herod's long-term paranoia, which results in the killing of boys "two years old and under" in Bethlehem (2:16). This indicates a more settled existence for Mary and Joseph in Bethlehem, giving Matthew's narrative a more reflective, broad quality.

Luke's narrative, on the other hand, heightens the dramatic tenor of the event with a frame of reference of only a few hours in a single night. Also, befitting an urgent delivery in a makeshift location, the shepherds "went with haste" (2:16 NRSV) to see the newborn on the very night of his birth. This cascade of events is part of Luke's rhetorical tone—the birth is urgent and miraculous, a tone that transfers to his message.

Conversely, in the central section, except for the precise indication of the beginning point in 3:1-2, there are almost no chronological markers other than the "next" and "then" sort (despite the careful attention given to chronology in 1:1—3:2). Is the Galilean drama one year, three, or five? This doesn't seem to matter within the narrative, because Luke is not focused on "what happened when" but on "who Jesus is."

Then, in the narration of his last week, time again slows to a crawl. Moments matter and intimate personal details of extreme anxiety, sleepiness, fear, and anger give color and emotion to the narrative. Rhetorically, Luke draws the reader deeply into the drama of the passion by slowing down time.

Most of the features of Jesus' birth in ch 2 are unique to Luke:
- the census and travel motif (vv 1-7)
- the announcement to the shepherds (vv 8-20)
- the circumcision and offering for purification in the temple (vv 21-24)
- the presentation to Simeon (vv 25-35)
- the prophet Anna's recognition of the "redemption of Jerusalem" (vv 36-38)
- the return to Galilee and intervening years of growth (vv 39-40) and
- the return trip to Jerusalem as a young boy who enthralls the local teachers (vv 41-51)

When compared to Matthew, the only other birth narrative about Jesus in the Bible, the difference in tone and substance is striking. Matthew's telling has no census/travel motif, nor does it have a homeless Joseph and Mary seeking urgent refuge in a manger for the birth. In Matthew, Bethlehem seems to be Joseph and Mary's place of residence, whereas in Luke it is the ancestral home they visit on the occasion of the census. Matthew has a star and no shepherds, but Luke has no wise men. Luke's political lens is global, emphasizing the birth in "the entire Roman world," while Matthew's is distinctly local, focusing on Herod, the client king of Palestine.

While quite different, these two birth narratives have become conflated in popular imagination. Wise men and shepherds kneel together in the modern crèche. This points to the broader folk context in which these stories reside in modern Christianity.

IN THE TEXT

■ **1-3** The historicity of the **census** (v 1, *apographesthai*, lit., **register** or **enroll**) has been questioned by modern interpreters. While large-scale census-taking was not unknown in this period, none encompassed the **entire world**, as Luke's phrase *pasan tēn oikoumenēn* implies when he uses it elsewhere (4:5; 21:26; Acts 11:24; 17:31; 24:5). The NIV renders the phrase as **the entire Roman world** (possible in Acts 24:5).

The importance of the census is the way it situates the birth of Jesus on the world stage. A worldwide census sets a broad geopolitical context for the nativity and asserts that the birth of the Messiah is of global importance. By invoking the will of **Caesar Augustus** (v 1) in the census, and the facilitation of the Syrian ruler **Quirinius** (v 2), Luke shows the significance of the birth in relation to the political power structures of the day—a significant issue, no doubt, for his readers.

But in the story-world, Luke shows that these rulers are only minor players in the drama of the Messiah, merely fulfilling the role assigned them by God. From the international affairs of Caesar, to the regional affairs of Quirinius, to an insignificant Judean village, it is the omnipotent God who rules in the Lukan narrative, not Caesar. Thus, this narrative carries over the emphasis from the first chapter that the Jesus story stands at the crossroads of history.

The census is also politically significant in Luke since registration establishes liability for taxation. A census invariably brought an increase in taxes for locals, which meant fewer crops for subsistence—a life-and-death issue for peasant farmers who lived on a razor-thin margin of survival (Crossan 1991, 126). It is not surprising, for example, that Quirinius' census in A.D. 6 caused a revolt among the people of Galilee and Judea.

That revolt was led by Judas the Galilean (Acts 5:37), who, in Josephus' telling of history, founded the Zealot movement ultimately responsible for the Great Revolt in A.D. 65-70. Thus, census-taking was one cause in the chain of

75

events that eventually culminated in the destruction of the temple. In view of these political realities, Luke's placement of Jesus' birth in the context of a census is significant. The message of a Savior at census time carries undertones of liberation from an oppressor and highlights, in a subtle way, the political implications of the Messiah's advent for Luke's first readers.

The Chronology of Jesus' Birth and the Census of Luke 2:1-7

The Gospels agree that Jesus was born during the reign of Herod the Great, who died in 4 B.C. (Matt 2:1; Luke 2:1-7). The passages on the chronology of Jesus' birth are Luke 1:5; 2:1-3; 3:1-2, 23; 9:7-9 (see Matt 2:1, 16; 14:1-12; Mark 6:14-16).

Luke 3:1 says the ministry of John the Baptist commenced in the fifteenth year of Emperor Tiberius, which was in A.D. 27-28. Since Luke tells us in 3:23 that Jesus was "about thirty" when he began his public ministry, we can surmise a birth date at the end of Herod's life (see Matt 2:16). The other political figures mentioned by Luke in 3:1-2 fit with A.D. 27-28 as the probable date when Jesus entered public life.

According to nonbiblical sources, a provincial census was ordered by Quirinius when Judea was annexed as a Roman province in A.D. 6. Josephus discusses this census in *Ant.* 18:1-10, §23-26, using the same Greek word used here by Luke, *apographō*, "register, record." He places the date of the census, however, in the thirty-seventh year of the victory of Actium by Caesar, or A.D. 6/7, nearly ten years after the birth of Jesus.

The majority opinion has gone against Luke's accuracy on the description of a worldwide census at the time of Jesus' birth (beginning in 1835 with the arguments of D. F. Strauss). Still, others defend his presentation as historically plausible (see Nolland 1989, 99-102; see the "enormous literature of controversy" on this issue in Schmitz 1992, 883-85; Brown 1979, 548-55; Safrai and Stern 1974, 1:372-74; and others). At the least, Luke's reference to the imperial policy of census-taking as a tool of governance shows his awareness of the political implications of such policy for Jesus' birth (Brown 1979, 549).

■**4-5** There is no evidence outside of Luke that Roman census procedures required repatriation to one's place of birth. Nonetheless, Luke asserts that **Joseph** and **Mary** did exactly this in order **to register** (v 5). Readers' questions arise about Joseph and his relationship to Bethlehem. He returns there to register, the text tells us, because his ancestral origin is **the house and line of David** (v 4; 1 Sam 16). But were his parents still living? Did he have other family in the area? Had he been born in Bethlehem or ever lived there? If the answer to any of these questions is yes, we can only guess why Joseph and Mary find themselves so alone in their hour of need.

The significance of the Bethlehem location in the narrative has to do with Jesus' identity as the Son of David. This is the essence of Jesus' identity in

Luke (1:27, 32-33, 69; 2:11; see Matt 1:1). The birth in Bethlehem reinforces this prominent theme from 1 Sam 16:1, where the town is called David's home. The "city of David" (*polin dauid*) usually refers to Jerusalem (e.g., 2 Sam 5:7; 2 Kgs 9:28). But here it is **Bethlehem the town of David** or "the city of David, which is called Bethlehem" (KJV).

Jesus' birth in Bethlehem demonstrates Luke's awareness of a passage understood by early Christians as a prophecy of the location of the Messiah's birth. "But you, Bethlehem Ephrathah, though you are small among the clans of Judah, out of you will come for me one who will be ruler over Israel, whose origins are from of old, from ancient times" (Mic 5:2, quoted in Matt 2:5; see John 7:42). This textual evidence makes the birth of the Messiah in Bethlehem a theological necessity for early Christians. It could take place nowhere else.

2. Jesus' Birth and Circumcision (2:6-21)

BEHIND THE TEXT

The announcement of the Messiah's reign comes to the most humble members of society, **shepherds** (v 8), mediated by exalted heavenly beings. A single **angel** (vv 9-12) is joined by **a great company of the heavenly host** (v 13). Contrasts heighten the dramatic tension of Luke's narrative. There is a juxtaposition of the mundane locale of the shepherds' field near Bethlehem, which means the "house of bread" (v 15), with the angelic host from the transcendent locale of "heaven" (vv 13, 15). The sacred geography of heaven invades the shepherds' field. The advent of the Messiah transforms the ordinary.

A further contrast is seen in the mundane activity of the shepherds. Their sleepy nighttime vigil is illuminated by the brilliant light of the "glory of the Lord" (v 9), and heavenly hosts sing God's praises. The full consciousness of spiritual illumination is contrasted with the unconsciousness of sleep.

This juxtaposition of the extraordinary and the ordinary has been a thread throughout the story: An ordinary priest and his wife, a humble maiden, and now common shepherds—all are visited by extraordinary cosmic beings. The repetition of the theme of the inclusion of "all people" (1:48; 2:10, 31; 3:6) further highlights the broad reach of this advent to common people.

IN THE TEXT

■ **6-7** Joseph, in urgent need of a place for his wife to give birth, finds no welcome in Bethlehem. Hospitality was a vital feature of Jewish culture at this time, yet not even *a home taking in guests* (v 7, *en tō katalymati*) can accommodate the desperate couple. Since Luke uses the technical term *pandocheion* for a commercial inn in 10:34, it seems likely that he refers to a private dwelling here.

The newborn baby is laid in a **manger** on the property (v 7, *phatnē*, a stall or animal's feeding trough; see 13:15). Luke is emphatic on this point, mentioning the manger three times (vv 7, 12, 16). Some suggest that the *kataly-mati* here is a nook off the crowded central room of a Palestinian home. That is, there was no room for the baby in the main room, so he was tucked to the side in a space for animals (Nolland 1989, 106; see Carlson 2010, 326-42). It was common for animals to be kept in houses in this culture.

Ironically, the one who will ascend the throne of David enters the world homeless. Likewise, Luke mentions twice the intimate detail that Mary **wrapped him in cloths** (vv 7, 12; NRSV: "bands of cloth"). She improvised a solution for the cool night. These details give Luke's infancy narrative immediacy and poignancy, a "paradox of divine condescension" (Nolland 1989, 106).

In any case, neither family nor friends are present to give the couple succor, although this might be expected in Joseph's ancestral home (Carlson 2010, 327). The narrative mood of this passage communicates the isolation, fear, and loneliness of the circumstances in the story. These intimate details serve to slow the narrative pace of action and dramatize the scene.

This homeless birth is prophetic of the lack of a permanent home for Jesus throughout the Gospel. Luke's Jesus is constantly on the move, from even before his birth. As an unborn child he travels from Nazareth to Elizabeth's home in Ain Karem, then back to Nazareth. Mary carries the unborn baby from Nazareth to Bethlehem. After the birth, Matthew records the flight of the holy family from Judea to Egypt before their return to Nazareth years later (2:14, 22-23)—a detail totally missing in Luke.

The homeless theme continues in Luke as Jesus travels throughout his ministry (e.g., 4:14, 30, 31, 42, 44; 5:11, 12; see the commentary on 9:1-7, 57-58). The desperate circumstances of his birth portend his lifelong itinerancy and homelessness.

■ **8-12** These verses report the third epiphany of the birth narratives (1:11-20, 26-38). Again, the normal pattern of human affairs is interrupted by a cosmic intervention. This time it is an unnamed **angel of the Lord** (v 9), who appears to the shepherds. As with both Zechariah and Mary, fear is the response of the shepherds to the appearance. Again, the angel brings the message of comfort: **Do not be afraid** (v 10; 1:13, 30).

The angel proclaims: **Today in the town of David a Savior has been born to you; he is Christ the Lord** (2:11; see 1:30-33). The Davidic theme (1:27, 32, 69) is again advanced as the angel proclaims the central assertion of the Gospel—Jesus is Savior, Christ, Lord, and Messiah (1:32, 35, 47, 69; 2:11). From the perspective of reader-response, readers must now bear the responsibility that comes with knowledge. Indifference becomes increasingly untenable as the narrator challenges the engaged reader either to accept or reject the claim. It is in the nature of a "Gospel" to call the reader from neutrality to decision; in this sense, Luke is indeed an Evangelist.

Repeating the location and circumstances of the child (v 7), the angel indicates that the Savior will be found **wrapped in cloths and lying in a manger** (v 12). This is to be a **sign** (v 12) to the shepherds that things are as the angel predicted. But it is also a sign that, contrary to popular expectations, they would find the baby in humble circumstances. This Christ is found in a manger, not a palace, a sign of his humility and identification with the common (see Craddock 1990, 52).

■ **13-14** The announcement of Jesus' birth is attested by the sudden appearance of **a great company of the heavenly host**. They were praising God and saying, *"Glory to God in the highest, and peace on earth to all on whom his favor rests!"* (v 14). This language of ascribing glory to God is not from the OT, but from the Second Temple Judaism (see Bar 2:18; 4 Macc 1:12; and *Pss. Sol.* 18:10 (Fitzmyer 1981, 1:410).

A textual variant in the latter part of the verse has significant theological implications. Peace on earth to those "on whom his favor rests" renders *en an thrōpois eudokias*. The predicate genitive noun *eudokias*, "favor, good pleasure," is difficult to interpret (see BDF, §165; Metzger 1975, 133; see Fitzmyer 1997, 1:102-3 on the Hebrew background of the phrase). Some ancient manuscripts have instead a nominative form, *eudokia*, followed in the familiar KJV expression, "good will toward men." But nearly all modern versions take the original text in the prior sense. That is, the angel announces God's favor *upon* people through the birth of the Messiah. He does not announce the creation of goodwill *among* people—a significant difference of meaning (Fitzmyer 1981, 1:411).

The Priene inscription (see Behind the Text comments on 1:26-38) suggests the influence of the imperial cult as a background for this language. Caesar Augustus is said to come as a "savior" (*sōtēr*) who brings an end to war and "good news" (*euangelion*), similar to this passage in Luke.

An angel had previously declared Mary "highly favored" (1:28). Now God's **favor** also rests on those to whom the angel appears (v 14). Messianic blessings are beginning to spread; this is their first announcement outside of the family. Blessings first appeared in the private lives of Zechariah, Elizabeth, Joseph, and Mary. Now the news of the coming Messiah is breaking out into the public realm.

■ **15-21** The shepherds **hurried off and found Mary and Joseph, and the baby, who was lying in the manger** (v 16). This is the third mention of the location of Jesus' birth in a **manger** (vv 7, 12, 16). The stall signifies that he could have been born in no lower social station. His birth could not have been met by greater indifference. The contrast of Jesus' circumstances and identity is another of Luke's dramatic juxtapositions.

The word of the angel and the heavenly host in the shepherds' field is the first public proclamation of the coming of the Messiah in the narrative (v 10). The second public statement is made by the shepherds at the manger, **and all who hear it were amazed** (v 18; see also v 33). "All the people" (usually *pantes*, sometimes *hoi ochloi*) are "amazed" (usually *thaumazō* or *existēmi*; see 2:47; 4:22, 32, 36; 5:25) with Jesus and the events of his life.

Here in v 18, they are "amazed" at the words of the shepherds. Later they are "amazed" at his understanding as a boy (2:47), his gracious words and teaching (4:22, 32), and his exorcisms (5:26, *ekstasis*; 8:56; 9:43; 11:14). Finally, the disciples are amazed at the report of his resurrection (24:22). Public affirmation demonstrates that all the common people understand and appreciate who Jesus is, something his opponents, it will soon be seen, cannot.

Luke's almost entirely positive characterization of the "people" and "crowds" plays an important theological role in his message. It is they who immediately understand and respond to his message, quite in contrast to the religious authorities. Even when the masses are in error, as in 3:7-10, when corrected, they immediately repent (3:10; the exceptions are the mob scenes in Nazareth [4:23-30] and the Garden [22:47]; see the commentary on Luke's characterization of the crowds at 5:12-16 and 7:11-17).

By establishing the contrasting perceptions of the crowds and religious authorities, Luke creates "paradigms of perception." These seek to influence his readers' response to the narrative (Darr 1992, 50-59). Readers are not left in doubt as to where their sympathy should fall.

Upon hearing the shepherds' words, **Mary treasured up all these things and pondered them in her heart** (v 19). Among the synoptic authors, Luke alone presents a personal portrait of Mary, referring to her fourteen times (six times in Matthew). He includes intimate information about her state of mind in his narrative. She is, by turns, greatly troubled (1:29), afraid (v 30), perplexed (v 34), faithful (v 38), ecstatic (vv 46-55), humble (v 48), grateful (v 48), and amazed (2:33). Endearingly, she *hurries* to see Elizabeth (1:39). These passages give a unique glimpse into the inner life of Jesus' mother and are useful in developing a theology about Mary as an example of faith and holiness. Clearly, any such effort must look to Luke as a primary source (see Perry 2006; Gaventa 1999).

3. Temple Prophets and the Consolation of Israel (2:22-40)

BEHIND THE TEXT

Up to this point, the birth narratives have been full of awe and joy. Angels have prepared the participants for the arrival of the Messiah and gloriously announced his birth. An ominous shadow now begins to darken the narrative. While Simeon and Anna will publicly prophesy of the child's anointing as "the Lord's Christ" who effects "the redemption of Jerusalem" (vv 26, 38), readers learn that tragedy looms in the pages to come (vv 33-35).

Key words in vv 34-35 set a tone of conflict: destiny, falling and rising, opposition, the piercing of the soul. The further afield the message travels in the public domain in the narrative, the greater the complexity of its reception. At first all rejoice at the news of the Messiah. But in each new public setting (temple, the devil in the desert, Nazareth, Capernaum, etc.), it becomes clear that the advent of the Messiah will create trouble with the current order.

IN THE TEXT

■ **22-24** Mary and Joseph present themselves for **purification** at the temple in Jerusalem, following the birth of the baby (v 22). A woman was considered ritually unclean for seven days after birth, until the child was circumcised on the eighth day (v 21; Lev 12:1-8). This offering cleansed the ritual impurity contracted by the woman from the birth process so she could reenter the temple. Even though Luke refers to **their purification** (v 22), this offering technically applied only to the woman (Marshall 1978, 116). Since they are poor, Joseph and Mary offer the least expensive offering for purification, **a pair of doves** (v 24; Lev 12:6-8; see Beale and Carson 2007, 269-71).

Consecration of the **firstborn**, on the other hand, was a separate offering (v 23). God had commanded in Exodus that all firstborn males in Israel were to be consecrated to Yahweh (Exod 13:11-15). In the case of animals, this meant slaughter, but firstborn humans were "redeemed" with a substitute sacrifice. Joseph and Mary sought both the purification of Mary and the consecration of Jesus.

This story resembles the consecration of Samuel by Hannah (1 Sam 1:21-28). Samuel, the prophet who would establish the Davidic line by anointing David king, was dedicated to the Lord from birth. Hannah brought Samuel to the temple as soon as he was weaned and left him to be raised by the priests. Jesus, of course, was not left at the temple by his parents, nor was he a Nazirite, as were both Samuel and John (see the commentary on 1:15*b*-17). Still, all three figures play important roles in the biblical drama of the advent of the Davidic Messiah.

■ **25-26** Angels made the first public proclamation of the birth to the shepherds of Bethlehem (2:8-14). These shepherds "spread the word" to "all who heard it" (vv 17, 18). Two more confirmations of Jesus' identity follow, one private and one public. Both occur in the precincts of the temple.

The first proclamation comes from **Simeon.** Luke indicates that the **Holy Spirit was upon him** (v 25). The Holy Spirit, who has filled Zechariah, Mary, and Elizabeth (1:35, 41, 67; see the comment on 1:39-45), is now **upon** Simeon (NRSV: "rested on him"). The Spirit is located *on* or *over* Simeon, similar to the way he will come "upon" and "overshadow" Mary (1:35). This reflects Luke's sense of sacred location and echoes the physicality of the Spirit's presence on the Hebrew Bible prophets (e.g., 1 Sam 11:6; 16:3, 14, 23; 2 Kgs 2:15; see the commentary on 1:67).

God had promised Simeon that he would see **the Lord's Christ** (v 26, *ton christon kyriou*), a unique expression found only here in the NT. Simeon's phrase, **consolation of Israel** (v 25), is also not found elsewhere in Scripture.

But it richly expresses Israel's expectation that suffering would end because of the child's advent.

The testimony of Simeon shows how the good news emerges from the privacy of the manger to the public square of the Jerusalem temple. Once again, Luke juxtaposes locales with dramatic effect. The baby carried from a barn in Bethlehem to the inner sanctum of Judaism is recognized as Messiah in both settings. This fully establishes Jesus' identity in the narrative.

■ **27-33** As he takes the baby in his arms, Simeon declares a psalm of praise, traditionally called the Nunc Dimittis. The song echoes passages of Isaiah, which emphasize "light to the nations." This is a key phrase in Isaiah's universal offer of salvation (Isa 9:1-3; 42:6; 49:6; 51:4; 60:3). This salvation, says Simeon, is one God has **prepared in the sight of all people, a light for revelation to the Gentiles and for glory to your people Israel** (vv 31-32; see Isa 52:10).

This is the first direct reference in Luke to salvation for the Gentiles, a theme that extends through the Gospel and culminates in the book of Acts (a possible allusion in 1:79; see the Introduction, Theological Themes in Luke; also Acts 13:47-48; 26:23).

With Simeon's psalm, Luke launches the main theological project of his Gospel—redefining the boundaries of **salvation** (v 30) from the historic covenant community of Israel to the nonnational community of the repentant. Luke's phrase for this new community is **all people** (v 30). In the chapters to come, the response of sinners to Jesus, including Gentiles, will be pitted against the response of those within the traditional boundaries of **Israel.** Those who recognize his messianic identity respond to God with repentance and receive forgiveness. Those who fail to repent, usually Luke's Pharisees, teachers of the Law and priests, "stumble" on the rock of Jesus' messianic identity (Isa 8:14; see the commentary on Luke 7:18-23; 17:1-4; and 19:40).

The new boundaries of salvation in Luke include Gentiles. They do not, however, exclude the nation of Israel. This salvation is also for the Jews: **for glory to your people Israel** (v 32). Luke's new theology of "universalism" embraces simultaneously both Israel and the Gentiles. The offer of salvation is to *all* who repent, regardless of national or ethnic identity. This is similar in nature to the offer of salvation to all in Paul's universalism. His theology operates with the declaration of Jesus as Lord as its main principle. Luke differs somewhat from Paul's formula by placing its key emphasis on the operational importance of repentance. Still, this idea of the offer of salvation to all is the connecting thread between the thought worlds of Paul and Luke.

■ **34-35** Jesus' appearance, according to Simeon, is also the harbinger of judgment. Simeon's message is a private word to Mary, which the reader is privileged to overhear. This reveals both the inner life of the mother and the child's troubling future. Jesus' life will not be peaceful, but one beset by conflict and opposition. **This child is destined to cause the falling and rising of many** in Israel (v 34). An apocalyptic shadow is cast over the baby's life. It points forward to Jesus' description of his life as one that will set father against son (12:51-53).

His life will divide the hearts of men and women against each other and bare their innermost lives—**the thoughts of many hearts will be revealed** (v 35). The revealing of thoughts and deeds is a theme characteristic of apocalyptic judgment (see Rom 2:5; 1 Cor 3:13; Rev 15:4).

And a **sword will pierce** Mary's own heart (v 35). Given the division Jesus' life will bring families, this is not a sword of judgment, as in Ezek 14:17, but a sword of sorrow (see Bock 1994, 1:248-50, for suggestions on how to interpret this passage).

Mary will feel the personal pain of a son who repudiates his own family ties and is eventually betrayed by all (Evans 1990, 220). "Simeon hints at the difficulty she will have in learning that obedience to the word of God will transcend even family ties" (Fitzmyer 1981, 1:430; see the comment on vv 48-52 below; and on 8:19-21; 9:59-62; and 12:51-53).

■ **36-39** Women continue to play a prominent role in the story. **Anna**'s piety and suffering eventually led her to a life of devotion within the temple. She was a **prophetess** (v 36), a status held by only a few women in the Bible (Exod 15:20; Judg 4:4; 2 Kgs 22:14; Neh 6:14). As with the powerless virgin Mary and the barren older Elizabeth, this aged woman was socially disadvantaged. In this case, she had been widowed after only **seven years** of marriage (v 36).

In the Hebrew Bible widows symbolize desolation and sorrow (e.g., Isa 54:4-5; Lam 1:1-2). They had little chance for normal lives. But widows have a special place in Luke's story. He alone records the widow stories found in 4:26; 7:11-17; and 18:1-8. Perhaps this sympathy leads Luke to select a widowed prophetess as one of the first to proclaim Jesus' identity.

Anna, now near death, finally finds joy: **she gave thanks to God and spoke about the child to all** (v 38). Her tribe **Asher** means "happiness." This seems fitting with the appearance of the baby, especially after Anna's long and difficult life as a widow. Asher was a northern tribe that responded to an invitation to celebrate the Passover in Jerusalem following the fall of Samaria (2 Chr 30:10-12).

Some suggest this reference is a precursor for Luke's mission to the Samaritans in Acts 8:1-25 (Beale and Carson 2007, 274). This seems a reasonable conjecture, given Luke's use of "a light for revelation to the Gentiles" from Isa 42:6/49:6 in Simeon's song, and his growing thematic concern with this motif (see Acts 13:47; 26:23).

■ **40** Luke's summary statement at the end of John's birth narrative (1:80) depends on 1 Sam 2:26. Again, almost identical to 1 Samuel, Luke summarizes the birth narrative of Jesus: **And the child grew and became strong; he was filled with wisdom, and the grace of God was upon him** (v 40; compare v 52; see the table below).

The theme of wisdom appears in Isaiah's description of the shoot from the stump of Jesse in Isa 11:1-3, a passage with Davidic messianic implications. The messianic figure will have "the Spirit of wisdom and of understanding, the Spirit of counsel and of power, the Spirit of knowledge and of the fear of the LORD" (compare *Pss. Sol.* 17:37; 1 En. 49:2-3).

Jesus' robust physical stature would have been regarded as a sign of God's blessing (see the commentary on Luke 1:80). This description of his growth and strength in 1:40 fits the expected profile of a Jewish leader. We should imagine a historical Jesus at twelve as precocious, energetic, ruddy, and inquisitive. Some authors have speculated on Jesus' "hidden years," mostly from the angle of psychological analysis (see Capps 2000, 129-63; Miller 1997, 31-54). The question often arises about Jesus' father and the likelihood of his early death. What sort of effect would this have had on the young Jesus, especially as the oldest male child in a Palestinian family? Our concept of the incarnate God is enriched when we consider such natural aspects of his human experience.

4. Young Jesus in the Temple (2:41-52)

BEHIND THE TEXT

Between vv 40 and 41 the narrator notes a twelve-year time gap. Jesus' life from infancy to boyhood is veiled in mystery. Among the canonical Gospels, only Luke preserves this one brief story from Jesus' boyhood. Apart from the fanciful and late "apocryphal" infancy and childhood gospels, readers are left almost completely without information on the first thirty years of Jesus' life.

In the story-world of the Gospels, the silence about Jesus' early life creates an aura of mystery. Against this backdrop, his sudden emergence as a prophet-like figure at his baptism is all the more intensely portrayed. This glimpse of the boy at twelve confirms the extraordinary claims of the birth narrative, demonstrates the child's "wisdom" (as asserted in v 40), and prepares readers for Jesus' emergence as an adult in ch 3. For Luke, the adult Jesus arrives on the scene as an almost completely unknown entity, just as he does in the other Gospels.

In the second century A.D. and later, many authors sought to fill the void in the canonical Gospels about Jesus' early life. The "apocryphal" gospels usually focused on the infancy and early life of Jesus. In these ancient narratives, palm trees bow reverently before Mary on the way to Bethlehem, and the boy Jesus brings clay pigeons to life (for a convenient collection of the infancy gospels see Barnstone 1984, 383-408). Although they are of no historical value, these fictional accounts present an interesting counterpoint to the almost militant silence of the canonical Gospels on the details of Jesus' early life.

In 1:5-7 we noted the flawless priestly pedigree of John's parents. Similarly, Joseph and Mary demonstrate respect for the Law and the temple, following prescriptions for purification and consecration (2:21-25), and annually presenting the child in the temple courts (2:27, 37, 41). Now, twelve years later, the careful observation of Law and tradition continues in the text as the parents take the boy up to Jerusalem "according to the custom" for the Feast of the Passover (vv 41-42).

All faithful Jews were commanded to "go up" to Jerusalem three times annually for holy days—Passover, Pentecost (or Feast of Weeks), and Feast of Booths (or Tabernacles; see Exod 34:23; Deut 16:16; as to the age of young attendees, see *m. Hag.* 1:1). The phrase "go up" derives from Jerusalem's altitude, situated high on a long ridge in eastern Palestine.

Passover was the principal annual feast. It attracted massive numbers of pilgrims from great distances each year. It seems reasonable that from "300,000 to 500,000" Jews inundated the city yearly. This would have required the sacrifice of 30,000 lambs, one for each ten people (Sanders 1992, 128; not the 255,600 lambs suggested by Josephus). Jerusalem's normal population was 30,000, but its temple could accommodate 400,000 worshippers, and Passover was the most popular festival (Sanders 1992, 128).

Such a journey was impossible for many Jews in distant locales. But Joseph and Mary undertook the arduous seventy-mile trek **every year**. This indicates their piety and the social importance of celebration in the spiritual capitol of Judaism. Pilgrims from the same region traveled together (v 44; see Sanders 1992, 125-38; Safrai and Stern 1974, 2:891-96).

Passover and the Second Tithe

In Deut 12:17-18 all Jews were enjoined to spend their "second tithe" in Jerusalem at the time of Passover (Jeremias 1972, 57; Sanders 1992, 128-29). This made the festival a time of great rejoicing and celebration. Food, song, and fellowship were the main activities, all in the shadow of the imposing Temple of Yahweh.

For residents of the small northern hamlet of Nazareth, the annual Passover trip to the Holy City would have been the highlight of the year. As Joseph and Mary returned home with a large contingent of family and friends, they presumed the young boy was somewhere in the crowd of pilgrims. To their dismay they discovered after leaving the city that the boy was missing.

IN THE TEXT

■ **41-47** At **twelve years old** (v 42) Jesus would have been close to the time of what Jews today call bar mitzvah, the "son of the commandments" (*m. Avot* 5:21). This is the age of transition from childhood to manhood. Youths were expected to take on the yoke of the Law. While coming of age is not mentioned in the text, age twelve has significance for Jesus' maturation and upbringing as a Jew. In Luke this is Jesus' "coming out" event.

It is not difficult to imagine a young boy awestruck by the Holy City and the **temple courts** (v 46), an architectural wonder of the world. The expectations of his parents might soon be forgotten. The boy's knowledge impresses the teachers of Jerusalem. The education for sons started at age five. Families who could afford it sent their sons to yeshiva (parochial school). Jesus must have had the benefit of studying under the best teachers of his village. Not the least expense of attending school was the absence of sons from their fathers' trades, a real burden to impoverished families. Luke's point was that the "Son of God" was required to learn. Nothing about his divinity relieves him of this human necessity.

The precocious twelve-year-old attracted attention in the courts of the Jerusalem temple. This is remarkable in itself, if the size of the crowds at Passover is considered. A full **three days** after the boy goes missing, he is still deeply engaged in conversation with the teachers in the temple. The boy Jesus was **sitting among the teachers, listening to them and asking them questions. Everyone who heard him was amazed at his understanding and his answers** (vv 46-47).

This scene looks backward and forward in the narrative. It looks backward, because his precociousness derives from his identity as "the Son of God" (1:35), and forward, because it presages his status as a great teacher and rabbi in his public ministry.

More specifically, this account foreshadows 19:47 and Jesus' next return to the temple, where "every day he was teaching." The extended teaching narrative in 20:1—21:38 is parallel to that of the boy Jesus in the temple. In an almost midrashic way, we hear how his initial experience at age twelve blooms in the life of the adult Jesus. This is complete with what he actually says and does in the temple, and how others react. Ironically, in every subsequent reference to the temple in Luke, Jesus is in conflict with its authorities (e.g., 20:1 ff.; 21:6; 22:52).

In Luke's characterization, from his earliest days as a boy, to the culmination of his ministry in Jerusalem, *Jesus teaches the Scriptures.* Even in his postresurrection persona on the road to Emmaus, Jesus' mind is immersed in the Scripture and its teaching. For Luke, this is who Jesus is. It must be considered one of the central facets of his characterization (see the comment on 24:13-49; Acts 1:3).

■**48-52** Jesus becomes separated from his family as they leave Jerusalem. Once they realize this, his parents search desperately to find him. The three days it takes to find him would include one day traveling out from Jerusalem, one back, and a day of searching in the city (Marshall 1978, 127). On being found in the temple, the scene of Mary and Joseph with their son introduces an element in the Gospel that will reemerge in his later life.

Mary gives voice to what any parent in a similar situation would feel: **Son, why have you treated us like this? Your father and I have been anxiously searching for you** (v 48). Jesus' reply to his mother hints at impatience: **"Why were you searching for me?" he asked. "Didn't you know I had to be in my Father's house?"** (v 49). The devotion to temple evinced by the parents is mirrored in the life of the young Jesus. But, more importantly, it demonstrates that the preeminence that allegiance to God's work will have in Jesus' life.

The genitive phrase *tou patros mou*, *of my Father*, has a sense both of location and of origin. Jesus views this house as more holy than any other; and he identifies with it as a representation of his relationship with his Father. This is a statement of self-identification in terms of sacred place.

Second, the phrase suggests patrilinear origin. The "house of the father" or *bet 'av*, is one of three levels in the kinship social system. Along with tribe and clan it identifies one's place in the society (see comments on 15:11-16). It is a physical location, where land, livestock, house, and family are found. But it is also a statement of lineage, establishing one's place across the generations.

Jesus is not the son of Joseph, he seems to say, but the son of the Father (compare Prov 4:3; Neh 1:6). As with Jacob and his ladder in Gen 28:18-22, his father's house is the place of fulfillment of promise, the place to which his heart will always long to return.

The tension between Jesus and his family will emerge in Luke's narrative during his adult years. Two events in the triple tradition (Matthew ‖ Mark ‖ Luke) show that Jesus experienced emotional distance from his family in his later years (Luke 8:19-21; Matt 12:46-50; Mark 3:31-35; and Luke 14:26; Matt 10:37; Mark 8:34). In the double tradition, or Q material (Matthew ‖ Luke), we have the difficult logion: "let the dead bury their own dead" (Luke 9:59-62 ‖ Matt 8:21-22), and the soliloquy on division within the family (Luke 12:51-53 ‖ Matt 10:34-36), both of which reflect emotional distance from his family. Other references on this subject occur in one Gospel only (Mark 3:21; Luke 11:27; and John 2:4). The Gospels would not have preserved such difficult evidence about Jesus' personal life, suggests one scholar, "without the warrant of fact" (Taylor 1952, 235; see Miller 1997, 31-54).

Luke concludes both the birth and youth narratives with summary statements in 2:40 and 2:52 (see 1:80). This is in conscious emulation of 1 Sam 2:26; 3:19, where a similar pair of summaries brackets the birth and youth narratives of Samuel.

Summaries in 1 Samuel and Luke

1 Sam 2:26	1 Sam 3:19	Luke 2:40	Luke 2:52
And the boy Samuel continued to grow in stature and in favor with the LORD and with men.	The LORD was with Samuel as he grew up, and he let none of his words fall to the ground.	And the child grew and became strong; he was filled with wisdom, and the grace of God was upon him.	And Jesus grew in wisdom and stature, and in favor with God and men.

Luke's familiarity with 1 Samuel continues to be obvious as he connects Jesus conceptually to the story of the emergence of the Davidic throne in 1 Samuel (see the commentary on 1:7, 15b-17, 27, 32-33, 54-56, 68-70; 2:8-12).

FROM THE TEXT

The human aspect of Jesus' experience of familial relationships teaches us a great deal about Christology and the nature of the incarnation. Jesus experienced the intimate bonds of family life and knew its joys and conflicts. Christology must incorporate this reality into the notion of incarnation. The Son of God bore the burden of being the eldest son, experiencing the poverty known to all villagers, the demands and costs of struggling to learn a trade amid these pressures, and the necessity to conform to the expectations of one's family and village in a multitude of ways.

Awareness of Jesus' mundane burdens should encourage all who struggle in life. Jesus experienced tensions and problems in his life that are not so different from ours. As is often the case with modern parents, Jesus' parents "did not understand what he was saying to them" (2:50). A fuller example of his humanity cannot be imagined. In the end, however, he was "obedient" (v 51) and returned home with Joseph and Mary.

Theologically, the human realities of the incarnation teach us that all our struggles are understood by God. He was "a man of sorrows, and familiar with suffering," and "although he was a son, he learned obedience from what he suffered" (Isa 53:3; Heb 5:8). Christ comes to us and stands beside us—sharing our humanity in the mundane suffering of daily life common to all. None who experience the brokenness of family and home or the desperation of poverty need feel alone. God himself is with us.

II. THE BEGINNING OF JOHN'S MINISTRY AND THE BAPTISM OF JESUS: LUKE 3:1-38

A. The Beginning of John's Ministry (3:1-20)

1. The Call of John (3:1-6)

BEHIND THE TEXT

The preaching of John the Baptist appears in all four Gospels and begins with the same basic message. The sources of John's preaching in the Gospels include the triple tradition (Matthew; Mark; and Luke), Q (Matthew || Luke); John 1:19-23; M, Mark, and L (the Synoptic Evangelists' independent sources: Matt 3:1-6; Mark 1:2-6; Luke 3:1-6; Webb [1991, 60-61] lists twenty-eight pericopae about John in Luke and Acts). All three Synoptic Gospels emphasize repentance and baptism (Luke 3:3). And all, including John, quote Isa 40:3 (Luke 3:4-6) as referring to the Baptist's role as a precursor to Jesus.

89

The message of John is presented by the Gospels as primarily religious, rather than political, in nature. The two worlds are, of course, inextricably intertwined. But the Evangelists downplay the political aspects of John's message, probably as a defense against charges of sedition. These fears were not unfounded: Herod Antipas felt sufficiently threatened politically by John's popularity to arrest and execute him (Luke 3:18-20). Josephus speaks of Herod's concern that John would incite "civic unrest" (*Ant.* 18.5.2, §118) as rationale for having John eliminated. In the early years of the first century, populist preachers who gathered crowds presented ruling authorities with political problems and challenges to the fragile Roman peace.

Luke's historical reconstruction of political events is not always flawless (see commentary on 2:1-5). Nonetheless, the political leaders named in the beginning of ch 3 provide a sound historical context for the commencement of John's ministry. By rehearsing the global and regional political context (see 1:5; 2:1-2), Luke shows that the messages of John and Jesus transcend the realm of local Jerusalem religion and politics (see Behind the Text on 2:1-7).

Luke provides little detail concerning John's movements at the beginning of his ministry. He says only that the word of God came to John in the desert in the region of the Jordan. The Gospel of John identifies the area of John's initial ministry as "Bethany on the other side of the Jordan" (John 1:28; see the commentary on 1:80 on the desert motif; on the Qumran connection, see Taylor 1997, 42-48). Tradition places this site six miles southeast of Jericho at el-Maghtas. The Fourth Gospel also reports that John and Jesus ministered side-by-side for a time in the area of "Aenon near Salim" (John 3:22-23). This is about twenty-five miles from the southern tip of the Sea of Galilee, on the western side of the Jordan River.

John the Baptist was also active on the eastern side of the Jordan River, that is, in Perea (Luke 3:3; Taylor 1997, 46). It was in this area that John angered Herod Antipas with his preaching against Herod's marriage to Herodias (3:18-20). Jews traveling south from Galilee often crossed to this area on the eastern side of the Jordan near Beth-shean to avoid the non-Jewish territory of Samaria.

IN THE TEXT

■ **1-3** The political leaders mentioned by Luke include: **Tiberius** (ruled A.D. 14-37), **Pontius Pilate** (A.D. 26-36), **Herod Antipas** of Galilee (4 B.C.-A.D. 39), **Philip** of Ituraea and Trachonitis (4 B.C.-A.D. 34), and **Lysanius of Abilene** (known only by this biblical reference).

Luke mentions as religious leaders the high priests **Caiaphas** (v 2, ruled A.D. 18-37) and **Annas** (A.D. 6-15), a former high priest. Deposed from office by the time of John and Jesus, Annas still exerted influence on Jewish affairs (see Acts 4:6) as Caiaphas' father-in-law. The **fifteenth year of the reign of Tiberius Caesar** (v 1) was A.D. 27-28. Thus, John would have been in his early thirties.

Careful attention to the political context of John's emergence echoes a theme from 1:5 and 2:1-7. There the birth narratives were given a similar geopolitical setting. Luke seems concerned to show that the political powers of the day are not at center stage in salvation history. They are present; they have obvious influence; but they are subordinate to God's power and plan.

Following the description of the powers of the current age (1:5; 2:1-7; 3:1-2), John appears in the narrative, seizes the initiative, and brings about God's plan. In this sense, Luke's references to political entities deal with the ultimate issue of true power in the affairs of the world. Although the consummation is yet to come and Caesar reigns, in Luke's story-world God remains finally and fully in control of the cosmic drama.

In 1:80, Luke reported that John was "in the desert until he appeared publicly to Israel." With vv 2b-3, the time has arrived: **the word of God came to John . . . in the desert** in **all the country around the Jordan**. Imperial power and wilderness are juxtaposed. The use of Isa 40:3-5 in vv 4-6, describing John's appearance in the "desert" echoes Israel's return from exile in Babylon. Perhaps it also evokes hopes for its future deliverance from a similar oppressor—Rome. As God restored Israel after the exile, he now brings a new restoration to his people. We have already learned, however, that this restoration will not be like the last, a reestablishment of the nation in its homeland. This restoration will include all the nations (1:79; 2:32; 3:6) and will be based on the transformation of the social order (Green 1997, 163).

John is **preaching a baptism of repentance for the forgiveness of sins**. Luke's wording of this phrase follows Mark verbatim (Mark 1:4b). Matthew's formulation is somewhat different: "Repent, for the kingdom of heaven is near" (3:2). They were "baptized by him in the river Jordan, confessing their sins" (v 6 NRSV).

The phrase "to preach baptism" is a "highly uncommon expression," evidencing a Christian interpretation of John's activity (Evans 1990, 235). It seems to conceive of the preaching (*kēryssōn*) of this baptism as a work of God in itself. Luke indicates that the Baptist movement was a significant force in its own right, reaching as far as Asia Minor twenty years after Jesus (Acts 19:1-4). Evidence of a robust independent Baptist movement abounds in Luke (5:33; 7:18, 33; 9:19; 11:1; 20:6; Acts 1:5, 22; 10:37; 11:16; 13:24-25; 18:25; 19:1-4). John's preaching of a "baptism of repentance" had its own cachet in the Baptist movement for years to come.

Interpreters look for the historical roots of John's baptism in several places. Bock offers three options: Qumran practice (so Fitzmyer 1981, 1:454), proselyte baptism of Gentiles by Jews (the *tevilah*, immersion of converts in ritual baths; so Wigoder 1989, 184), and a baptism of repentance unique to John (Bock 1994, 288-89). To these options, a fourth should be added: the traditional practice of OT ablutions associated with cleansing, both ritual and

3:1-3

moral (Evans 1990, 236; e.g., Lev 11:36; 15:16; 22:1-6; Pss 26:6; 51:2; Isa 1:16; Ezek 36:25; Zech 13:1).

Repentance by converts was already known within Judaism (Webb 1991, 184-85). But John connects water baptism with an ethical imperative of repentance—an important development. The association of these two ideas blurs the line between ritual impurity, for which water is adequate, and moral impurity, for which repentance is the solution. This was a step the sectarians at Qumran had already taken (Klawans 2000, 75; see the sidebar Sin, Impurity, and Disease in Luke in ch 5). But it was not common in the Judaism of this time. This makes the Qumran practice the most fruitful line of investigation for understanding John's baptism.

The Qumran ablutions had two functions: purification and initiation (Webb 1991, 161-62). John's baptism has aspects of both. The purification is twofold, moral *and* ritual. It is also initiatory, because John preaches this act as an induction into the community of the Messiah (v 17). The implications of this view will expand in chs 5 and 6. There, sin, impurity, and disease are considered in the context of Jesus' healing and teaching activity.

John's baptism is further described as **for the forgiveness of sins.** This aligns with Luke's overarching presentation of repentance and forgiveness as the only means of entrance into the new community of the Messiah—for both Jews and Gentiles. In chs 5—19, six exemplars of this experience will demonstrate to readers the efficacy of repentance for sinners (see below From the Text; and Behind the Text for 5:1-11). John's baptism has existential, moral, and ritual imperatives (3:10-14). All of these prepare the way, not only for the Messiah, but for Luke's presentation of how salvation operates in the new age.

■ **4-5** Isaiah 40:3 is quoted in various forms by all four Gospel writers (Matt 3:3; Mark 1:2-3; Luke 3:4-6 [who alone adds Isa 40:4-5]; John 1:23). The Gospels treat the text as a midrash. They offer a pesher-like exposition of Isa 40 as interpreting the mission of John as a return from exile. As the return was a time of national restoration, so John's message will bring restoration. This time, however, it will be based on repentance rather than political hegemony.

The reference the "desert" (v 2) echoes Isaiah's prophecy in Isa 40:3: **voice of one calling in the desert** (Luke 3:4). In Isaiah, the desert refers to the land between Babylon and Jerusalem, traversed by the returning exiles (see Isa 35). Isaiah calls for the road through the desert to be made "straight." The Gospels reapply this to John, who will "prepare" Jesus' path (Fitzmyer 1981, 1:452-53).

Only Luke among the Synoptics quotes also Isa 40:4-5. Isaiah promises that **every valley** along this path **shall be filled in.** Luke takes the Greek verb *plērōthēsetai*, **filled in,** to have a double meaning here. *Plēroō* is used twenty-one times in the Gospels (seven in Luke) and Acts to indicate the fulfillment of prophecy. John's preparatory ministry metaphorically fills in valleys, smoothing the way for the Messiah. But his coming also *fulfills* prophecy.

Likewise, the verb *tapeinōthēsetai*, in the phrase **every mountain and hill made low**, elsewhere in the NT always means "humbled." John's ministry of baptism for repentance calls sinners to *humble* themselves before God. So again, Luke employs a double entendre based on the Isaiah passage.

Crooked roads shall become straight, the rough ways smooth. In Luke's midrash, this phrase from Isa 40 refers to the ethical demands of John's message. The crooked path is the path of the wicked (Prov 2:12-15); the straight path, that of the righteous (Prov 3:6). In Luke 3:10-14, John explicitly advises the "crowds" as to how crooked paths might be made straight. In order to avoid the ax of judgment the crowd must give to the needy and live honest lives.

■ **6** By the inclusion of the quotation of Isa 40:5, Luke has gone beyond his fellow Evangelists to highlight Jesus' promise of salvation for the Gentiles: ***all people will see God's salvation*** (Luke 3:6; see 2:30-31). This salvation finds its culmination in the final verses in Acts: "Therefore I want you to know that God's salvation has been sent to the Gentiles, and they will listen!" (28:28).

2. John Warns the Crowd of Judgment (3:7-9)

■ **7-9** With John's first spoken words, the narrative darkens. Earlier, Mary's hymn alluded to apocalyptic judgment, since God "has scattered those who are proud" and "brought down rulers from their thrones" (1:51-52). That idea reemerges in John's harsh words about those who come out to hear him. He calls them all a **brood of vipers**. His anger seems to arise from the apparent self-interest of the crowd—**Who warned you to flee from the coming wrath?** (v 7). There is a disparity between their words of repentance and the attitudes of their hearts.

In this instance, the "crowd" represents those currently excluded from salvation or from comprehending John's message. Other examples of the "crowd" as a literary category, alongside the "Pharisees" and "tax collectors and sinners" will emerge in subsequent chapters. These characters are "paradigmatic": through them the narrator establishes a "hierarchy of perspectives" (Darr 1992, 57; see 50). Readers, under the influence of the narrator's persuasion, sympathize with those in the narrative who can understand the message (the repentant crowd, v 10) and judge those who cannot.

The **viper** (v 7), a venomous snake, is a symbol of evil in the Bible. Its use here is a provocative insult. In a parallel passage about the beginning of John's ministry in Matt 3:7, John's words are uttered against the *Pharisees* (see Matt 12:34; 23:33). Luke broadens the audience to include everyone: **the crowds coming out to be baptized by him** (v 7). Luke's application of vipers to the whole crowd makes the saying doubly harsh. John castigates those searching for deliverance. John sees the crowd as not yet demonstrating the ethical conduct expected of those who confess repentance.

The **coming wrath** (v 7) sounds a familiar OT theme. Here for the first time in Luke 3:7-9 (see Zeph 1:14-15; 2:1-2; Mal 3:2-3), apocalyptic warning calls Israel to account. Often directed at Israel by her prophets, repentance was required whenever she relied on ritual rather than covenant faithfulness for a right relationship with God.

John confronts the interior dialogue he suspects some in his audience bring to the scene: **And do not begin to say to yourselves, "We have Abraham as our father." For I tell you that out of these stones God can raise up children for Abraham** (v 8). John challenges Israel's self-understanding as the chosen people of God (see Green 1997, 175-77). Ethnic purity is meaningless, if righteous conduct is not in evidence. God could make even **stones** serve him, if he chose (Isa 51:1).

John does not totally reject the temple, tradition, and law. But John's words are a corrective to the practice of placing these features at the center of Jewish religion. Instead, John calls for righteousness, both personal and corporate, based on **repentance** (v 8).

The Primacy of Faith in Judaism

Faith has always been central to the proper practice of Judaism. In Luke's extensive use of the Samuel tradition, faithfulness of the heart is crucial to the story. David was acceptable to God because of the state of his heart, not because of his position as king within the nation or his scrupulous observation of the Law.

This emphasis on interior faith is at the center of the Deuteronomistic tradition of the OT. What one *does* indicates the condition of the heart. In the NT, James is well-known for its emphasis on this idea; but the Gospels identify the same principle as pivotal in the teaching of Jesus. Inward faith is evidenced in outward action; anything less is hypocrisy.

Paul traces the roots of justification by faith back to Abraham, who was justified not because he fulfilled the external requirement of circumcision, but because of his faithful heart (Rom 4:9-12; Gal 5:6).

In emphasizing the importance of ethical action, John speaks as a reformer, one who calls Jews back to the roots of their tradition of faith and right practice. His words are not a criticism of Judaism per se, but a "prophetic critique" of Judaism. This is a vital distinction (Evans and Sanders 1993, 8; see Taylor 1952, 127-32). The main figures of the Gospels, John and Jesus, do not oppose Judaism but call into question the corrupt practices of then contemporary Judaism.

John exhorts his audience: **Let your penitent hearts produce worthy fruit** (v 8). Israelites must not presume that their status as sons and daughters of Abraham will protect them from the coming wrath. If the "fruit of repentance" can trump lineage, then outsiders to Judaism can also be saved.

This is not a new idea, of course. Genesis 17:4 says of Abraham, "You will be the father of many nations." And Sarah will be "the mother of nations" (Gen 17:16; see 49:10). Likewise, in Isaiah all nations will stream to God (2:2; 5:26; 11:10; 42:1; 45:20a; 51:4; 55:5; 56:6-8; 62:2). The point is subtly made in Luke, but the open call of salvation to all is on solid biblical ground. Acts pursues this theme by portraying Paul as the champion of salvation for the Gentiles (Acts 15:12-18; 18:6).

Every tree that does not produce good fruit will be cut down and thrown into the fire (Luke 3:9*b*). John warns that prophetic fire will sweep away all who fail to produce **good fruit**. The shift to an apocalyptic tone is abrupt and, perhaps, intentionally unsettling in the narrative flow. Suddenly, according to John, the present order is threatened—"menaced at its very roots," by the inbreaking power of God (Eichrodt 1961, 345).

Preexilic prophecy tended to focus on the immediate political and religious context of the prophets. The purview of postexilic prophecy shifts to a longer, more orderly view of national restoration. There, temple and its cultus are highly regarded as stable, intergenerational institutions at the center of the restoration (see, e.g., Ezra and Nehemiah). But here, John's apocalyptic perspective portrays impending doom—judgment that will sweep away the unproductive trees, soon and at once. The axe is **already** laid to the root of the tree (see Luke 13:6-9).

The present tense verbs of v 9 give the warning a powerful immediacy. These things are happening now, but the line between the present and future is blurring. Luke's Baptist expects a cataclysmic end in the near future—so near as to be "already" present. From a narrative perspective, this is a sobering turn of events in what has been, to this point, a hopeful and positive story.

FROM THE TEXT

A modern example of corruption demonstrates the importance of inner faith in Judaism. Recently, a Jewish financier bilked trusting investors of billions of dollars in a vast fund scheme. Many of these investors were charitable organizations, schools and universities, including Yeshiva University of New York. The financier was the treasurer of the board; and the University lost millions. Rabbi Benjamin Blech, Yeshiva's professor of the philosophy of law, said this unfortunate incident was "an opportunity to convey to students that ritual alone is not the sole determinant of our Judaism, that it must be combined with humanity, with ethical behavior, with proper values, and most important of all, with regard to our relationship with other human beings"—a poignant description of the Jewish values of inner faith (*New York Times*, December 22, 2008).

3. Ethical Demands (3:10-14)

■ **10-14** The setting of John's instruction to the crowd is a stylized characterization of his preaching in general, rather than a historical description of a single event. Acts uses this device in Peter's sermon at Pentecost. There the crowd verbalizes a nearly identical response, "Brothers, what shall we do?" (Acts 2:37 ‖ Luke 3:10). This type of speech is a variety of indirect discourse. The precise words are the narrator's, characterizing John's typical message.

Luke's severe characterization of John's message can be partially explained on literary grounds. His harsh words produce a penitential response from the crowd. This highlights Luke's focus on repentance as the path to salvation (see vv 3 and 8; 5:32; 13:3, 5; 15:7; 16:30; 17:4; 24:47; see Acts 2:37). In response, the crowd pleads, **"What should we do then?"** The question is repeated twice more for emphasis, first by **tax collectors** (v 12), then by **soldiers** (v 14). The readiness of the crowd to repent creates a persuasive rhetorical effect on Luke's readers, closing the gap between them and the narrator.

In each repetition there is a question, reply, and ethical instruction. The common thread in the exhortations is the responsible use of resources and the importance of equity in communal life. In the first exhortation, John speaks to the **crowd** about communal responsibility with material goods (v 11). In the second, he addresses **tax collectors**, and speaks of fairness in the gathering of taxes (v 13). Third, to the **soldiers,** he speaks of avoiding extortion and violence, bidding them to be content with their wages (v 14). These ethical deeds constitute the fruit of repentance (v 8; on John's preaching of repentance, see further Nave 2002, 146-59).

Narrative Structure of John's Ethical Instructions (3:10-15)

		QUESTION	REPLY	ACTION
vv 10-11		The crowd asks . . .	In reply he said . . .	Whoever has two coats must share . . .
vv 12-13		Tax collectors ask . . .	He said to them . . .	Collect no more than the amount prescribed . . .
vv 14-15		Soldiers also ask . . .	He said to them . . .	Do not extort . . . be satisfied with wages

The conscientious use of money as a sign of spiritual integrity is a special feature of Luke's Gospel. Here it finds expression in John's preaching to the crowds (see the commentary on 9:1-6; 11:39; 12:13-34; 16:10-15, 19-31; 19:13-27, 45-46; 21:1-4).

Following the radical apocalyptic tone in vv 7-9, it is ironic that John counsels nothing more than ethical conduct in the disposition of goods and participation in the local economy. He does not, for example, call on the crowd to rise up against Rome or the corrupt Jerusalem temple aristocracy. Neither does he condemn tax collectors for serving the oppressive powers. And Roman soldiers are encouraged only to be honest, rather than join a rebellion against the empire.

In spite of John's fiery apocalyptic rhetoric, the actual content of his preaching in Luke is apolitical. His is a moral vision rather than a political one.

There seem to be variant strands of traditional material here, some fiery and political, and some quiescent and accommodating. Luke brings these strands together, but not in an entirely convincing way. John's message is an odd combination of fiery judgment and moral persuasion.

As we will see in vv 19-20, John's preaching is certainly not taken as politically benign by the Roman client king, Herod. Nevertheless, Luke presents an apolitical John, probably in the interests of the community context of his readers. This Gospel was written in the painful years following the destruction of Jerusalem occasioned by an ill-fated revolution. The issues that sparked it were taxation and Roman occupation. These probably are still politically sensitive in Luke's community; and this explains Luke's portrayal of John as politically neutral.

4. "Are You the Messiah?" (3:15-17)

■ **15-17** Returning to the tone of vv 7-9, Luke again portrays John as an incendiary prophet of doom. The shift in tone is once again an indication of the complexity of apocalyptic material in the Synoptic Gospels, and evidence of Luke's attempt to tread the middle way. John *was* viewed as a revolutionary by Herod and died in a Perean jail as a political prisoner (Matt 14:3-12; Mark 6:17-29). Luke, in contrast to Matthew and Mark, does not comment on John's death.

John's relationship to Jesus' message of love is complex in Luke. The two traditions seem to be in a certain tension. John's question from prison about Jesus' identity, "Are you the one who was to come, or should we expect someone else?" (7:18), hints that John had misgivings about Jesus' approach to his messianic ministry.

The **people** in v 15 are presented as a more sympathetic group than the self-interested "crowd" in v 10. **The people were waiting expectantly and were all wondering in their hearts if John might possibly be the Christ.** The sense of expectation shows the excitement John's preaching produces in the crowd. His message raises hopes of deliverance in a time of political confusion and religious turmoil. This was probably just as true of Luke's community as it would have been in A.D. 27 when John preached. There is a subtext in Luke's portrayal of John: Should the voices of accommodation and appeasement to Roman hegemony win out? Or, is resistance the right path? This question was relevant to both periods.

In v 16 John turns to the subject of baptism. The juxtaposition of the baptism of **water** and the baptism of **fire** highlights the contrast between humble repentance and apocalyptic judgment. The water of baptism for repentance is personal and signals interior change. The baptism of fire, conversely, will sweep away the present order and change the course of history.

As biblical symbols, water and fire are both purifying elements, but by very different means (see Isa 4:4; Dunn 1970, 12). Water symbolizes moral purity (Pss 26:6; 51:2; Isa 1:16; Zech 13:1), and fire represents the purifying presence of God himself (Gen 15:17-18; Exod 3:2; 19:16-21; Isa 6:6-7; Mal 3:2). Water and fire were "purgative and refining for those who had repented, destructive . . . for those who remain impenitent" (Dunn 1970, 13).

The Messiah's advent, according to John, will come with the baptism of the **Holy Spirit**, described as a baptism of **fire** (v 16). John, Zechariah, Elizabeth, Mary, and Simeon have all been described as "full of the Holy Spirit." They were individuals upon whom the Holy Spirit rested (1:15, 35, 41, 67; 2:25). John's message offers this filling as available to the general populace: **he will baptize you** [plural, *hymas*] **with the Holy Spirit and with fire.**

This baptism **in** [*en*] **the Holy Spirit** is an expansion of the sacred community to include the common people. Along with that inclusion comes the experience of intimacy with God through the Holy Spirit, an intimacy formerly reserved only to the main characters in the drama: John, Zechariah, Elizabeth, Mary, Simeon, and Anna. John's message says there will be a sudden "democratization" of intimacy with God at the appearance of the Messiah. This is classic Lukan theology: The common people may share immediately in the Spirit-filled life through repentance (v 3).

The Baptism of the Holy Spirit in Luke

The language of the "filling of the Spirit" appears in 1:15, 35, 41, 67; and 2:25. Here in 3:16 it is a baptism *in the Holy Spirit*, a phrase that appears again in Acts 1:5. Does the usage in Acts refer to initiation into the community, as it seems to do here in the Gospel? Or, is it a reference to an empowering subsequent to initiation?

Arguments have been made in both directions (see Ervin 1984, Stronstad 1984, Dunn 1970). (Bock [1994, 322-24] lists four interpretive options on the baptism of Spirit and fire.) From a narrative perspective, it seems plausible to interpret this baptism in 3:16, and in Acts 1:5, as simply the doorway into the new holy community. If this is the correct interpretation, then the "baptism in the Spirit is not something distinct from and subsequent to entry into the Kingdom; it was only by means of the baptism in the Spirit that one could enter [the sacred community] at all" (Dunn 1970, 22).

The debate on the issue of subsequent empowerment later in Acts and throughout Paul is a matter of such complexity as to be best explored in those contexts. But here, in Luke 3, the language of Spirit baptism refers to induction into the Christian community.

There is a clear disjuncture between John's apocalyptic vision in ch 3 and the coming of the Spirit to the early Christian community at Pentecost in Acts 2. The language of Spirit baptism is the same, but the tone and substance are quite different. In Luke 3, John speaks urgently of impending doom. Baptism by fire and the Holy Spirit is the only way of escape. In Acts, by contrast, a new age has begun and the coming of the Spirit is both an initiation into the sacred community and an initiation into a lifetime witness and practice. Luke seems to weave these themes together in his larger two-volume work.

At v 17, John's voice once again takes on a severe tone. The "good news" of v 18 is counterbalanced by bad news for the **chaff**. Those people represented by chaff will be burnt **with unquenchable fire**, a terrifying image of destructive judgment. The Messiah will **gather the wheat into his barn**. This is a metaphor for final judgment but also refers to induction into the new messianic community. The interpretive framework of the rest of Luke's Gospel will be shaded by the apocalyptic threat introduced in Luke 3:7-17. The advent of the Messiah is to be accompanied by joy and expectation, but also by the threat of judgment.

The Wheat and the Chaff in the Old Testament

There are numerous references to chaff, wheat, and fire in the Bible. On a threshing floor, harvested wheat is thrown in the air with a large shovel (v 17). The light, outer husk of the grain, the chaff, is blown entirely away. The heavier straw drifts to the edge of the platform. And the grain, the densest part of the plant, falls directly to the floor. The wind blowing the chaff away from the grain represents the Spirit's separating the worthless from the worthwhile in biblical parlance.

In the OT, this imagery is applied to the covenant community during periods of infidelity to Yahweh. For example, those Israelites who offer idolatrous human sacrifices are like "chaff swirling from a threshing floor" (Hos 13:3). Those threatened with exile to Babylon are "like chaff driven by the desert wind" (Jer 13:24).

This imagery of chaff is also applied to the "wicked" outside the Israelite community, those beyond the pale of salvation (Ps 1:4; Job 21:18). Zephaniah 2:1-2 associates this imagery with the "Day of the Lord," a time of all-consuming judgment: "Gather together, gather together, O shameful nation, before the appointed time arrives and that day sweeps on like chaff, before the fierce anger of the Lord comes upon you, before the day of the Lord's wrath comes upon you."

Fire imagery is naturally associated with chaff, which connects it to the motif of judgment. Malachi 4:1 says of Israel: "'Surely the day is coming; it will burn like a furnace. All the arrogant and every evildoer will be stubble, and that day that is coming will set them on fire,' says the Lord Almighty." John uses this rich imagery of judgment to characterize the coming of the Messiah. It will be a time when the good will be separated from the wicked, like the wheat from the chaff.

Jesus uses similar imagery in his teachings. In the parable of the tares and the wheat in Matt 13:24-30: "Allow both [wheat and weeds] to grow together until the harvest; and in the time of the harvest I will say to the reapers, 'First gather up the tares and bind them in bundles to burn them up; but gather the wheat into my barn'" (v 30 NASB). In Matt 12:33-37, both the tree and fruit imagery and the "brood of vipers" language are found on Jesus' lips. In Luke 13:6-9, the unproductive fig tree is to be cut down.

5. Herod Arrests John (3:18-20)

■ **18-20** The **good news** (v 18, *euangelizō*, a verbal form) is announced by a variety of people in Luke. First, it is proclaimed by angels (1:19; 2:10), now by John the Baptist (3:18). Throughout the remainder of the Gospel the proclamation of the "good news" is central to the message of Jesus. (See 4:43 and the comment on 8:1-3.)

Herod Antipas (v 19) is the tetrarch of Galilee (as in 3:1; ruled 4 B.C.- A.D. 39). He is not to be confused with King Herod of 1:5. His son, Herod Antipas, rules on the west side of the Jordan in Galilee and in Perea on the east side, a region that extended from the river Arnon in the south to the Yarmuk River at the Sea of Galilee. Herod Antipas was married to the daughter of Aretas IV, king of Nabatea (9 B.C.—A.D. 40), the kingdom south of Perea.

This liaison produced a long period of peace between the two rulers. But Herod Antipas fell in love with **Herodias** (v 19), the wife of his half-brother Philip (Luke 3:1; Mark 6:17). Herodias demanded that Antipas divorce his Nabatean wife and marry her, which he did. This angered Aretas, to whom Antipas' first wife fled. Aretas and Antipas eventually went to war over the issue, a war in which Aretas prevailed.

John objected to the union of Herod Antipas and Herodias, because Jewish law forbade marriage to a brother's wife while the brother was living (see the commentary on Luke 15:11-16 and 20:27-40; compare Mark 6:18). John apparently asserts that such a liaison rendered Herod ritually impure and made him a lawbreaker (Webb 1991, 33, 367). Such preaching in the region of Perea would have damaged Herod's interests there.

It is not surprising that Herod did not tolerate such conduct from a populist who was gathering large crowds. Nabateans living in Perea took great offense at the snub of their royal household and no doubt supported John's agitation against Herod. This led to political instability in the area. Nevertheless, Herod adds insult to injury by ***throwing John in prison*** (v 20). Josephus says Herod moved against John because he feared an uprising led by John (*Ant.* 18.5.2, §118).

FROM THE TEXT

A baptism of repentance and an emphasis on ethics go hand-in-hand in John's message. The two form an inseparable bond in his preaching about religious experience. The proof of personal repentance is ethical reform; and reformed behavior is the hallmark of true repentance. The thrust of John's message is that ethical reform is an imperative of redemption and that Jewishness (or being descendants of Abraham) is meaningless if personal (and corporate) behavior is "crooked."

Personal holiness is the foundation of corporate holiness. And it is this corporate holiness that makes a people prepared for the Messiah. John will "prepare the way of the Lord" by preparing the hearts of people for the appearance of their Savior. They must exhibit personal and corporate holiness in order to be prepared for the Messiah's coming. Furthermore, implicit in John's message is the conviction that repentance and ethical reform should be reestablished as the center of Israel's self-understanding.

Zechariah prophesied that John's ministry would enable God's people "to serve him without fear in holiness and righteousness before him all our days" (1:74-75). He further prophesied that John would go before the Lord "to give his people the knowledge of salvation through the forgiveness of their sins" (v 77). *Then* the light from on high will appear. By extension, repentance begins to open the door to the community of the Messiah for Gentiles who also repent.

The central section of Luke conveys the message of salvation for the penitent. In chs 5—19, all the major figures act out ethical reforms and personal repentance—all of them are sinners: Peter the fisherman (5), the tax collector Levi (5), the sinful woman who anoints Jesus' feet (7), the prodigal son (15), the tax collector (18), and Zacchaeus the tax gatherer (19). In all these cases the characters are perfect examples of **penitent hearts producing worthy fruit** (3:8).

The main body of the Gospel is, in a sense, a showcase for the differences between penitent sinners and proud religionists. With unexpected irony, only those lost in sin recognize and respond to the message of Jesus. The inclusion of Gentiles in this salvation is the focus of the second volume of Luke's work, the Acts of the Apostles. But its seeds are here in the Third Gospel.

B. The Baptism of Jesus (3:21-22)

BEHIND THE TEXT

Angels and prophets announce the birth of Jesus and John in the first two chapters. But the status of Jesus as the Son of God is announced by a voice from heaven at his baptism. The birth announcements are prophetic; but the voice from heaven is supraprophetic—it is the voice of God himself. This lends a new level of narrative authority, one that challenges Torah-based faith. If fundamental issues such as the identity of the Messiah can be confirmed by a voice from heaven, Torah as the bedrock of Judaism is called into question.

The identity of Luke's community is a matter of surmise, but he makes this significant move away from Torah as the sole authority of faith without explanation. This implies that Luke's audience is not a traditional Jewish one, but more likely one for whom such an abnegation of Torah would be acceptable, as in a community of Diaspora Gentiles.

IN THE TEXT

■ 21-22 Luke, unlike Matt 3:13 and Mark 1:9, does not explicitly state that John baptized Jesus. **When all the people were being baptized, Jesus was baptized too** (v 21). Nor is it clear who hears the voice from heaven. In Matthew, it is a public event—"This is My beloved Son" (3:17 NASB). In Mark and Luke it seems to be a personal epiphany—"You are my Son." There are sparse details in Luke's report compared to Matthew and Mark. While deemphasizing its public nature, he retains the essence of the event—a divine authentication of Jesus' status.

This divine affirmation introduces no new information into the narrative. Readers already know Jesus' identity as Son of the Most High (1:32, 76), Son of God (1:35), and Savior of the house of David (1:69; 2:11). We already know about baptism (3:3, 7). And the Holy Spirit has been an active force throughout the narrative (1:15, 35, 41, 67; 2:25, 26; 3:16). All these features are already present in the narrative before Luke narrates Jesus' baptism.

What *is* different is the way all of these narrative features are brought together in a summative scene; and theological consolidation takes place here. From this location, the story moves aggressively forward into the ministry of Jesus (see Green 1997, 186). Two further things are to be observed.

First, in the scene where an inference of Trinitarian theology can first be discerned in the Gospel, the event is authenticated by a voice from heaven (*Bat Qôl*). The Father speaks from heaven; Jesus the Son is baptized on earth; and the Holy Spirit mediates God's presence. The heavenly voice is the ultimate, incontrovertible witness to a revelation by God. This is a *new* word from God, over and above past forms of revelation. Ironically, it confirms the truth of past OT pronouncements about the Messiah's advent.

Second, the Trinitarian theme, never overt in the Gospels, can be further developed in Luke, based on this foundational event. For example, readers are prepared to view the Son as the representative of the Father in the coming age (9:26). The intimate description of the Father/Son relationship in 10:21-22 seems a natural part of the developing theology, given what we know of Jesus' beginnings (also 22:29, 42; 23:34, 40). At the end of the Gospel, all three personae are present at the Ascension: "I am going to send you what my Father has promised; but stay in the city until you have been clothed with power from on high" (24:49). An implicit Trinitarian theology has been indirectly forged in the narrative.

The *Bat Qôl*

The *Bat Qôl*, literally the "daughter of a voice," was a well-known convention in Judaism (Gen 21:17; 22:11). As prophecy declined after the exile, the heavenly voice was considered by some to be the new form of prophetic communication. The voice from heaven represented the ultimate in revelation for matters beyond the reach of reason. The rabbis would only listen to an ostensible *Bat Qôl* when they "could not and never would, reach a conclusion by the force of [their] argumentation and reasoning" (Urbach 1987, 301). If accepted as authentic, such a voice was an authority against which no argument could be raised.

Still, sages wondered if a heavenly voice could legitimately settle disputes. After all, the prophets had received the seed of their teachings at Sinai through Moses. A *Bat Qôl*, by its very nature, challenged the view that the writings of the prophets were inviolable. If the prophetic tradition could be superseded by a *Bat Qôl*, then the permanence of Torah-based Judaism was obviously called into question.

In one rabbinic story Yahweh himself appeared at the back of a room full of sages who were arguing a point of Torah. When he raised his voice to offer an interpretation, the rabbis told him to hold his peace saying, "You gave Torah to us, now leave us to interpret it!" The Torah was from God, but the interpretation of it was the birthright of his children! It is easy to see why the Christian assertion about a voice from heaven designating Jesus as Messiah would have been controversial for traditional Jews, and why rabbinic stories to this effect came into being in the postdestruction period.

The descending **Spirit** (v 22) is described by Luke as *sōmatikōi*, **in bodily form**. This bodily form **descended** (*hōs peristeran*) **like a dove**. That is, the Spirit came, not in the image of a dove, but floating down as would a dove. In Luke there is a general tendency to describe the Spirit in terms of physical location. The Spirit will "overshadow" Mary (1:35). Now the Spirit descends (3:22) as an angelic being, floating down from above to alight on Jesus.

3:21-22

This descent of the Holy Spirit should be read in context with the passages in which Zechariah, John, Elizabeth, and Mary have been filled with the Holy Spirit. There, angelic visitors announced the Christ and imparted the Spirit (1:15, 35, 41, 67; 2:25). But here, at Jesus' baptism, the Spirit was seen to invade him bodily, a much more intense image. We cannot know whether this experience *inaugurated* Jesus' sense of his sonship or whether it was a *culmination* of a long process (see Dunn 1975, 62-67). But from a narrative perspective, it is the cessation of John's ministry and the beginning of Jesus' ministry.

The Voice from Heaven

Ps 2:7	Isa 42:1	Luke 3:22
You are my Son; today I have become your Father.	Here is my servant, whom I uphold, my chosen one in whom I delight.	You are my Son, whom I love; with you I am well pleased.

The voice from heaven says: *You are my beloved son; I rejoice in you!* (v 22). Two OT texts seem to inform the expression of the voice. Psalm 2:7 is considered by many to be one of the key texts underlying the NT usage of "Son of God" in general and Luke 3:22*a* in particular. But the phrase in Psalms is far from the profound title it becomes in the NT. Genesis 6:2; Deut 14:1; 2 Sam 7:14; Job 1:6; 2:1; 38:7; Pss 29:1; 82:6; 89:6; Hos 2:1, and other texts may also have influenced NT usage (Fitzmyer 1997, 2:103-7).

Under the influence of Ps 2:7, some scribes of the Western text altered Luke's text to say, "today I have begotten you" (Metzger 1975, 136). Luke 3:22 seems also to reflect the language of Isa 42:1*a*: "Here is my servant, whom I uphold, my chosen one in whom I delight" (also 2 Sam 22:20). The combination of ideas brought together by Luke is "not unparalleled in Judaism" (Marshall 1978, 156). But most likely it represents a bold departure by Christians to appropriate a profound title for Jesus (Fitzmyer 1997, 2:103, quoting Bousset).

Green captures the panoramic significance of the expression: "Here Luke demonstrates Jesus' reception of his divine vocation; his empowerment by the Holy Spirit; his status as a representative of David, Abraham, and indeed, all humanity; and his uncompromising solidarity with God's purpose" (1997, 184).

C. The Genealogy of Jesus (3:23-38)

BEHIND THE TEXT

There are two genealogies in the NT. Both occur in the introductory sections of their respective Gospels, Matthew and Luke. Both are derived from sources only available to that author; and they are quite different. Modern genealogies provide information about ancestry to satisfy the curiosity of descendants. The purpose of biblical genealogies is more specialized. Primarily, they connect individuals to their ancestry in order to establish their status and rights of inheritance and to secure legitimacy within a community. Such issues were important in cultures where kinship was the organizing principle of society (see 15:11-16 on kinship). In terms of historical value, ancient genealogies can range from factual to largely symbolic constructions, which take substantial liberties with succession and dating.

There are two types of genealogies, segmented and linear. The former is like a family tree and tends to span four or five generations. This type establishes either equality or superiority of rank among those of recent generations. The genealogies of Jesus are of the second, or linear type. They are simple lists that establish deep connection to ancestors. In the case of Matthew, it connects Jesus to Abraham. In the case of Luke, the connection penetrates all the way to "Adam, son of God." As such, both genealogies have great depth, or penetration into history, but they offer little in the way of verifiable historical content.

IN THE TEXT

■ **23-38** As an introduction to his genealogy, we are told that Jesus was **about thirty years old** when he began his ministry (v 23). Twelve was the age of manhood in Jewish culture. Thirty was the age for authority (*m. Avot* 5:21; Luke 4:6).

This chronological marker echoes the mention of Jesus' age of twelve in 2:42. Luke does not shift the temporal scene quite as abruptly as Matthew, who has a thirty-year gap between Jesus' birth and adult ministry. Still, Luke's jump of even eighteen years in time is significant. We might expect to find such liberties in epic literature from the period. But the Gospel genre takes similar literary liberties, unconcerned that the gap might diminish our understanding of the message.

Many have studied biblical genealogies. Attempts to reconcile their contents with history have proven unsuccessful (see the survey in Fitzmyer 1981, 1:488-98). Marshall calls the problems within genealogies "insoluble with the evidence presently at our disposal" (1978, 159). Johnson considers explorations of the historicity of genealogies "futile or even fatuous" (1991, 72).

In general terms, Luke has seventy-six names; Matthew has forty-two. Luke's names are listed in ascending order; Matthew's, descending. Where the lists cover the same period of biblical history, they agree in twelve names from Abraham to David, but only two from David to Joseph. Marshall reviews the various proposed solutions to these discrepancies without settling on a solution (1978, 157-61).

Wesley observed that, in spite of the technical difficulties of the genealogies, the "grand point in view" is that Jesus is the promised one from the seed of Abraham (Wesley 1981, vol. 1, notes on Matt 1:1). Both Matthew and Luke trace Jesus to **David**, and so on to **Abraham**. These connections are central to the claims of heritage that have been important to Luke in the story so far. Recall the care Luke took to establish the familial and priestly credentials of Zechariah and Elizabeth (1:5). Here Luke concludes his genealogy with the memorable phrase **the son of Adam, the son of God** (3:38).

The purpose of Luke's genealogy is to connect the ministry of Jesus to the broader generations of Adam, the father of *all* humanity, rather than just to the children of Abraham (3:6; Brower 2005, 17). This is one of the more significant points that can be made about Luke's extension of Jesus' genealogy back to the origins of the human family.

In his larger narrative structure, Luke's genealogy has another function. While the genealogy seems to interrupt the narrative flow, it actually solidifies the pedigree Luke has carefully set out: Jesus is born within the Jewish nation. He is a faithful member of that community, as are all around him. His credentials as a prophet and heir to David (through Joseph) are impeccable. In the wider scope of the story, this pedigree justifies Jesus' role as critic and

105

reformer of the faith. That is, his call for reform comes from within the community.

The location of Jesus' heritage within the human family also has significance for the incarnation. Jesus' human, physical roots extend deep into the ancestral family of Abraham. This witnesses to his humanity and identifies Jesus as one who participates fully in our human condition (see Brower 2005, 47, 51). Theologically, all Christology proceeds from this foundation.

III. JESUS' MINISTRY IN GALILEE: LUKE 4:1—9:50

A. The Beginning of the Ministry (4:1—5:11)

1. The Testing of Jesus (4:1-13)

BEHIND αTHE TEXT

Throughout the biblical story God has tested the loyalty of his servants. The names of these individuals evoke different images in the reader's mind: Adam and his "apple," Noah and his absurd ark, Abraham and the sacrifice of his son, Job and his suffering, Moses and his insurmountable odds, Elijah and his nemesis Jezebel and her prophets of Baal, Isaiah and his implacable opponents, Jonah at the bottom of the sea, and the nation of Israel itself, lost in her own wilderness for forty years.

All of these are pivotal figures in biblical history and provide valuable intertextual context for the testing of Jesus. Most have some sort of desert/wilderness motif, either literal (Moses, Elijah) or figurative (Adam, Job, Noah, Jonah). Most eventually "pass" their test of fidelity to God, but not without periods of failure. Others seem to fail outright. In most of these stories, the future of God's community hangs in the balance (excepting Job). Some of these elements are present in the testing of Jesus. Yet, none of these stories provides an exact parallel to his wilderness experience.

Jesus is "tempted" in the wilderness after his baptism (v 2). The NIV translates *peirazō* as **tempt;** but the context of this story suggests *test* as a better translation here. A test is any sort of analytical procedure designed to measure performance; and in any real test there is the possibility of failure. Jesus undergoes three such tests of fidelity to God at the hands of the devil. Each test comes from an external source not an "inner conflict" (Fitzmyer 1981, 1:510).

The point of the narrative is not that Jesus can resist temptation to sin; he never seriously waivers, as far as the narrative indicates. He has just been baptized and anointed by the Spirit; and a voice from heaven has proclaimed him the Son of God (3:21-22). In this context, the point seems to be that Jesus must demonstrate his readiness to take up his role as Messiah. The wilderness experience is not a test of Jesus' morals, but a test of his "performative competence" (Green 1997, 191). Fidelity to God is the primary qualification. It is in this sense that the story of Jesus' testing aligns itself intertextually with other biblical characters.

Jesus' identity as the Son of God does not exempt him from testing and suffering. His identity is rather the cause of testing. Luke has presented Jesus' advent as an integral part of God's purpose in history. But his incarnation exposes him to the fall of humanity, including the potential for sin and disobedience.

At no point in the testing does Jesus seem in danger of succumbing to the devil's test of his loyalty. Nevertheless, the test is a real one. That is, it can be failed. If this is not the case, there is no merit in passing it. If passing is inevitable, the narrative presentation of Jesus' humanity is reduced to mere appearance. On all these matters Luke is silent, leaving the theological work to his readers.

In 3:21—4:13 Luke briefly creates a parallel story-world in which spiritual powers come to the fore of the narrative. This parallel world is a world in which Jesus is a recessive figure. His personage is overshadowed in a contest arranged for him by the dominating spiritual powers.

The intervening genealogy (3:23-38) seems out of place inserted into such a spirit-centered segment of text. On the one hand, the purpose of the genealogy is to establish Jesus' ancestral pedigree, rights of inheritance, and legitimacy within the community of Abraham. On the other hand, the presence of the genealogy here in the narrative is intended to indicate that Jesus is not *just* a charismatic prophet. He is the prophet of the house and lineage of David in whom both heritage and the divine imprimatur converge. Unlike Matthew, who traces the genealogy of Jesus to Abraham (Matt 1:1), Luke traces the pedigree as far back as **son of Adam, son of God** (3:38). This is the potent combination all Israel has been awaiting.

As with all tests, Jesus' wilderness test is administered by others. He is delivered to the devil by the Holy Spirit (4:1) for a test of his fealty to the

108

purposes of God. This recessive identity indicates that Jesus is, at least temporarily, portrayed as God's agent rather than an independent entity. That he is God's agent in his "central, active role" in the Gospel and the "root of Jesus' identity in Luke-Acts" (Green 1997, 191).

As much as it might appear otherwise at points in the larger Gospel story, the question remains: Who is the real protagonist, the leading actor? Is it the Spirit (as in 4:1) or God (as in 1:19) or Jesus, or even the devil (as in 4:3)? Ultimately, God is the prime protagonist in the story-world. But he is also deeply veiled most of the time in the narrative. As here in the testing, other protagonists step forward at points to assume the leading role temporarily.

The language of 4:1-13 concerns the balance of power. Jesus does not decide to enter the wilderness; he is "led" there by the Spirit. Mark 1:12 (NRSV) goes so far as to say the Spirit "drove him out" (*ekballei*). Once in the wilderness, Jesus is "led" by the devil, who controls the encounter throughout.

Luke employs a flat characterization of Jesus here. There is no ambiguity or the tension of a wavering purpose. He is a stoic, impassive figure in a cosmic struggle. The devil is also flat in characterization. He wants only one thing—to shift Jesus' loyalty from God to himself. Moreover, both Jesus and the devil are agents representing the interests of their unseen and conflicting spiritual realms; they do not act as independent entities.

The devil has his grand moment in the wilderness testing. But his personal presence soon recedes in the narrative. He does not withdraw from the story, but goes "underground" working through Jesus' human and spiritual antagonists, ironically, including his disciples Judas and Peter (22:3, 31; compare also Matt 16:21 ‖ Mark 8:31). He reemerges in the passion narrative at the seduction of Judas (22:3; see Pagels 1995, 90).

The temptation of Adam has been proposed as an interpretive lens for Jesus' wilderness testing (e.g., Neyrey 1985, 165-84; Evans and Sanders 1993, 36-45). If the encounter with the devil is viewed as enticement to sin in a seductive sense, Luke (it is claimed) casts Jesus as the new Adam. He endures a garden-like test of his obedience to God. The serpent tests Eve in the garden: "Indeed, has God said, 'You shall not eat from any tree of the garden'?" (Gen 3:1 NASB). Jesus is *tempted* to sin, as the new Adam with a new "apple." The forbidden fruit is not knowledge, as with Adam, but hegemony over the world.

Jesus' successful passing of the test secures the redemption of humanity from the original fall by leading him to the cross, and so conquering Adam's sin that binds us. In this reading, Jesus, the second Adam, reverses the grievous error of the first man by his righteous resistance to the devil. "But unlike Adam, whose failure resulted in defeat and death at the hands of Satan, Jesus' success results in life (cf. 1 Cor 15:45)" (Evans and Sanders 1993, 45).

Other authors have seen the narrative of Luke through the lens of the story of Israel (Tannehill 2005, 125-44). Abraham's sacrifice of Isaac is a significant intertext (Gen 22:1-14). Abraham's commitment to God is tested by the command to offer his son as a sacrifice: "Some time later God tested Abraham" (Gen 22:1; Heb: *nsa*, LXX: *peirazō*). God tests Abraham to ascertain whether his commitment is genuine, whether he is qualified to be the father of many nations. After preventing him from killing his son by a heavenly voice (*Bat Qôl*, suggestive of Luke 3:22), God reaffirms his promise to make a great nation of Abraham (Gen 22:15-19). The patriarch of Israel overcomes a test of his loyalty at the inauguration of the covenant.

Jesus' wilderness experience is an inaugural testing of his loyalty and fitness for his sonship. Abraham inaugurates the first covenant by means of a sacrificial test of his son, and God inaugurates the second or new covenant by means of a test of his own Son (see 1:55, 73; 3:8, 34, where the Abraham story is foundational to Jesus' advent).

The wilderness wandering of Moses and the people of Israel is another instance of a "test" of a biblical figure (Deut 8:2; again Heb: *nsa*, and LXX: *ekpeirazō*; see Green 1997, 192). Israel is God's "firstborn son" (Exod 4:22) just as Jesus is God's Son. Both are tested by the Father. Deuteronomy 8:2 says, "Remember how the LORD your God led you all the way in the desert these forty years, to humble you and to test you in order to know what was in your heart, whether or not you would keep his commands." The themes of being led into the desert, forty years/days (see Exod 16:35; 24:18; 34:28) and testing are present in both stories. Jesus himself quotes Deut 6:16 to the devil (Luke 4:12: "Do not put the Lord your God to the test") comparing his own testing to that of Israel's trials in the desert.

The dissimilarities between Jesus and Israel are just as striking. Luke's point could well be that Jesus passes his test in the wilderness, whereas Israel did not. Thus, Jesus shows himself obedient to God's call and prepared to assume his duties as Messiah (Green 1997, 193; Fitzmyer 1981, 1:510). Furthermore, Israel's wilderness wandering is a punishment for her guilt of disobedience (see Josh 5:6). This is not the case for Jesus or Abraham; both are innocent.

Job is another figure that may provide some intertextual background for Jesus' testing. (Bock [1994, 364] calls Job the "closest OT parallel." But he insists that Jesus' testing is an "unprecedented" incident in biblical literature.) Job is one of the Bible's pious pagans, similar to Melchizedek, Jonah's sailors and the king of Nineveh, and Cyrus, king of Persia. The overarching question of the book of Job is philosophical in tone and represented by the adversary's question: "Does Job fear God for nothing?" (Job 1:9). Both Job and Jesus are innocent figures, presumed pure by God. Both emerge from the test vindicated; but Jesus more so than Job.

Most striking is the "deal" struck between the adversary (Heb: *stn*, Satan; LXX: *diabolos*) and God in Job. Have the Holy Spirit and the devil (*ho diabolos*) similarly cooperated in Luke? In Job, the deal is explicit (Job 1:6-12). In Luke it is implicit. That is, the negotiation between God and the devil is held off the stage, prior to the encounter with Jesus. But the Spirit clearly leads Jesus into the wilderness. Jesus' conduct in his desert testing could be considered the supreme example of selfless piety. Job faltered somewhat (Job 3), but Jesus stood firm in his loyalty and obedience to God.

In terms of the structure of Luke 3:1-13, Luke used two features. The first is a series of contrasts used to heighten the drama in the testing scene. The second feature is an event, saying, and response structure.

Narrative Contrasts Used by Luke in the Testing Scenes

Jesus led by Spirit (v 1)	Jesus led by devil (v 5)
Jesus full of Holy Spirit (v 1)	Jesus tested by devil (v 2)
The Jordan River (v 1)	The wilderness (v 2)
Jesus "full" of the Spirit (v 1)	Jesus' stomach "empty" (v 2)
Bread (v 3)	Stone (v 3)
Forty days (v 2)	An instant (v 5)
Up (vv 5, 9)	Down (v 9)

Structure of Tests in Luke

Event	Saying of the Devil	Response from Scripture by Jesus
vv 1-2	v 3	v 4
v 5	vv 6-7	v 8
v 9	vv 9b-11	v 12

The presentation of the testings is formulaic. Despite the mystical nature of the tests, the style of the narrative is matter-of-fact. Luke gives no indication that this is a dream or vision. The events of forty days are compressed into a brief passage; and there is a sense of being swept along in a chaotic experience. Time cascades rapidly. This narrative treatment is quite different from the slow-motion pace Luke used in the Mary and Elizabeth texts.

From a synoptic perspective, Matthew and Luke have used their Q source to expand Mark's brief treatment of the tests in Mark 1:12-13 (see Fitzmyer 1981, 1:506-8). Matthew and Luke vary the order of the three trials. Matthew places the challenge to test God by leaping from the pinnacle of the temple second; Luke places it third. This allows Luke, as usual in the Gospel, to conclude the scene in Jerusalem. Beyond this, the treatments in Matthew and Luke are essentially the same.

IN THE TEXT

■ **1-2** Jesus **returned from the Jordan** (v 1), the region southeast of Jericho where his baptism took place (see 3:3). A seventh-century tradition locates the testing in the arid desert mountains above Jericho, northeast of Jerusalem. The so-called Mount of Temptation towers in the distance above Jericho. With its themes of wilderness wandering and fasting, the testing of Jesus has long been a traditional text for the season of Lent, a time of fasting for forty days before Easter.

The narrative setting contrasts the lushness of the **Jordan** River with the barrenness of the **desert** mountain. We recall that John had just prophesied that the paths of the Lord would be straightened in the "desert," the mountains leveled and the valleys filled in (3:3-6). John's metaphorical call for a conquest of mountains and valleys is followed by Jesus' battle with the devil. This occurs in the desert wilderness and mountains surrounding Jericho, a partial fulfillment of John's words.

Jesus is said to be at once *full of the Holy Spirit* and *led* by him. Yet, he is also *tested by the devil.* The narrative presents these two polarities: Holy Spirit and devil. They appear as actors on a cosmic stage, waging a battle with Jesus in the middle. Readers know nothing about the person of Jesus at this point in the text. He is described in spare terms—we know only that he "hungers" and "answers" the devil. His character only becomes more complex in the narrative as the desert testing is complete and he enters Nazareth.

The test is conducted by the devil. But it is not a dualistic event in the sense that the powers of good and evil are equal. It is a monotheistic event, in that the contest is overseen and permitted by the Spirit, God's representative in the story. As in Job, God's supremacy is not in doubt in the narrative. Nor does there seem to be a serious possibility that God's plan will be derailed by defeat at the hands of the devil (Kingsbury 1991, 14). Still, theologically, the potential failure of the Messiah must be real, as with any true test (see Brower 2005, 51). Otherwise, the narrative is drained of moral force.

The *diabolos* is not a high priest of evil here. He is rather an antagonist after the style of Satan in the OT:

- In the story of Job (1:6), he is the slanderer or adversary, the one who serves the function of the court skeptic and troublemaker (Job 1—2). He is like the devil's advocate [Latin: *advocatus diabolic*] in Roman Catholicism's beatification process, whose job is to raise objections to the granting of sainthood (Cline 1989, 25).
- We might also compare Zech 3:1-5, in which Satan stands to "accuse" the high priest Joshua in the presence of the angel of the Lord.
- Similarly, in 1 Chr 21:1, Satan "incited" David to take a census. These three incidents represent Satan's activity in the OT: he "tests, he accuses, he leads astray" (Garrett 1989, 39).

In Job, *the satan* stands *within* the heavenly court as an official cynic. For him the preeminence of good is not an accepted fact. The *diabolos* in the testing of Jesus does not accept that good is incorruptible. He believes that even Jesus can be corrupted by vulgar rewards. He is dangerous to Jesus, not simply because he is supernatural, but because he is so intelligent (Pagels 1995, 39).

What he says makes perfect sense, especially to those whose experience tells them that good is in short supply in the world.

In Job 2:4, Satan plays this role perfectly, "'Skin for skin!' Satan replied. 'A man will give all he has for his own life.'" Just as in Job, Jesus' testing is orchestrated by God. It is a test in which *God* must demonstrate the Son can pass. The devil is merely an instrument in the procedure. In the Abraham narrative, the function of the test is much the same. But the important difference is that God himself assumes the role of the adversary.

Luke uses the term *ho satanas* as a proper name five times in his Gospel (10:18; 11:18; 13:16; 22:3, 31). But he uses *ho diabolos* here in ch 4 (vv 2, 3, 5, 9, 13). This usage seems closer to the impersonal accuser/adversary/slanderer, **the satan**, of Job and the OT generally.

In the so-called intertestamental period, the earliest known use of *satanas* as a proper name is *Jub.* 23:29 and *As. Mos.* 10:1 in the second century B.C. But in the OT Apocrypha and Pseudepigrapha, references to these types of figures increase in number. This was likely under the influence of Persian religion, with which Jews came in contact during the exile (Hamilton 1992, 988). In this literature, a wide variety of terms are used to describe demonic characters, and Satan as a proper name is only occasionally found. The term occurs only three times in the Qumran literature (1QH 4:6; 45:3; 1QSb 1:8; see further Hamilton 1992, 987-89) and never as a proper name.

Tested in the Desert: Real or Scripted?

Is Jesus' testing in the wilderness a real test or merely some preordained script he must act out in the divine plan? The portrayal shows not a hint of wavering on Jesus' part. But a fully incarnate Jesus must have been at real risk of failure in the test of obedience. In order to have theological and practical importance for the church, Jesus' choice to live in holiness must have been real. And it is real only if the testing was real.

This has implications for the role of Jesus as an example for Christians. Jesus becomes for us a model of holiness *within* his human experience (see Brower 2005, 18). He calls his followers to holiness from his place within humanity, not from a place above it or beyond it.

Jesus passed his test by virtue of his messianic identity (3:22b) but also by his oneness with the Spirit (4:1, 14). This calls disciples to persevere in the contest of loyalties we face through reliance on the Spirit. Such a view changes the challenge of the holy life from one focused on resistance to the seductions of temptation (as necessary as that is at times) to a life of active affirmation of the will of God. Our every decision calls for loyalty to God and the desire to tread the path to which he calls us.

The **Holy Spirit** is not mentioned in vv 5-13. In contrast to the **devil**, he stands quietly offstage as Jesus struggles alone with his protagonist. Indeed, the

Holy Spirit is upon him (3:22), fills him, and leads him (4:1). He will soon fill Jesus with power (4:14). But the contest with the devil seems to be Jesus' to win or lose. Yet, it is not his struggle alone. As God's agent, the Spirit is also present with Jesus, but only in a secondary, supporting role. The dignity of free will is given to Jesus. At the same time he feels the strength of the Spirit's presence.

Also found in the narrative is a contrast between **full** (v 1) and **hungry** (v 2). Jesus is full of the Spirit but empty of stomach. Hunger is one of the most visceral of human needs, and Jesus must have been at the limit of human endurance. Survivalists say that in extreme conditions a human being can go three hours without shelter, three days without water, and three weeks without food. Coming at the end of the forty days, the temptation to turn a **stone** into **bread** (v 3) comes to Jesus in a time of absolute physical need. It is, thus, the ultimate test of his incarnation. His passing of this test shows that incarnation has not compromised the divine presence in Jesus. He, in fact, shows himself to be above the corruption that comes with humanity. The test is real and so is the moral force of Jesus' choice to remain loyal to God's will.

■ **3-4** The Greek of v 3 is spare and the devil's words have the power of simplicity: **If you are the Son of God.** This is the first of three questions introduced by the conditional conjunction, "if" (vv 3: *ei*, 7: *ean*, 9: *ei*). Verses 3 and 9 pose the question of sonship in identical language. This taunt is a direct challenge to the *Bat Qôl* of 3:22 and seems calculated to wound and provoke a weak man.

The devil is astute. As Jesus is experiencing Exodus-style hunger, the devil proposes a divine solution similar to manna, **bread** from **stone** (see Green 1997, 194). How could the Son object to creating bread for himself? After all, God saved the Israelites miraculously, why should not the Son be saved as Scripture promises (Ps 33:18-19; Deut 28:1-14)? But Jesus refuses to use his divine status for self-preservation. That is, his refusal is sacrificial in nature. Is his prayer for God's day-by-day provision later in 11:3 informed by his desert experience of hunger? The need for sustenance cannot lead him (or us) outside of God's will.

Given Jesus' hunger, satiation is the perfect test of his will. But to contravene the laws of nature by turning a stone into bread, as the devil proposes, would require Jesus to violate the reality of his incarnation, and thus fail God's test. Jesus' refusal to act out of self-interest demonstrates that his experience of the Spirit is never turned to his own advantage. He walks in the Spirit to bring good news to the poor, not glory and food to himself (4:18). This is a significant lesson for the Spirit-filled church (Acts 8:18-20).

Jesus quotes Deut 8:3 to the devil: "Man does not live on bread alone but on every word that comes from the mouth of the LORD." This passage comes from Moses' sermon to Israel on the eastern banks of the Jordan, not far from the Mount of Temptation. There Moses warned the Israelites of the dangers of the conquest they were to attempt in Canaan. The progeny of the nation and the occupation of the promised land were dependent on obedience to Yahweh's commandments. In the same way, the inauguration of Jesus' ministry, his own Jordan crossing, must stand the test of loyalty to God's commandments.

■ **5-8** The **high place** (v 5, *anagagōn*, lit., "led him up") to which the devil takes Jesus is a summit, a place from which one can see afar. The narrative uses the imagery of ascension to build to a climax in the scene. Here again is the formula of event/devil speech/Scripture response of Jesus.

The heavenly tour of Jesus and the devil has a contemporary intertext in a pseudepigraphic narrative from the end of the first century A.D., the *Testament of Abraham*. There, the archangel Michael is sent by God to gather Abraham's soul to his fathers in death. Abraham refuses to go and demands a tour of the "inhabited world." Michael puts him in a chariot and they soar above the world where they see all the activities of humanity on display (*T. Ab.* 10:1-15).

Apparently, the devil takes Jesus on a similar whirlwind tour of **all the kingdoms of the world** (v 5). The offer of the gift of **all their authority and splendor** (v 6) parallels what God has already promised Jesus: "of his kingdom there will be no end" (1:33 NRSV; see Ps 2:7-8). This is the "event" portion of the threefold structure. The condition for this gift of authority and splendor is stark: **So if you worship me, it will all be yours** (v 7). But Jesus remains true to his identity as the "Son" (3:22). He draws from the fullness of the Spirit in him (4:1) and refuses to take this shortcut to exaltation.

In his response to the conditional offer Jesus quotes Deut 6:13: **It is written: "Worship the Lord your God and serve him only"** (Luke 4:8). This refers to the warning to the Israelites to refuse to follow other gods in the land of Canaan, which they are about to enter. The "authority and splendor" on offer by "the devil" are compared, figuratively, to the false gods of Canaan. It is not that these powers are less than real. But Yahweh is jealous of the affections of his people, just as in the Exodus.

FROM THE TEXT

The danger of evil is sometimes found in its similarity to good: a false prophet's predictions come true (Deut 13:1-3); 666 is just less than the divine perfection of 777 (Rev 13:18); the false messiah appears outwardly to be the genuine figure and is easily misidentified as the real Messiah (Luke 21:8; 2 Cor 11:13-15). The danger of evil is the way it masquerades as the right path.

The devil tempts Jesus to circumvent the constraints of his humanity by taking an easier path to his rightful heritage than the one required by his incarnation. The destination is the same; the devil simply and reasonably suggests, "Why not take another path? The only cost is small—just worship me." The path of the highest good often involves suffering and difficulty in the biblical story. Such was the case with Jesus. And so it may be with us.

IN THE TEXT

■ **9-12** The devil takes Jesus to the pinnacle of the temple to test him with another act of self-preservation. The temple was the symbol of all that was holy in first-century Judaism. The devil's position on its **highest point** (v 9) amplifies the blasphemy of his taunt. It also reiterates the "high place" of v 5 and echoes the devil's dubious claim to authority and exaltation.

In a duel of Scripture citations, the devil quotes Ps 91:11-12: **For it is written: "'He will command his angels concerning you to guard you carefully; they will lift you up in their hands, so that you will not strike your foot against a stone'"** (Luke 4:10-11). Jesus' response is from the same Deut 16 passage he quoted in the second test. This time, the response is from v 16: **"Do not put the Lord your God to the test."**

The Deuteronomy text refers to the testing of God by the people of Israel at Massah in Exod 17:1-7. There the people were dying of thirst and "tested" the Lord, demanding to know, "Is the LORD among us or not?" Perhaps Jesus' use of this passage reflects an understanding that the sin of Massah was the failure to trust Yahweh explicitly, no matter how desperate the situation. At issue for Jesus, as earlier for Israel, is fidelity to God.

■ **13** The devil now leaves Jesus **until an opportune time**. The comment seems to refer to his reappearance in the passion narrative at the seduction of Judas (22:3). Otherwise, there is only the brief reference to him as a character in the parable of the sower (8:12). From a narrative point of view, the devil is decisively and handily dismissed as a less than formidable opponent in the story. As Milton put it, the devil is "quite at a loss, for all his darts were spent." The contest of the cosmos was not even close to being lost in these tests. Jesus passed his Exodus-like test with unswerving fidelity to God and a genuinely selfless, Job-like piety.

FROM THE TEXT

In Dostoevsky's *Brothers Karamazov*, the Grand Inquisitor argues that Christ could have solved all of humankind's problems had he only yielded to the devil's tests. Miracles, mystery, and authority—this is what base and ignorant people really require, the devil argues. Give them miraculous bread to quiet their stomachs, mystery to still their confused minds, and authority to relieve them of the painful responsibilities of freedom. Meet these needs, he argues, and humankind will happily surrender freedom for tyranny.

Christ resisted the arguments of the Inquisitor, believing the greater good was the freedom of people to have faith. The Inquisitor's certainties could not be used to circumvent a fundamental right of creation—the freedom to choose (as in Gen 3:1-7). Yes, hunger, confusion, and the uncertainties of self-determination are burdens shared by all humans; but to rescind human freedom would be tragic, argues Dostoevsky's Christ.

Jesus shows his fealty to God in resisting the devil in the Gospel narrative. But, more importantly, he shows us a better path in life—one to which we are called. Ours is not a predetermined life, but one in which we are free truly to engage the world created by God. The Inquisitor argues that humankind could have been truly happy with miracles, mystery, and authority. But Jesus instead gives us freedom, a higher and more profound calling.

It is the freedom to doubt or have faith, to hate or love, to go one's own way or follow in the steps of another. This freedom brings with it the burdens of the thinking life and its attendant moral responsibilities. But this life of freedom, though complex, difficult, and sometimes painful, is to be desired more than certainty.

2. Jesus Returns to Nazareth (4:14-30)

BEHIND THE TEXT

Jesus' visit to Nazareth is found in the triple tradition (Matt 13:54-58 || Mark 6:1-6 || Luke 4:14-30). This scene demonstrates how Luke typically shapes his story from traditional material. This passage reveals Luke's distinctive hand in numerous ways: *First*, Luke places the incident at Nazareth at the beginning of Jesus' Galilean ministry. Mark and Matthew mention the visit only incidentally, and at the midpoint of the Galilean ministry. In Matthew, the visit follows an extensive presentation of Jesus' teachings. Matthew notes only that they "took offense" at him in Nazareth so that he could do no miracles there (13:57-58). Mark's treatment is even more brief and incidental (6:1-6). Most importantly, it follows an extensive period of ministry in Capernaum (Mark 1:21; 2:1).

Luke is aware of Jesus' previous activity in Capernaum (4:23). Nonetheless, he makes the visit to his hometown in Nazareth the inaugural event of his public ministry. This sets a definitive tone of conflict and rejection for the entire ministry. Only Luke mentions that, after reaching out to his own community, Jesus finds himself threatened with death (v 29). This theme foreshadows the crucifixion and will be repeated frequently in the Galilean ministry (9:44, 51; 13:31; 17:22; 18:31-34; 19:47).

Second, distinctive of the Nazareth narrative in Luke's composition is its unique structural arrangement. Jesus enters two synagogues back to back in vv 14-15 and 16-30. The results are diametrically opposed at the outset of the narrative (Tannehill 2005, 8, 12). In the surrounding synagogues, Jesus is "praised by everyone" (v 15 NRSV), while the people of Nazareth reject him.

The juxtaposition of different synagogue receptions is expanded by the addition of the story of the synagogue at Capernaum in vv 31-37. The people of Capernaum are amazed and proclaim his authority. This further highlights his rejection by the Nazarenes (Fitzmyer 1981, 1:528-29). One's response to Jesus is the key to entering the community of the penitent in Luke. These synagogues serve as paradigmatic representations of possible responses to Jesus and his message within the Gospel. Choice is the emerging theme.

Third, the conflict in Nazareth foreshadows the civic rejection of Jesus and alienation from his family (see 2:34; 10:13-16; 12:52-53). Luke alone omits the humanizing reference to Jesus' siblings included in Mark 6:3 and Matt 13:55. In Luke, Jesus is alone from the beginning of the ministry. He is never portrayed as a man of family.

Fourth, only in Luke (vv 18-19) does Jesus read from Isa 61:1-2. This passage touches on the themes of poverty, liberation, and blindness mentioned earlier in the songs of Mary and Zechariah (1:52-53, 71, 79). This distinctive Lukan concern for the disadvantaged will reappear in 6:20b; 12:33; 14:13, 21; 15:14-19; 16:19-30; and elsewhere.

Fifth, other unique features arise from Luke's substantial expansion of two aspects of the synoptic material. Matthew and Mark note only that the inhabitants of Nazareth "took offense" at Jesus (Matt 13:57; Mark 6:3), whereas Luke supplies a long digression on the cause of the offense (4:23-30). Matthew and Mark simply note that Jesus could do no great miracles in Nazareth and marveled at their unbelief (Matt 13:58 || Mark 6:6). Luke again extends the narrative with an account of the attempted stoning of Jesus for heresy (4:28-30). Thus, for Luke, the Nazareth incident is the source of conflict in the story.

There is an intimacy in the writing style of Luke's narrative treatment of the Nazareth scene. Time moves slowly and we feel as though we are present in the crowded synagogue. We can hear his neighbors at first respond approvingly of their favorite son, only to become angry and violently reject him.

Luke gives readers insight into the close-knit community of Nazareth, a hamlet of about four hundred people. We feel the pain of alienation in Jesus' rejection (Reed 2000, 152). The peace of the town is shattered by religious turmoil. Its intensity points to the deeply troubling nature of the disagreement over the words and identity of their native son.

The Synagogue in the First Century

The incident at the synagogue in Nazareth is one of few pre-A.D. 70 references to early synagogue practice in Judaism. It is considered the oldest description of what actually took place in a first-century synagogue (Kimball 1994, 101). In fact, here and Acts 13:13-15 are our primary sources for the way synagogue was conducted in Jesus' day. Curiously, the term "synagogue" never appears in the writings of Paul.

Synagogue services consisted of readings from the OT, perhaps in the local dialect, here Aramaic. There would also be the recitation of set prayers, a homily by one of the prominent members in the community, and a benediction (Kimball

1994, 101). The readings would have customarily been from the Law and the Prophets. This is the case with Jesus here and with Paul in Acts 13:13-15.

The use of the Psalms was also common in the synagogue. Paul quoted from the Psalms three times in his synagogue sermon in Pisidian Antioch in Acts 13:16-41. Psalms is the most quoted book in the NT. We know that the use of the Psalms was, at one point, prohibited in synagogues, since it was thought to detract focus from the Law and the Prophets (*m. Sabb.* 16.1; see Neale 1991, 77).

IN THE TEXT

■ **14-15** Luke uses a summary formula to make the transition from one stage of the story to the next. The summary has:
- a geographical aspect (he **returned to Galilee** via Capernaum)
- a supernatural aspect (**in the power of the Spirit**)
- a public aspect (**and news about him spread through the whole countryside**)

Jesus' power in the Spirit is already manifesting itself in mighty deeds as reports about him spread (see 4:23).

From a narrative perspective, the ministry of Jesus is now fully launched. We are prepared as readers for the next stage of work—his teaching, exorcism, and healing activity in Galilee. Verse 15 indicates that Jesus **taught in their synagogues**. It introduces two synagogue scenes in sequence; one in Nazareth (vv 16-30) and one in Capernaum (vv 31-37).

He taught in their synagogues, and everyone praised him (v 15). Crowd approval is a theme Luke will mention again in v 22. It sets the coming rejection in Nazareth in higher narrative relief. The narrative will return to this approbation after the violent interlude in the Nazareth synagogue (4:32, 36; 5:26; 8:56; 9:43; 11:14; see the commentary on 2:15-21).

■ **16-19** Jesus quotes Isa 61:1-2 as a self-reference in his home synagogue. For the first time he publicly declares his self-understanding as the **anointed** of God. And he does this to the people among whom he was **brought up** (v 16). There is little evidence that assigned readings from the Prophets were used in synagogues in this period. When Jesus was handed the Isaiah scroll the selection of this specific text was his choice (v 17, see Fitzmyer 1981, 1:531-32).

The quotation itself is a conflation of Isa 61:1-2 and 58:6 (see 6:20-21; 7:22; Acts 4:27; 10:38 for other allusions to this passage in Luke). Since Jesus is said to "read" the text (v 16), some interpreters describe the synagogue scene in Nazareth as a Lukan composition. That is, the appropriation of the Isaiah texts has "programmatic" or "typical" significance in defining the purpose of Jesus' anointing. (Marshall [1978, 178, 180] does not dismiss the "historicity" of the event. See Tannehill 2005, 4.) Other interpreters suggest that such mixed texts were not unusual in synagogue readings. Readers would often select mixed texts by "word tallying." That is, two texts, Isa 61:1 and

58:6, sharing a common word such as *aphesis* here, were linked for the reading (Evans and Sanders 1993, 21). Even so, the Nazareth scene was no doubt subject to shaping by Luke toward a programmatic end.

Jesus declares that **the Spirit of the Lord is on me** (v 18). Luke has repeatedly noted how the leading characters in his narrative have been touched by the Spirit. They have been "filled" (1:35, 41, 67; 2:25) with the Spirit. He has "revealed" something to them (2:26), "guided" them (2:27 NRSV), or will "baptize" them (3:16, 21). This theme culminates for Jesus in 3:22. There, the Spirit descends "on" him, as a dove. Now, the Spirit is also said to rest "on" Jesus, anointing him for his mission. Luke's sense of a sacred location for the Spirit, upon people, is similar to the presence of the Spirit on the ancient prophets (see the commentary at 1:67 and 2:25-26).

The text defines Jesus' ministry in terms of compassion and **good news** for the **poor, prisoners, blind,** and **oppressed** (4:18; see the commentary on 8:1). In what one calls "likely the most important passage in Luke-Acts" (Kimball 1994, 97), compassion for the disadvantaged is placed at the center of this Gospel.

Isaiah 61:2, **the year of the Lord's favor** (v 19), refers to the year of the Jubilee and its attendant ideas of the forgiveness of debts, the repatriation of property, and the release of slaves (Evans and Sanders 1993, 21-22). This would have been, Sanders suggests, one of the favorite passages of the congregation. They, no doubt, viewed themselves as the referents for whom deliverance was promised. Upon hearing Jesus' interpretation, which identified Gentiles as the referents, their admiration turned to offense.

In chs 5—19 the story returns again and again to this theme of the compassionate treatment of the disadvantaged. The definition of "poor" is to be understood in terms of a range of issues relating to status in Mediterranean culture rather than simple poverty. This broader understanding of the "poor" accords well with the range of individuals represented as sinners in Luke. While some are economically poor, others are poor in "education, gender, family heritage, religious purity, vocation, economics and so on" (Green 1997, 211; see 209-13).

Luke's social vision is one in which the present societal structures will be upended. Oppression and need will be abolished by the reign of God. Joy will replace the suffering of the lowly (see Isa 58:6-9; see the commentary on 1:46-53; 6:17-26, 27-31; and 7:18-23).

Luke and Isaiah

Luke believes that the understanding of Scripture is the key to interpreting the life of Jesus. He has "a deep-seated conviction that a correct reading of Scripture, Moses and the Prophets, give one the ability to see what is going on in the real world" (Evans and Sanders 1993, 18).

There are five hundred ninety references to Isaiah in twenty-three books of the NT. These references cite sixty-three of Isaiah's sixty-five chapters (Evans and Sanders 1993, 14). This inaugural quotation from Isa 61 sets the agenda for Jesus' ministry. This may be seen in the culminating reference to the importance of Scripture in understanding Jesus' identity and purpose emphasized in 24:44-47 (see 16:29-31; see Evans and Sanders 1993, 14-25). These two references form a parenthesis around the ministry, placing the correct interpretation of Scripture at the center of a correct understanding of Jesus.

■ **20-22** The moment of Jesus' self-revelation has a dramatic literary setting. With every eye in the synagogue **fastened** on him (*atenizō*: "look intently"), Jesus announces: **"Today this scripture is fulfilled in your hearing."** Significantly, the Lukan Jesus does not complete the Isaiah text, which refers to the "day of vengeance." This is an announcement of hope, not judgment. So Luke downplays the Deuteronomistic bent of Isa 61:2*b* (Fitzmyer 1981, 1:532). The presentation of Jesus' self-concept here focuses on compassion, not judgment (see John 3:17).

All in the synagogue initially **spoke well of** Jesus. They **were amazed at the gracious words that came from his lips** (v 22). But his interpretation of their favorite text changed their attitude. In other settings in Luke, "amazement" is a term of genuine approbation (2:18, 47; 4:22, 32, 36; 5:26). But here its purpose seems to be to set the coming rejection in particularly high relief.

■ **23-30** The next significant Lukan digression from Mark and Matthew is contained in vv 23-27. There Luke explains how Jesus offends his fellow villagers. At v 23 Jesus' visit home takes a dark turn. Just as "all spoke well of him" (v 22), Jesus seems intent on provoking his hometown residents.

Jesus refers to **Elijah**'s provision of food to the Gentile woman of **Zarephath** during a drought (v 26; 1 Kgs 17:8-24). He also mentions **Elisha**'s healing of **Naaman the Syrian**, a Gentile leper (v 27; 2 Kgs 5:1-19; see the commentary on Luke 5:12-16). Jesus' reference to these two prophets implies that they set the precedent for his prophetic ministry. Like theirs, his mission will be reserved for Gentiles, not God's elect, Israel (see further the Introduction, Theological Themes in Luke).

One of the distinctive concerns of Luke/Acts is the issue of Jewish and Gentile relations. The inclusion of Gentiles in salvation finds repeated expression in Luke/Acts (see 7:1-10, Behind the Text). To suggest God will favor Gentiles over Jews in the plan of salvation was to reject the central tenet of Judaism: Israel's primacy as the covenant community of Yahweh.

Such a critique of Israel's narrow-mindedness was a common theme in the message of the prophets of Israel and Judah (see 1:32; 3:8, 16-17; 13:24-30) and always nettlesome to a temple-based Judaism. No wonder his hometown neighbors were spurred to anger at this interpretation of Isa 61 (see Evans and Sanders 1993, 22-25)!

The crowd was so violently stirred that they took him to the brow of a hill to cast him over. If his neighbors found Jesus guilty of heresy, they may have felt a civic obligation to drive him from the town and stone him (Deut 13:6-18; *m. Sanh.* 6:4; see Neale 1993, 90-100). With an Elijah-like departure (1 Kgs 18:46), Jesus simply walked through the crowd and left, likely never to return (9:58).

3. The Synagogue at Capernaum (4:31-37)

BEHIND THE TEXT

The narrative now moves the activities of Jesus to **Capernaum** (v 31). The name means the "village of Nahum" (an unknown individual). The town was located on the western shore of the Sea of Galilee. Its population is estimated to have been between six hundred and fifteen hundred (Reed 2000, 152).

The area is now barren, although in Jesus' day it was well-forested. The village existed as early as the middle Bronze Age (1900-1550 B.C.); but it was eventually abandoned after the Muslim invasion of the Holy Land in the seventh century A.D. The site lay buried and unknown until rediscovered in 1894 by the Franciscans.

In 1968, the ruins of two buildings were uncovered by archaeologists at Capernaum. One is a fourth-century synagogue apparently built on the foundation of the synagogue of Jesus' day. The other is the so-called house of Peter. This large residence consists of several courts with adjacent rooms. Its excavated ruins are visible today.

The identification of this home as the domicile of Simon Peter is speculative. But if it is correct, he must have been a well-to-do fisherman and prominent citizen of Capernaum. John 1:44 identifies the nearby village of Bethsaida as the hometown of Peter. The house of Peter is the setting of the events in Luke 4:38-41.

IN THE TEXT

■ **31-37** Continuing the pattern of teaching in local synagogues on the **Sabbath** (v 31; see 4:16, 44), Jesus commenced his ministry in the prosperous fishing village of Capernaum. The **authority** (v 32) of Jesus over the cosmic realm is the emergent theme in the story of demon exorcism in vv 33-36. Testing by the devil in the first part of the chapter sets the background for the cosmic struggle of Jesus against demonic forces in the villages of Galilee.

In the wilderness, the devil claimed to have dominion over "all the kingdoms of the world" (4:5). In the chapters to come, Luke records four stories of individuals possessed by demons (4:33-37; 8:26-39; 9:37-43; 11:14-23). Numerous passing references and summary statements refer to Jesus' ministry as an exorcist (4:41; 6:18; 7:21, 33; 8:1-3; 9:1, 49-50; 10:17-20; 11:24-26; 13:31-32).

The stories are exemplars of the overarching cosmic struggle in Luke's theology. The struggle for cosmic dominance is "mammoth in significance" for understanding Luke (Garrett 1989, 37). It culminates in the Beelzebub controversy in 11:14-23. After Jesus was accused of casting out demons by Beelzebub, he asserts, "if it is by the finger of God that I cast out the demons, then the kingdom of God has come to you" (11:20 NRSV).

Luke's point at this stage of the story is not about compassion or individual salvation. His concern is to demonstrate the victory of God over the temporal master of the earthly kingdom, the devil himself and his associates (see the commentary on 9:1-6).

The exorcism story in 4:33-37 is representative of this emerging cosmic victory. Whereas the ascendancy of the kingdom was proclaimed by angels (1:32-33; 2:11), it is now proclaimed by the opposing powers of the cosmic world, the demons (see Behind the Text on 8:26-39).

The man in this story is **possessed by a demon, an evil spirit** (v 33). That is, more accurately, he had "the spirit of an unclean demon" (NRSV). Luke's use of the adjective *akathartos*, **unclean**, to describe the **demon** is unique. It may arise from Greco-Roman culture in which demons are simply the spirits of the departed (Grundmann 1964, 6, 9-8).

The demon speaks in the plural: **"Ha! What do you want with us, Jesus of Nazareth? Have you come to destroy us? I know who you are—the Holy One of God!"** (v 34). This indicates the plurality, or perhaps quantity of evil in the man. The demon speaks as a representative of his realm, an ambassador of the cosmic community of Satan. The point of the incident is to reinforce the understanding of Jesus as the absolute authority over the cosmic realm.

The demon calls Jesus **the Holy One of God**. This is Markan material (1:23-28); Luke follows his language. The phrase refers to God in 1 John 2:20 and Rev 16:5. It is not commonly used of Jesus in the Gospels. In the OT, Aaron, Samson, and Elisha are called holy men of God (Ps 106:16; Judg 13:7; 16:7; 2 Kgs 4:9; see Beale and Carson 2007, 291). Here the phrase echoes Luke 1:35: "So the holy one to be born will be called the Son of God" (see 4:41). It has Davidic undertones in Acts 2:31 and 13:35, which cite Ps 16:10.

Jesus' method of exorcism is simply to speak to the demons. ***Be silent and come out!*** (v 35). The absence of magical procedures in Jesus' exorcisms is a departure from accounts of other exorcisms practiced in the period (e.g., Tob 6:1-9; Josephus, *Ant.* 8:45-49, §8.2.5). Jesus' effectiveness as an exorcist depends on his identity as the Son, not popular methods.

In his typical style, Luke summarizes the story with a report of the crowds' response: **All the people were amazed and said to each other, "What is this teaching? With authority and power he gives orders to evil spirits and they come out!"** (v 36). Again, with his characteristic broadness, Luke indicates that the report of Jesus began to reach **throughout the surrounding area** (v 37). All the characters in the narrative now agree. Angels have proclaimed Jesus' divine role. Demons have identified him as the Son. And the people are amazed at his authority and command over the spiritual powers.

4. Peter's House and Beyond (4:38-44)

BEHIND THE TEXT

The healing of Peter's mother-in-law is triple tradition material. It is a touching scene in the style of Mark. Luke adopts Mark's basic formulation (Luke 4:31-44 ‖ Mark 1:21-39). The connection between demon possession and illness is not explicit for the Gospel writers. But Mark's placement of the healing of Simon's mother-in-law between two exorcisms is suggestive. Similarly, Luke lists demonic possession within a series of ailments (Luke 7:21). He seems untroubled by this implicit, if subtle, connection of physical illness with a sinister spiritual cause.

IN THE TEXT

■ **38-44** People crowded around Peter's house seeking healing from **various kinds of sickness** (v 40) and demon possession. Verses 40-41 function as another summary statement of the initial events of the Capernaum ministry. They reinforce the motif of Jesus' hegemony in the cosmic realm. Readers are meant to understand that the demon exorcisms and their proclamations of his sonship were characteristic of this inaugural period of work. The cumulative effect confirms a sense of the inevitability of Jesus' success in his role as the Son. Demons exclaim, **You are the Son of God** (v 41).

The success of the mission is such that it cannot be confined geographically to one village (see Tyson 1992, 24-26). The story is bursting out in terms of geography. Jesus must move on to other villages and towns to proclaim the good news. He reiterates the Isa 61 quote in v 18: **I must preach the good news of the kingdom of God to the other towns also, because that is why I was sent** (v 43; see Nave's [2002, 13-24] treatment of divine necessity in Luke).

What is **the good news of the kingdom**? The verb "to bring good news" (*euangelizō*) is first found on the lips of the angels in Luke 1:19 and 2:10 refers to the births of John and Jesus. John preached "good news" (3:18), which was, among other things, a "baptism of repentance for the forgiveness of sins" (3:3; see the commentary on 3:15-18).

Similarly, in 7:22 Jesus advises John's disciples to tell John that the "good news is preached to the poor." In Acts, "good news" refers to Jesus' identity as the Christ (Acts 5:42; 8:12, 35). Thus, the "good news of the kingdom of God" has a wide range of meanings in Luke.

Jesus proclaims the kingdom, not from a stationary geographic position, but in motion. This is the antithesis of a temple-based theology. His teaching has no walls, no sacred geography. The kingdom must be physically spread about and cannot emanate from one location. It must be taken to the towns and villages (see 9:2, 60).

The relationship of Jesus to the towns and villages of Galilee is a key component in Luke's Gospel. He was often welcomed initially, but eventually disavowed by many. References to towns and villages in Galilee and Samaria are found in 5:12, 17; 7:11; 8:1; 9:10, 57; 10:1, 10, 13-15, 38; 13:22; 19:1.

The story takes its first dramatic turn onto the broader public stage as Jesus departs to enter the **synagogues of Judea** (4:44). This identification of the villages as in **Judea** is problematic, since Luke 4:14; Matt 4:23; and Mark 1:29 all indicate Galilee as the provenance of Jesus' early activity. Unlike the synoptics generally, John's Gospel presumes that Jesus moved back and forth between the two regions. Later copyists changed Luke's text to "Galilee." But Judea is retained by modern translators, because it is the more difficult reading. Thus, it is more likely the original text of Luke.

FROM THE TEXT

What shall we say about demons? In the language of the NT story-world there is a cosmic tension, even equilibrium of good and evil. Wesley observed, "The whole of the spiritual life is a subtle equilibrium that is always susceptible to imbalance" (Oden 1994, 339). The good news asserts that one day the forces of good will overcome the forces of evil. The gospel also recognizes that this day has not yet fully arrived, and thus our need of the gospel. Demonic forces are a natural and necessary part of Luke's story-world. It is also the lens through which all NT authors see the world and organize their understanding of life in it.

In the gospel (and in almost all forms of religion) these forces are personified. There is a son of God and a devil. There are angels; and there are demons. There is a heaven and a hell. All of these represent their position in the cosmological structure of the created world.

This worldview, by personifying good and evil, transforms the cosmological universe into a moral universe. The respective powers want, love, stray, punish, dictate, persuade, do good, and do evil, just as people do. These polarities of good and evil lie at the foundation of ancient Christian beliefs. And by extension, they constitute the foundation of traditional Christian faith.

In the mid-twentieth century, Rudolf Bultmann declared the death of this as NT "mythology." "Modern men take it for granted that the course of nature and of history . . . is nowhere interrupted by the intervention of supernatural powers" (1958, 16). This view sounds dated in our postmodern world. But it still describes today's widely held scientific view that the world is nothing more than a nexus of causes and effects, both natural and rational.

Whatever modern readers may believe about the realities underlying the NT language of angels and demons, it would be a mistake to dismiss such language as irrelevant. Bultmann thought all language of supernatural powers was merely metaphorical. Nevertheless, he said NT language of evil powers expresses this insight:

> that evil is not only to be found here and there in the world, but that all particular evils make up one single power which in the last analysis grows from the very actions of men, which form an atmosphere, a spiritual tradition, which overwhelms every man. The consequences and effects of our sins become a power dominating us, and we cannot free ourselves from them . . . a power which mysteriously enslaves every member of the human race. (21)

Our experience of life in the twenty-first century hardly disavows this description of the powers of evil. The gospel story provides us with the cosmological lens through which we may view modern life. It may seem archaic to some. But the world of absolute spiritual realities empowers us to live meaningfully, and to pursue the good we believe will eventually overcome all (see Lane 1996).

5. The Catch of Fish and a Call to Follow (5:1-11)

BEHIND THE TEXT

In ch 5 Luke begins to teach that sin, impurity, and disease dominate life in his story-world. The chapter functions as a parable about these fundamental issues of the human condition. A fisherman, a leper, a paralytic, and a tax collector all encounter Jesus and experience transformation. Each character represents the experience of one or more of these realities. Each finds deliverance from their condition: sin gives way to righteousness, impurity to purity, and disease to healing.

These conditions are found in a variety of combinations among Luke's characters. The fisherman, for example, is sinful in his own eyes, but neither ill nor ritually impure. The leper is ritually impure and diseased, but not sinful. The paralytic is ill, but not impure, either morally or ritually. Levi is morally impure and possibly ritually impure.

The encounter with Jesus by each character highlights a distinct aspect of his mission. At the end of ch 5, we find that Luke has dealt with the various struggles of the story-world through these typical figures. One is forgiven, one rendered ritually pure, another made physically whole, and one abandons a life of sin.

All these characters experience salvation through their various kinds of faith, the unifying theme among them. Peter has the faith to put the boats out again (v 5). The leper falls to the ground, begging Jesus, "make me clean" (v 12b). The friends of the paralyzed man have faith and let him down through the roof (vv 19-20). Levi has the faith to leave his tax table (v 28).

Juxtaposed in stark contrast, the Pharisees, a sect famous for its ritual purity and rigorous practice, are portrayed as morally impure. They fail to respond in love to the lost. Their glaring faithlessness is the moral of the story. Luke teaches: Be like the fisherman and his friends, not like the Pharisees.

Sin, Impurity, and Disease in the Stories of Ch 5

	Sin	Ritual Impurity	Disease	Full of Faith
Fisherman	✓			✓
Leper		✓	✓	✓
Paralytic			✓	✓
Tax Collectors	✓			✓
Pharisees		✓		

More broadly in Luke, we now enter that part of the narrative (chs 5—19) in which sin, impurity, and disease are conquered in the lives of numerous characters. Six individuals are highlighted by Luke, with a special emphasis on repentance. Each character has an existential crisis leading to repentance:

- Peter in 5:1-11
- Levi in 5:27-32
- the sinful woman in 7:36-50
- the prodigal son in 15:11-32
- the tax collector in 18:1-8
- Zacchaeus in 19:1-10

These individual stories are all unique to Luke's Gospel.

Peter is the first of Luke's penitents. As Jesus' leading disciple, he is a fitting archetypal penitent (see the Introduction, Theological Themes in Luke). All the Synoptic Gospels make the call to repentance a central feature of Jesus' preaching (Matt 3:2; 4:17; Mark 1:4, 15; 6:12; but not John). Luke structures his narrative and theological message around the stories of these penitents.

Luke summarizes his theology in two key passages: The first is in 24:46-47: "This is what is written: The Christ will suffer and rise from the dead on the third day, and repentance and forgiveness of sins will be preached in his name to all nations, beginning at Jerusalem." The second is Acts 11:18. In response to Peter's baptism of Cornelius, his colleagues admit, "So then, God has granted even the Gentiles repentance unto life."

The story of Luke 5:1-11 has a format similar to that used in the testing by the devil in 4:1-13: event (5:1-7), saying (5:10b-11), response (5:8-10a). This pattern is found in various permutations throughout the chapter in vv 12-16, 17-26, and 27-32.

Verses 4-11 contain the story of the miraculous catch of fish. This scene serves as a precursor to the more formal commissioning of the disciples in

6:12-16. Luke conflates two passages in Mark, 4:1-2 and 1:16-20. He then expands the tradition by the addition of the story of the great catch in vv 4-9. Matthew and Mark record only that Simon, Andrew, James, and John left their nets at his call (Matt 4:18-22 ǀǀ Mark 1:16-20). Neither mentions the miraculous catch. But all three Synoptic Gospels contain the logion about "fishers of men" (earlier in Matt 4:19 and Mark 1:17).

This passage is a rare instance in which the Gospel of John and Luke include a story otherwise absent in the synoptic tradition. Luke's account is similar to John's postresurrection draft of fish (John 21:1-11; see Brown 1970, 1090). This raises the possibility that Luke has preserved a form of that same tradition, placing it early in Jesus' ministry. If Luke predates John, there is no question of direct dependence. But perhaps Luke knew the story in another form, simply as one of Jesus' miracles.

The story introduces the "sinner" motif in the third Gospel. Throughout his story Luke introduces "good, healthy sinners." They are not the irredeemably "wicked" of the OT (Heb: *reshaim*; usually *hamartōloi*, "sinners" in the LXX). In Luke, sinners are, irrespective of their past lives, plain and honest members of the common people, quick to express faith and renounce the error of their ways. Luke's archetypal sinners are spiritually genuine and heroic figures. They *always* evince good religious conduct (see the commentary on 6:32-36).

Verses 1-11 introduce the character Simon to the story. Simon has a special relationship with Jesus throughout Luke (see 9:28-36; 22:54-61). It begins here in ch 5. Luke is careful to develop the character of Simon as the leading disciple, the one who interacts with Jesus on their behalf. Jesus stays in his home, uses his boat, and has extended conversations with Simon (4:38; 5:3, 4, 5, 8-10). This is all material unique to Luke.

Peter's call has been compared to OT call narratives (Exod 3:1-22; Josh 1:1-9; Jer 1:4-10; esp. Isa 6:1-10; Beale and Carson 2007, 292; Green 1997, 233). But none of these stories provides a satisfying intertextual connection. The story stands on its own as a unique call narrative to Jesus' disciples.

IN THE TEXT

■ **1-3** The call of the disciples begins with Jesus **standing by the Lake of Gennesaret**, the people crowding around him listening to **the word of God** (5:1). Here, Luke begins to build his characterization of Jesus as a teacher. He already teaches "in their synagogues" (4:15) and in Nazareth with "authority" (4:32). All are "amazed" at his words (4:22, 32). As in all the Synoptic Gospels, teaching will be the main activity of the Galilean ministry (see Matt 4:23; Mark 1:39). Interspersed with this activity are healings and controversies. But, above all, Jesus is portrayed as one who brings the word of God.

Luke conjoins text from Mark 4:1-2 and 1:16-20 to create a single teaching scene at the shore of the Sea of Galilee. People were **crowding around** him and listening to the word of God (v 1). The phrase **the word of God** is a favorite expression of Luke (here; 8:21; 11:28; and eleven times in Acts; compare only Matt 15:6; Mark 7:13). The setting is idyllic, with Jesus seated in a boat teaching those around him. In the audience are Simon and his partners, quietly **washing their nets** (v 2).

■**4-9** At Jesus' request, Simon and his partners put out into **deep water** to make a second attempt at taking a catch, even though they had worked fruitlessly all night (vv 4-5). **Deep water** connotes the new life direction they are about to undertake. To work fruitlessly in darkness is an allusion to their current spiritual position. To call this allegorical would be overdrawn. But there is a parabolic quality about it (Bock 1994, 455). In a single morning these men are invited to embark on a new mission that will dominate the rest of their days—deep waters indeed.

"Simon" and "Simon Peter" are used interchangeably until 6:14. This miracle causes Peter to proclaim his own sinfulness. As a result of the catch, he **fell at Jesus' knees and said, "Go away from me, Lord; I am a sinful man!"** (v 8). Peter experiences guilt or a sense of unworthiness in response to the event. His penitential response is curious; we would expect amazement or joy, not guilt.

As a "sinful man," Peter's instinct is to flee from the holy. In this literary context, Peter's response functions as an example of sin in the presence of the holy. This is similar to Moses' experience at the burning bush. Moses "hid his face, because he was afraid to look at God" (Exod 3:6; compare Gen 3:10; 15:1; 21:17; 28:17; Exod 34:30).

The call of Isaiah (Isa 6:1-10) has similarities in form: epiphany, reaction, reassurance, commission (Green 1997, 233). Peter is not presented as an actively wicked individual. Rather, he is merely a normal man whose sense of moral failure overwhelms him in the presence of the holy. This normalcy keeps his character accessible to the reader. As a typical character, Peter brings a persuasive force to bear on the reader's response. "Be like Peter," Luke seems to encourage his audience.

Peter and the other fishermen are **astonished** (v 9). The noun *thambos* is used in the NT only by Luke. **Astonishment** is the same word used for the response of the witnesses to Jesus' exorcism of the demoniac in the synagogue at Capernaum in 4:36. It also describes the response of the crowd at the healing of the man lame from birth in Acts 3:10. The word connotes not just amazement but fear, a response that would seem justified at witnessing a miracle.

Jesus exhorts Peter and the disciples, **Don't be afraid** (v 10). This is the same exhortation given Zechariah, Mary, and the shepherds in their epiphanies (1:13, 30; 2:10; see Nolland 1989, 222). The exhortation is a connecting sinew, demonstrating that all these events are divine manifestations. For Luke, the point of the encounter is humility, fear, and penitence. These are key features of his emerging paradigm of salvation by repentance.

The response of Jesus to the disciples is found in all the synoptics: *"Do not fear! From now on you will catch people"* (v 10; see also Matt 4:19; Mark 1:17). Luke's insertion of the great catch in 5:4-9 creates a stronger focus on the logion than the parallels in Matthew and Mark. Jesus' comment about his disciples "fishing for people" identifies the catch of fish as a metaphorical or allegorical act. The metaphor of fishing as a symbol for gathering Israel has parallels in Jer 16:14-16; Hab 1:13-17; and Amos 4:2.

Similar examples of metaphorical acts by Jesus in Luke include the stilling of the storm (8:22-25), feeding the five thousand (9:10-17), and possibly even the transfiguration (9:28-36). Similar symbolic acts in the Gospels certainly include the cursing of the barren fig tree in Mark 11:20 and turning water into wine in John 2:1-11.

■ **10-11** The core disciples are introduced into the story here. Besides Peter, they are **James and John, the sons of Zebedee, Simon's partners.** Andrew, Simon's brother mentioned by Mark, does not appear in Luke until 6:14. In response to the miracle of the second catch they docked their boats, **left everything**, and **followed him** (5:11).

It has been observed that Luke's account provides a more "psychologically plausible" scene than that found in Matthew and Mark. There, the disciples simply drop everything to follow Jesus at their first meeting. In Luke's story, Simon already knows Jesus and has seen him at work in Capernaum (4:31-39; Fitzmyer 1981, 1:560). Perhaps, this was one of the reasons Luke added the material about the catch to the initial call of the disciples.

The theme of homelessness and poverty as a condition of discipleship begins here. Many will be called to leave all and "follow" Jesus (v 11, including the disciples, vv 11, 27-28; would-be disciples, 18:22; crowds, 7:9; 9:11; see Behind the Text on 9:1-6 and 23-25; and the commentary on 9:57-62 and 14:27). Jesus will eventually cap this theme with the assertion that those who have left all will be compensated many times over in the world to come (18:28-30).

Henceforth in Luke, Jesus will operate his ministry with a coterie who accompany him everywhere. These disciples, ordinary working-class fishermen, will be his constant companions in the narrative until they dissolve into the background following his arrest. At the point of denial and betrayal they cease to "follow"—the primary condition of discipleship (22:54; see Mark 14:50; Matt 26:56 where the disciples instead "flee"). Even so, the Jesus movement has been transformed in the narrative from the work of a single traveling rabbi to that of an entourage.

B. Conflict Arises as Jesus Heals and Teaches (5:12—6:16)

1. A Leper Healed (5:12-16)

BEHIND THE TEXT

In the OT "leprosy" was a term applied to a wide variety of skin diseases (see Wright and Jones 1992, 277-78). By the time of Jesus, the NT term *lepra* probably included the disease known today as Hansen's disease. But this is not certain.

Leprosy in Jesus' day was a disease with complex social and religious implications, which blurred the line between physical sickness and sin (Wright and Jones 1992, 279-80; see, e.g., Num 12:10-15; Deut 28:27; 2 Chr 26:16-21). In the OT, the disease is sometimes a punishment for pride or disobedience (Num 12:1-16; 2 Sam 3:29; 2 Kgs 5:27; 2 Chr 26:19). But on the whole, the connection between leprosy and sin does not seem to be in view in the relatively few references to the disease in the Gospels, except perhaps in Luke 4:27.

The most extensive narrative on the disease is found in Lev 13—14. Leviticus 13:45 prescribes that a leper must wear ragged clothes, live outside the camp, and cry out to others who approach, "Unclean, Unclean!" (see Luke 17:12). The leper was excluded from the community to prevent the spread of the disease and to quarantine a potential source of ritual impurity. Such isolation amounted to pariah status for the unfortunate sufferer—"He shall live alone; his dwelling shall be outside the camp" (Lev 13:46 NRSV). It was a physical illness that resulted in ritual impurity and communal and religious exclusion. It was often, but not always, thought to have been caused by moral impurity.

The similarities between the Peter incident in vv 1-11 and the leper incident create a rhythm in the narrative.

- Both prostrate themselves in humility and need (vv 8, 12).
- Both cry out plaintively (vv 8, 12).
- Jesus speaks a defining word to each (vv 10, 13).
- Both leave the scene with a new life (vv 11, 14).

The key difference in the two stories is that:

- Peter self-identifies himself as a "sinner."
- This leper is simply a man with a disease.

This healing sets the stage for two other narratives about lepers, which Luke alone records: The stories of the leper Lazarus in 16:19-31 and of the healing of the ten lepers in 17:11-19. The second story again highlights Jesus' healing and inclusion of outcasts. Both stories further develop this theme in the Gospel.

■ **12-16** This story of the cleansing of a leper introduces an important theme in Luke: the restoration of the marginalized to family, society, and temple. Lepers experienced a double curse of physical contagion and ritual impurity. They occupied an extreme position among those excluded from society. Early in Luke these individuals are healed and welcomed into the new kingdom. Their healing is cited as evidence of Jesus' identity as the Christ in 7:22: "Go back and report to John what you have seen and heard: The blind receive sight, the lame walk, those who have leprosy are cured, the deaf hear, the dead are raised, and the good news is preached to the poor."

In 4:27, Luke mentions Naaman, the Gentile leper who symbolized the extreme in physical and social marginalization. Jesus' citation of his healing signals that the ostracized *within* and *without* ethnic Israel will be included in his new community. Luke's use of the leper story in vv 12-16 expands his theme of salvation for the excluded.

The man is **covered with leprosy** (v 12), a phrase that highlights the misfortune of his condition. He lives in a permanent state of ritual impurity, caused by his natural condition rather than sin. He falls to the ground and **begged** Jesus to cleanse him. His cry is **"Lord, if you are willing, you can make me clean"** (v 12). As with other characters in ch 5, he is humble, falls to the ground, and is full of faith. The leper requests a cleansing not a healing. This suggests the unitary nature of his condition in his mind. His impurity and illness are one to him.

Jesus reached out his hand and touched the man (v 13). In so doing he does not break the law of Moses, since Lev 13 does not say a leper cannot be touched (see Green 1997, 237; Nolland 1989, 227). But the act would have communicated ritual impurity to Jesus. This is not particularly significant in itself. Once healed, the impurity of the leper is easily cleansed, as demonstrated by Jesus' instruction to the leper to visit the local priest (v 14). Likewise for Jesus, it would have required a routine matter of cleansing. But the contact between Jesus and the leper has a deeper significance here.

Contrary to expectations, Jesus' touch reverses the normal path of the contagion conveyed by leprosy. Purity rather than impurity becomes contagious (Blomberg 2005, 137). Thus, he says to the leper, *Be purified!* (v 13, *Be cleansed*). His word and touch remove both illness and ritual impurity. There is no distinction in the narrative between ritual impurity and disease. The language of cleansing serves the purposes of healing both conditions.

There is a subversive motif here with regard to the temple. In the normal course of affairs, priests do not heal or cleanse lepers. They only proclaim them clean once the condition is removed. The priest is only the mediator of the holiness that emanates from the temple, not its source. But Jesus conveys purity by direct action. In effect, he supplants the mediating activity of the priesthood.

The role of ritual is made obsolete and the purity of the temple is, in effect, synonymous with contact with Jesus' hand. This is a radical innovation.

The injunction **Don't tell anyone** (v 14) is underplayed in Luke compared to Mark. There Jesus "sternly" warned the leper to keep silent (Mark 1:43 NRSV). Jesus **ordered** the already cleansed and healed leper to show himself **to the priest and offer the sacrifices that Moses commanded for your cleansing, as a testimony to them** (v 14). Is this a defiant act comparable to 5:22-26? That is, does Jesus heal in order to confront his contemporaries with his identity? or, Is his command simply an act of compliance with the Law? The context suggests it may well be more than simple compliance.

Commanding discretion fuels the spread of the news of the healing: **Yet the news about him spread all the more, so that crowds of people came to hear him and to be healed of their sicknesses** (v 15). Not just a single crowd, but "many crowds" (NRSV) begin to seek out Jesus. From a narrative perspective, the stakes are being raised as Jesus' ministry becomes more public.

As the crowds grow, so does Jesus' need to withdraw to **lonely places** where he **prayed** (v 16; 4:42). He is not physically alone again in the narrative until 22:41, the scene in the Garden (John 18:1) of Gethsemane (Matt 26:36; Mark 14:32; Luke mentions neither aspect of the location).

Sin, Impurity, and Disease in Luke

The relationship between ritual impurity and moral impurity has been the subject of recent study by scholars of ancient Judaism (see Klawans 2000). In ancient Judaism, did the presence of ritual impurity imply the presence of sin? The OT and literature of Second Temple Judaism do not, in general, portray ritual impurity as sinful. Nor, conversely, is the defiling force of sin ritual in nature (Klawans 2000, 136-38). There were exceptions to this among the diverse "Judaisms" of the first century A.D. Qumran is the obvious example. In the Qumran literature, moral impurity and ritual impurity are for the "first time . . . merged into a single conception of defilement" (Klawans 2000, 75; Blomberg 2005, 79). This observation leads us to a salient point for NT studies: issues of the relationship of ritual impurity and moral impurity were, as with many aspects of first-century Judaism, a topic of sectarian debate (Klawans 2000, 138).

Ordinary ritual impurity could be contracted through a wide range of natural activities, particularly those involving an emission of bodily fluid. The condition was innocuous and easily remedied, often in the course of a single day (see Lev 11—15 and Num 19). In the more severe types, seven days of purification were required to remove the condition. Ritual impurity was neither a sin nor uncommon. It was unavoidable in life and of temporary duration ("permitted impurity" vs. "prohibited impurity," caused by immoral behavior; Wright and Hübner 1992, 729-30, 733). In fact, to become ritually impure was occasionally obligatory, as in fulfilling one's responsibilities to the dead (Klawans 2000, 137).

The language of "moral impurity" arises from Lev 18 and 19. There sexual sin, idolatry, and murder "defile" (Lev 18:24-30; 19:31; Num 35:33-34; compare

Mark 7:20-23; see Klawans 2000, 21-31, 148; Wright and Hübner 1992, 729-30). This defilement is "distinct" and "grave," but not *ritual* in nature (Klawans 2000, 21). That is, it does not prevent the individual from entering the temple or present any physical impediment in life.

This runs counter to a number of earlier NT studies. From Jeremias to Borg, sinners are identified in ways ranging from one who is ritually impure, to one who engages in particular professional activities, to one who evinces extreme moral failure. Borg describes first-century Judaism as a "purity society," which generated "sharp social boundaries" based on ritual impurity. His views have had wide influence (Borg 1994, 111-12). But if ritual impurity was not considered sinful, as Klawans argues, it is difficult to claim there were social boundaries between sinners and the righteous based on purity alone in Jesus' day.

2. The Paralyzed Man Is Healed and Forgiven (5:17-26)

BEHIND THE TEXT

The healing of the paralyzed man is the next event in Luke's collection of parables of the human condition in ch 5. This man was paralyzed. Paralysis is not so much a disease as a disability. There is no indication of moral failure in the man; and the cause of his paralysis is not discussed. In this story, the emphasis is on his faith rather than his humility.

This story introduces another suite of related events in the early part of Luke. The healing of the paralytic is the first of five conflict stories in 5:17—6:11. These set out a pattern of opposition from the Pharisees. They are:

- the healing of the paralytic (5:17-26)
- the calling of Levi (5:27-32)
- the question on fasting (5:33-39)
- the plucking of grain on the Sabbath (6:1-5)
- the Sabbath healing of the man with a withered hand (6:6-11)

All five have a common event-opposition-saying format:

- A healing or provocative event occurs in the ministry.
- Jesus' opponents take exception and challenge him verbally.
- Jesus responds with a saying that brings resolution to the passage.

Luke follows Mark in this material (Mark 2:1—3:6). The narrative purpose of these conflict stories is to compare and contrast Jesus' ministry to the Pharisees'.

IN THE TEXT

■ **17-19** The healing of the paralytic is a complex and dramatic story in Luke. Important spectators, including **teachers of the law** and **Pharisees**, have come **from every village of Galilee and from Judea and Jerusalem** (v 17). This description raises the level of conflict, because the opposition to Jesus is seen to represent a broad geographic area. Also, the crowds are a counterpoint to the secrecy enjoined in the previous story (v 14). The drama is further heightened by the observation that the **power of the Lord was present for him to heal the sick** (v 17). The scene has the feel of a highly volatile event.

In Mark's setting of this scene, Jesus was simply "at home" (Mark 2:1 NRSV). The scene is also less than public in the parallel in Matt 9:1 and 3. But in Luke, the healing is staged as a crucial public event. The same tendency to adjust the setting is seen in Luke 6:17 compared to Matt 5:1.

The **Pharisees** (vv 17, 21) are introduced here for the first time as Jesus' chief antagonists. They will serve that role consistently throughout the remainder of Luke. Their doubt and opposition in this incident will become the characteristic response of all Pharisees in the narrative. Readers, privy to inside information about these opponents (v 21), become disinclined to consider them sympathetically. They are "a caricature of morality to be avoided" (Darr 1992, 92).

The **crowd** (v 19) is Luke's designation for the "normal" people present. It is so large that a chaotic mass of people restrict physical access to Jesus. One can imagine noise, pushing, and tension as people jockey for position. The event has a catalytic feel, especially with reference to the presence of power brokers from across the region.

The **paralytic** (v 18) and his friends are determined to gain access to Jesus. **When they could not find a way to do this because of the crowd, they went up on the roof and lowered him on his mat through the tiles into the middle of the crowd, right in front of Jesus** (v 19). In this scene the paralytic and his friends are contrasted to the Pharisees and teachers of the Law who are passive and full of doubt. They simply watch and oppose Jesus by questioning his actions in their hearts (v 21).

This juxtaposition of eagerness and passivity tells readers that the supplicants have the right attitude; and the religious authorities, the wrong attitude. The omniscient author offers readers access to the hidden thoughts of the Pharisees. "Ideas about characters, events, settings, ideology, etc. are continually being reaffirmed, negated, revised, and supplemented . . . . [T]he mental constructions are sequential, cumulative, and subject to change" (Darr 1992, 30). Luke builds a characterization of Jesus' sympathizers and opponents sequentially and cumulatively.

■ **20-26** In response to the great faith of the paralytic and his friends, Jesus says, **"Friend, your sins are forgiven"** (v 20). It is the equivalent of saying, "Your faith has made you well" (as in 17:19). It was commonly understood in Judaism that God alone forgives sin (Ps 130; Isa 43:25). Here the passive voice—"your sins are forgiven"—was a conventional way Jewish teachers sometimes implied an action by God (Sanders 1995, 213). But vv 21 and 24 belie this interpretation. Jesus grants forgiveness on God's behalf, and the declaration is shocking to at least some present, who describe it as **blasphemy** (v 21).

LUKE

5:17-26

The theology of forgiveness of intentional sin in the OT is straightforward. It involves confession, restitution, and an offering (see sidebar). Here, the dispute with the Pharisees is Jesus' appropriation of the right to declare something normally granted only by God. As with Jesus' cleansing of the leper by his direct touch, this also makes a radical claim for Jesus.

Why does a paralyzed man need forgiveness of sins? There was a subtle blurring of the line between sin and disease in the OT and contemporary Judaism. This is another situation in which the two issues brush together. Jesus seems to reinforce the sense of causation by discussing forgiveness with a paralyzed man (Marshall 1978, 219). This is Luke's first reference to **faith** (v 20; Green 1997, 240). The man is not simply paralyzed and made to walk. He is full of "faith" *and* receives "forgiveness." *And* he receives healing based on that faith. Thus, the complex of issues around impurity, sin, and disease converge in this story.

Luke's purpose is not to explain the relationship between disease and sin but to demonstrate the power of Jesus to restore a man to wholeness. The line between impurity and disease is blurred, because it does not matter to the man. His struggle against sin, impurity, and disease is all one problem to him.

This may have theological implications as well. By his action of faith, he acquires forgiveness and healing. This result shows the unitary nature of salvation in Luke. By faith, a man whose world is shattered by the disorder of impurity and disease is restored to "holiness"—what anthropologist Mary Douglas once eloquently called the "unity, perfection and integrity" of life (1970, 68).

At still another level, the declaration of forgiveness carries a christological implication for Luke's broader narrative: the one who declares forgiveness in this chaotic scene is the crucified Messiah, mediating forgiveness through his sacrifice (Acts 10:39-43).

The Pharisees raise a reasonable question, **"Who can forgive sins but God alone?"** (v 22). In response, Jesus poses a legal (*halakhic*) question to his fellow experts: **"Which is easier: to say, 'Your sins are forgiven,' or to say, 'Get up and walk'?"** (v 23; see also 6:9).

In rabbinic disputation, such a question is called a *boruth*, "a vulgarity," designed to embarrass one's opponents by posing an unanswerable question. The method is used against Jesus in Luke 20:22 and Mark 12:18-27. The paralytic's immediate healing leaves no doubt that the **Son of man has authority on earth to forgive sins** (v 24). The people were **amazed** (v 26, *ekstasis*, "bewilderment, ecstasy, astonishment"). They said they had seen **remarkable things today**. This demonstration of authority further establishes Jesus' messianic character in the narrative.

This is Luke's first reference to the **Son of Man**. It is a phrase he will use often (twenty-five times), but with varying meanings. It is, at times, a simple form of self-reference, one with particular roots in the Ezekiel tradition (Ezek 2:1 and often thereafter; e.g., see Luke 5:24; 6:5; 7:34; 11:30; 19:10). On other occasions it refers to one who will suffer (9:22, 44; 22:22, 48, 69; 24:7), to Jesus as a figure of conflict (6:22; 12:8, 10), and to one who returns eschatologically (as in 9:26; 12:40; 17:22, 24, 26, 30; 21:27).

In 21:27, Luke quotes Dan 7:13, where the use of "son of man" certainly has an apocalyptic connotation. But this influence is not always clearly present in Luke's use of the phrase. While it seems to be a rather benign term of self-reference here in 5:24, the Dan 7 passage cannot be far from the ancient reader's mind as a stirring subtext. (See 17:22-23 and the comment on 18:31-34 and 21:27.)

The Theology of Forgiveness in Judaism

The theology of forgiveness in ancient Judaism was derived from Lev 6:1-7. Those who sin intentionally find forgiveness by confession, restitution, and a guilt offering (see also Num 5:5-7). Forgiveness is a relatively straightforward matter and available at all times, if these conditions are met.

The requirement of confession in Leviticus is most like Luke's paradigm of repentance. All six exemplary sinners of his Gospel evince something like confession. Peter confesses: "I am a sinful man!" (5:8). The sinful woman weeps (7:38). The prodigal says, "I have sinned against heaven" (15:21). The tax collector beats his breast (18:13). Zacchaeus offers, "If I have cheated anybody, . . ." (19:8).

There is some evidence of the second requirement, restitution. Levi leaves his tax table, which could be a form of restitution, for example. Zacchaeus agrees, "I will pay back four times the amount" (19:8).

There is less evidence of the third requirement, a cultic guilt offering. The lepers are required to make an offering (5:14; 17:14). But otherwise no cultic requirement is mentioned. On this point, E. P. Sanders was right to suggest that this was one of the offensive aspects of Jesus' career (see Blomberg 2005, 25). This is where the two paradigms of Leviticus and Luke diverge.

The Levitical paradigm sees "sin" as a communal transgression, involving property and rights. Thus, material restitution is essential. Luke's paradigm is more existential, viewing sin as a condition of the soul that, in itself, needs remedy. There is in Luke a dominating aspect of personal responsibility for sin and a corresponding freedom of choice to move toward redemption and holiness on a personal level. That is, while God's saving action is always and fully gracious, as the "orienting concern" of Wesleyan theology holds, without our responsible participation, grace will not save (Maddox 1994, 19; see also Newman 2010, 28-31).

Later, in Acts, a community property aspect emerges again in the sin of Ananias and Sapphira (Acts 5:1-11), a representation more akin to a Levitical approach. In this sense, the Gospel of Luke is more conducive to a Wesleyan reading than Acts.

Jesus' response to the paralytic introduces a new aspect to Luke's characterization of his identity. He appropriates a prerogative to declare God's forgiveness. This assertion of "authority" by the "Son of Man" is a turning point in the narrative. Thus, it is a turning point for the reader. The lines of conflict have been drawn and readers must decide: "With whom will I side in this conflict?" This is the rhetorical purpose of a gospel text. Indifference is not an option; one must decide how to respond to this presentation of Jesus as the Son of Man. One can side with the Pharisees, the stereotypical opponents of Jesus' work. Or, they can side with the sinners, who accept Jesus and his healing.

The narrator is not a disinterested party; and readers are subject to the "sequential and cumulative" mental constructions the narrator has created—a "hierarchy of perspectives." The narrator is viewed as reliable, as are the sympathetic characters in the story. The opponents, by contrast, are unreliable because of their transparent lack of faith and hostility to Jesus. This leads to a "rhetoric of perception" in the narrative to which the readers are subject (Darr 1992, 30, 53-59).

Within this process, pertinent questions arise for a reader. Who, indeed, can forgive sins but God? And who among us can easily tolerate, as the Pharisees are challenged to do, the deconstruction of cherished beliefs? Is a miracle sufficient cause to abandon sacred convictions? And, would that be wise in any case? In what way does adherence to tradition blind us to new truth? These are the suggestive questions that arise from the healing of the paralytic and Jesus' declaration.

On a more pragmatic level, the actions of the friends of the paralytic reflect the communal burden created by paralysis in this culture. The immobility of a community member taxed the resources of the entire village. A paralytic had to be cared for, could not work, and took up the time of those who had to carry him or her about. The men carrying this victim of paralysis sought not only the healing of the individual but also liberation from the burden of his care.

The picture of the man being lowered directly into the middle of the crowded house is a wonderful scene of chaos and creativity, but it demonstrates their desperation and determination as much as their faith. Clearly, the paralytic and his friends typify the faith the reader is encouraged to adopt.

3. Levi Follows Jesus and Gives a Banquet (5:27-32)

BEHIND THE TEXT

Levi is the inaugural representative of the tax collector as a type in the Gospel (5:27-32; 7:28-35; 15:1-2; 18:9-14; 19:2-10). His story is one of a matched pair: one at the beginning of the central section (5:31-32), and one at the end (19:9-10). Both contain a paradigmatic statement of the purpose of Jesus' mission.

In this chapter Luke sets out the conceptual framework for the central chapters of his Gospel. We have noted the four archetypal persons who respond to Jesus in ch 5. Now, other themes of this framework are enhanced or introduced: increased conflict, forgiveness, and inclusion of the marginalized in the new community.

The narrative in ch 5 has been building step-by-step toward this important decision of Levi:

- The crowds press around Jesus to hear his teaching (v 1).
- The miracle of the second catch of fish occurs (vv 4-7).
- Peter proclaims his sinfulness and he and his partners follow Jesus (vv 8-11).
- Prominent teachers come from all around the country to hear Jesus (v 17).
- A paralytic is healed and forgiven (vv 18-26).
- The crowd exclaims, "We have seen remarkable things today" (v 26).

Now, the repentance of an ordinary tax collector is the climax to this series of miraculous events.

The tax profession was held in contempt by the general Jewish population for obvious reasons. Tax collectors were subcontractors to the Roman government. They collected tolls at transit junctions between jurisdictions. A native Israelite who undertook this service to Rome alienated himself from his compatriots (see Derrett 1970, 178-85; Michel 1972, 88-105). Readers already know the honesty of tax collectors was in question, because of John's admonition to them to collect no more "than required" (3:13).

There were, no doubt, honest tax collectors in Palestine. So we are dealing again here with a stereotypical characterization, just as with the Pharisees, the soldiers, and the crowds. But in the Gospels, the tax collector is a category of individual who is subject to a special disapproval. Thus, the encounter has various layers of complexity. An irenic encounter between Levi and Jesus is as amazing as any of the preceding events of ch 5.

IN THE TEXT

■ **27-28** The **tax collector** Levi, as is characteristic of all tax collectors and sinners in Luke, responds positively to Jesus' invitation to **follow** him. He **left everything** and followed Jesus immediately, just as did Peter and his fellow fishermen. For Levi it is a complete break with his former life and occupation, a concrete action of repentance (Nave 2002, 167, 169). This builds on Luke's comment in 3:12 concerning the tax collectors who came to be baptized by John the Baptist. Archetypal sinners were eager to respond to John and Jesus. A gravitational attraction of sinners toward Jesus is building in the narrative, along with a corresponding alienation of the religious elite.

■ 29-32 Then Levi held a great banquet for Jesus at his house, and a large crowd of tax collectors and others were eating with them (v 29). This lively scene at Levi's house is a paradigm of Luke's program of the forgiveness and inclusion for sinners. The scene is a **great banquet**, hosted by Levi. The phrase is otherwise used only in Luke's description of a banquet in 14:13. In Matthew, Jesus is simply "at dinner in the house" (9:10 NRSV). This is not necessarily Levi's house at all (Matt 9:10 ‖ Mark 2:15).

Levi's banquet as a planned event is heightened by the presence of a **large crowd of tax collectors and others** (v 29*b*). The other synoptics refer simply to "tax collectors and sinners" (Matt 9:11; Mark 2:15).

Who were these "others" also in attendance? From a literary point of view they are people considered beyond the pale of inclusion by the religious elites. The passage does not establish the historical identity of Jesus' companions, only that he consorts with those outside the mainstream of religious acceptance. He is at odds with his coreligionists about the status of outsiders in the covenant community (see the Introduction, Theological Themes in Luke).

The Pharisees *egongyzon*, **complained** (v 30), about Jesus' table habits. This Greek word is often used in the LXX for the murmuring of the children of Israel in the wilderness (e.g., Exod 15:24; 16:7-12; 17:3; Num 11:1; Beale and Carson 2007, 293). They asked his disciples, **"Why do you eat and drink with tax collectors and 'sinners'?"** (v 30). Jesus' opponents consider his commensality with these people inappropriate.

The charge against Jesus is not treason, as in eating with Roman collaborators. Else the Pharisees would have said, "Why does your master betray Israel?" This would have been a much more effective charge; but they do not seem to object to Jesus' association with tax collectors and sinners until he *eats* with them (see Blomberg 2005, 98-103; Adams 2008, 115-17).

Jesus would have been at risk of consuming *demai*, or untithed food, at the banquet. A portion of the harvest was always to be reserved for the priests according to the biblical laws of tithing. Those who wished to be polite *and* observant would simply separate the tithe on their plate, if they were unsure of its status. But people often violated tithing laws in this period; and most were ritually impure most of the time. The Pharisees, however, were scrupulous on both counts. This could have been the basis for their affront.

Jesus would surely have contracted ritual impurity from his hosts. As a result, he would have been barred briefly from admission to the temple. But this was Galilee, so none except the sectarians who undertook a supererogatory level of observation would have been concerned (Neale 1991, 24-26). Such were the concerns of the Pharisees, not the general society. This could hardly have been a cause for public scandal.

Still, table fellowship had a profound significance in this culture (see Borg 1984, 82-86; Blomberg 2005, 17-30; and esp. Thompson 2007, 79-92). *M. Avot* 3:3 says,

But if three have eaten at one table and have spoken over it words of the Law, it is as if they had eaten from the table of God for it is written, "And he said unto me, This is the table that is before the Lord."

To eat together had a connotation of a sacred bond. The scene finds its meaning in the simple, but potent, cultural symbol of communion. Whatever the historical cause of offense, in this context its explanation is probably as much literary as historical.

In response to the Pharisees' criticism of his behavior, Jesus replies: **It is not the healthy who need a doctor, but the sick. I have not come to call the righteous, but sinners to repentance** (vv 31-32). Only Luke appends **to repentance** to the call. This logion further defines the declaration of ministry in 4:18-19 at the synagogue in Nazareth and recalls the proverb of 4:23. Again, Luke conflates the categories of sickness and moral impurity in the proverb in 5:32. This reinforces the idea that such distinctions are not clearly drawn in the minds of either the ancient narrator or his first readers.

Verse 32 operates on the basis of an analogy: sinners are metaphorically sick; and repentance makes them well. Put another way, repentance cures moral impurity. In Luke, it is the universal solution to what ails sinners.

Jesus' reference to the "righteous" is usually understood as ironic. It is the Pharisees "as they thought themselves to be" (Marshall 1978, 220) or a "parody" of their true condition (Green 1997, 248). It is a "rhetorical" characterization of how they see themselves (Bock 1994, 498). Luke, in fact, shows a careful hand by having Jesus call his banquet guests "tax collectors and others," whereas the Pharisees call them all "sinners." The meaning of the term is, after all, always determined by the lips on which it is found.

Thus, the proverb could be interpreted literally: "If you are well, you don't need the cure." That is, if you are humble and repentant, you've no need of the physician's cure. But the "sick" do need this remedy. And Levi is the case at hand. In this reading, Jesus' opponents are the righteous; and he justifies his ministry to sinners as his basic responsibility. This runs counter to Luke's uniformly negative characterization of Jesus' opponents, however. The irony in the term "righteous" in v 23 is hard to escape.

Even so, Jesus' call to the sinners is neither radical nor heroic. It is the biblical responsibility of the shepherd to seek the lost sheep of Israel (Ezek 34:4-16). This is a responsibility the Pharisees abrogate as shepherds. By extending grace to the tax collector Levi, Jesus simply does what the servant of God is supposed to do. The Son of Man *must* call the wayward back to relationship with God.

Jesus calls Israel back to her fundamental values of love and compassion for the lost and to the seminal law to love one's neighbor as oneself. Thus, he shows himself to be a true and faithful shepherd of the sheep of Israel. His call is radical, however, in the *degree* of grace he extends to those described by the term normally reserved for the irredeemable—sinners.

The LXX OT background of the term "sinners" is the "wicked" (Heb: *reshaim*; Greek: *hamartōloi*), the irredeemably lost (see the comment on 6:32-36). Here, sinners are incorporated into the new community. The use of the term in this way is a NT innovation; the irredeemably lost are readily saved (Neale 1993, 94-95).

FROM THE TEXT

Israel's prophets called Israelites back to the fundamental values of monotheistic Judaism when they had lost their way. The prophetic criticism of the shepherds of Israel in Ezek 34:4-24 is a good example. There, the religious authorities are accused by God of not caring for the lost: "You have not strengthened the weak or healed the sick or bound up the injured. You have not brought back the strays or searched for the lost. You have ruled them harshly and brutally" (v 4). In Ezek 34:8, 16 (NRSV), God himself said, "Because my shepherds have not searched for my sheep . . . I will seek the lost."

This passage was probably well-known among Jesus' contemporaries. His use of the language of Ezek 34 suggests he was charging these particular Pharisees with dereliction in their sacred duty. They had a sacred trust to watch over the lost sheep of Israel. These were the Jewish tax collectors and sinners they despised. It was the *duty* of the Pharisees to seek out these lost sheep, but instead they had scorned them as sinners.

In this narrative, Jesus and his Pharisaic opponents differ on the location of the boundary for exclusion from the covenant community. Luke has already shown us a Jesus who believes that even Gentiles are within the scope of God's care (4:26-27). Now he also encompasses those on the furthest margins of the covenant community (5:29-30). In Acts, Luke will extend those boundaries even further to the distant reaches of the Gentile world, to Rome itself.

In 5:31 there is an echo of the moving account of the redemption of Manasseh, the worst sinner in the history of Israel. Manasseh was guilty of a long list of sins, but he eventually repented (2 Kgs 21:1-18; 2 Chr 33:12-13). His prayer of repentance is recorded in the apocryphal *Prayer of Manasseh*: "You therefore, O Lord, God of the righteous ones, did not appoint grace for the righteous ones, such as Abraham, and Isaac and Jacob, those who did not sin against you; but you appointed grace for me, who am a sinner" (v 8). The similarity with Jesus' logion in v 31 is striking. Did he know of this evocative prayer by Israel's greatest sinner and use Manasseh's repentance as a model for those considered irredeemably lost by the religious elite?

4. The Parables of Cloth and Wineskins (5:33-39)

BEHIND THE TEXT

Luke's account of the controversial banquet of Levi is followed by two parables that deal with the nature of change and the challenge it presents to traditional expectations. First, Jesus' antagonists ask why his disciples do not fast like the Pharisees or the disciples of John. Some Pharisees evidently fasted twice a week (Luke 18:12). It was a common practice in the OT, especially during times of crisis and mourning among Israel's leaders (2 Sam 12:16; Ps 35:13).

The story of the patches and wineskins introduces an abbreviated form of the parable genre in Luke (see 6:4-49, the first full example; see Snodgrass 2008, 333; Matt 9:16-17 ‖ Mark 2:21-22). A parable can have multiple layers of meaning. This is part of the genius of the genre. The placement of these two parables here allows the larger context of 5:27-35 to influence their interpretation. The mission to marginalized tax collectors and others (vv 27-32) and feasting and fasting in the presence of the bridegroom (vv 33-35) are criticized by Jesus' contemporaries. They cannot accept his fellowship with the marginalized as a cause for joy. Nor can they celebrate his prophetic status as the bridegroom.

■ **33-35** Jesus and his coterie will be criticized about their open commensality throughout the Gospel (5:30; 11:37-41; 14:12-14, 15-24; 15:1-2; 19:1-10). The eating and drinking habits of Jesus are questioned in 7:33-34, again in connection with the disciples of John. John was famously ascetic. As a Nazirite, he abstained from wine (Luke 1:15; 7:33). No doubt, John's disciples had similar habits of self-denial, which must have fueled their criticism of Jesus and his disciples.

Against the backdrop of John's asceticism, Jesus' indulgence in food and wine appeared like dissipation to some of his contemporaries. His response to this criticism is an interesting window into his inner sense of identity. He has a jubilant approach to his life and mission. Fasting was associated with times of sorrow in Jewish tradition (see 1 Sam 31:13; 2 Sam 1:12; 1 Chr 10:12; Beale and Carson 2007, 293). **Jesus answered** the objections of his opponents. It simply was not the time for abstention: **"Can you make the guests of the bridegroom fast while he is with them?"** (v 34). Jesus identifies himself as the "bridegroom." The wedding celebration, as one of the most joyous aspects of Hebrew culture, represents a strong counterpoint to fasting.

Marriage was the key social institution of the Jews. The process of betrothal signified the joy and anticipation of the oneness of the couple. The wedding itself was an exultant procession with music, food, and laughter. That Jesus conceived of himself as the bridegroom in this role is an intimate portrait of the joyous relationship he shared with his followers. Mourning would come in time; the days would come when **the bridegroom will be taken from them,** Jesus said (v 35). But now was the time for celebration. This is the first time Luke alludes to Jesus' death (see Luke 2:35; so Snodgrass 2008, 480; Fitzmyer [1981, 1:599] disagrees).

■ **36-39** The parable of the patches and wineskins is a commentary, not on the incompatibility of the old and new covenants (as some suggest: Fitzmyer 1981, 1:601). In Luke, its concern is with the difficulty of accepting a different way of looking at a familiar issue. In this case, it is the change from ethnicity to repentance as the method of entry to the new community that is in contention. This is not the replacement of Judaism with a new religion. The parable invites Judaism to embrace again the inclusion of Gentiles, along the lines of the universal salvation foreseen by the prophets of old.

The parable causes us to reflect on how a change in perspective strains and challenges tradition. A new and old **garment** cannot be pieced together—the new won't match the old and the new will be destroyed (see Lev 19:19; Deut 22:11). On the one hand, Jesus seeks to reform the flawed practice of Judaism (the old garment). On the other, he will reconstruct a renewed Judaism on the foundation of the old (the new garment). This reform movement brings violence and change as well as renewal and growth. Jesus' reformation of Judaism will have elements of both deconstruction and construction, the cloth will certainly tear and the wineskin will certainly burst.

The symbolic meaning of **wine** in biblical narrative aids in the interpretation of the two parables. Wine is the symbol for the blessing of God in the covenant land, both now and in the eschatological order (e.g., Gen 27:28; Joel 3:18). Jesus recognizes how difficult it is going to be for the old cultic/pharisaic order to embrace the new messianic order, especially given the mounting opposition that has been in evidence in the previous verses.

Luke alone includes the logion in v 39: **And no one after drinking old wine wants the new, for he says, "The old is better."** Marcion omitted this verse from his revisionist text, because he thought it affirmed the rightness of the old ways of Judaism and the Law over the new path of the Gospel (Green 1997, 250; Metzger 1975, 139).

The comment is more likely a simple statement of fact, and a particularly compassionate observation by Jesus. He acknowledges how comforting the old ways are to people, and how many prefer the old, no matter how wonderful the advent of the new.

5. "The Son of Man Is Lord of the Sabbath" (6:1-5)

BEHIND THE TEXT

The final two of the five conflict stories of Luke 5:17—6:11 appear in ch 6. They, like the earlier stories, have the event-opposition-saying format. Both stories involve Pharisees as antagonists and both take issue with strict Sabbath work laws as interpreted by some Pharisees (see Gen 2:2-3; Exod 16:22-30; 20:8-11; 31:14-15; Deut 5:12-15).

Sabbath rest was the defining practice differentiating Jews from their pagan neighbors. It was a cultural expression of a religious ideal, similar to circumcision. These cultural practices defined Jewish identity in a hostile society and functioned as a "sign" between God and his people (Ezek 20:12; Green 1997, 252).

The idea of the Sabbath originates in the creation story where God rests after six days of labor (Gen 2:1-3). Reference to the Sabbath is found throughout the OT, especially in the Pentateuch and Prophets, less so in the Writings (only in Ps 92:1). First-century Jews emphasized the Sabbath (like circumcision and kosher laws) as a significant boundary marker separating Jews and Gentiles.

In the NT, the Sabbath is mentioned often in the Gospels and Acts (twenty-six times in Luke/Acts; nine times in Matthew; seven times in Mark). Elsewhere it is mentioned only in Col 2:16 and Heb 4:9 (as part of a major discussion on entering God's "rest").

At the cultural level, Sabbath observance originated as a social-humanitarian aspect in allowing rest from labor. It also, according to Amos 8:4-6, had a moral purpose: to control greed in commerce. Perhaps most importantly, the practice of Sabbath rest signaled to the broader society the "otherness" of Jewish life. As such, its observance was a sensitive and important topic among Jews. Any diminution of strictness in the keeping of Sabbath was construed as a challenge to Jewish identity. A lenient position on its observance was more than a subject of idle theological debate. Jesus' activities on the Sabbath were likely viewed as a litmus test of his self-understanding as a Jew. The text makes it clear that some considered his views subversive to the Jewish social-political agenda.

IN THE TEXT

■ **1-5** Jesus' disciples were picking heads of grain in a farmer's field; and Pharisaic observers objected to the propriety of this behavior. The presence of Pharisees, apparently at Jesus' elbow, continues the sense of high drama begun in 5:17. There "Pharisees and teachers of the law" from every corner of the country had come to observe Jesus. From a narrative perspective, the private phase of Jesus' ministry has ended. For this reason, readers are not particularly surprised by the presence of Jesus' opponents at his side.

There is a narrowing gap between the narrator, the characters, and readers in this scene. Readers, as it were, look over Jesus' shoulder, as if present in the field. We observe the interaction, watching the disciples rub the grains between their palms. Such is our closeness to the narrator and characters, and we identify with Jesus and his disciples and repudiate the harsh views of his opponents (see Darr 1992, 31).

The harvesting of grain as described in v 1 was allowed in Deut 23:25 (see also Lev 19:9-10; 23:22; Ruth 2:1-7). But it did violate laws against reaping and threshing on the Sabbath (Exod 34:21; see *m. Sabb.* 7:2 for the thirty-nine classes of work prohibited on the Sabbath: ". . . sowing, ploughing, reaping, binding sheaves, threshing, winnowing, cleansing crops . . ."). This concern can be seen in the Pharisees' question: **"Why are you doing what is unlawful on the Sabbath?"** (v 2).

Jesus compared the ad hoc harvest with the eating of the holy bread by David in 1 Sam 21:1-9. In that passage, David disobeyed the prohibition against the consumption of food reserved for priests. It is an unexpected use of that passage. First Samuel 21 does not concern Sabbath observance, but a quite different issue—ritual impurity based on sexual congress (1 Sam 21:4-8; see Lev 24:9).

The disciples of Jesus, however, do break an extrabiblical Sabbath commandment (*halahkah*) on reaping and harvesting. Jesus argues this "unlawful" behavior was justified by the human necessity of survival (see 2 Kgs 4:42-44). The conflict in both stories, 1 Samuel and Luke, is about the tension between the strict observance of law and a more lenient view of the Law as a guide to conduct. Neither David nor Jesus argues for the breaking of the Law; but both reserve the prerogative to interpret and judge prescriptions based on their own liberal interpretation of the Law.

Mark, in fact, includes a comment by Jesus that indicates he thought the Sabbath prescriptions had gone too far in this instance: "The sabbath was made for humankind, and not humankind for the sabbath" (Mark 2:27 NRSV). Apparently, in Jesus' thinking, the principles of compassion and human need trumped whatever dangers interpreting God's law more humanely might occasion.

In Luke, the Markan logion about the Sabbath being for humans is omitted. Only the summary statement remains: **the Son of Man is Lord of the Sabbath** (compare 5:24). This subtle redaction makes the comparison of Jesus to David the *point* of the Lukan story. This is not simply a dispute about Sabbath or purity laws. Jesus describes himself as the "Son of Man," the "Lord of the Sabbath." This description becomes a comment about his kingly identity and prerogative. Jesus seems to say, "Since David bent a law for human need, *I* can bend a law for human need." Jesus assumes the prerogative of the hero-king to make judgments about holiness and law.

The citation of the David story evokes an even deeper level of intertextual meaning in the argument. David was a righteous king, duly anointed by Samuel, but persecuted by corrupt Saul. While in flight, David found an ally in Ahimelech, the village priest of Nob, who had set out the holy bread (1 Sam 21:2) and gave it to David and his hungry men. The compassion of Ahimelech is contrasted to the figure of Doeg the Edomite, a Gentile mercenary who stepped forward to massacre the eighty-five priests at Nob in retribution for Ahimelech's mercy toward David. Saul's own soldiers had refused the king's order to kill the priests (1 Sam 22:18); but Doeg did the will of the king.

When Jesus refers to this story in response to the Pharisees' objection to the ad hoc harvest, he does three things:

1. He identifies himself as the Son of David with the same kingly prerogatives, including discretion in the use of that which is ritually holy.
2. By describing himself as "Lord of the Sabbath," he appropriates to himself the role of arbiter of the Law, valuing compassion and human

need over the strict observance of the Law. This growing independence of thought on matters of legal interpretation (see 5:22, 30-31) is an emerging aspect of Luke's characterization of Jesus.

3. He casts his opponents in a disagreeable light with reference to the Samuel story by subtly aligning them with the opponents of David. Doeg implemented the cruel retribution of Saul who opposed David's action. In a similar way, the Pharisees are seen in opposition to Jesus, showing they are more like Saul and Doeg than the compassionate Ahimilech. Jesus' opponents would have been offended by this insinuation.

6. Jesus Heals the Man with the Withered Hand (6:6-11)

BEHIND THE TEXT

In response to the inner thoughts of his critics, Jesus poses a classic legal question on the matter of healing on the Sabbath (see 13:13-17; 14:1-6). Such *halakhic* prescriptions were, by nature, the product of a long process of debate among rabbis and sages. Over time, a majority opinion prevailed on a disputed point of Jewish practice. The purpose of such disputation was to give guidance to Jews on how to avoid breaking the Law, especially on topics not directly addressed in the OT.

In this particular case, the point of contention is whether healing constitutes work forbidden on the Sabbath. Jesus does not abrogate an OT law per se by healing on the Sabbath. But his position does contravene a *halakhah*, which his opponents consider authoritative on the matter. The Mishnah postdates the time of Jesus; but at least some of its arguments derive from issues and debates with roots in the first century. *M. Yoma* 8:6 discusses the propriety of healing on the Sabbath and records a *halakhah* that would seem to support Jesus' more lenient position: "Whenever there is doubt whether life is in danger this overrides the Sabbath." Matthew includes a similar argument in Jesus' defense of his healing: "If any of you has a sheep and it falls into a pit on the Sabbath, will you not take hold of it and lift it out? How much more valuable is a man than a sheep! Therefore it is lawful to do good on the Sabbath" (12:11-12).

Jesus' opponents adhere to a stricter interpretation, which sought to preserve the Sabbath even from the "work" of healing. Jesus' position is the more liberal, lenient one. We do not know if it was actually a minority position in his day. But it certainly ran counter to the NT's portrayal of the Pharisees' position on this matter.

The need for preservation of Jewish ethnic identity and culture argued for strict observance of law to differentiate Israel from her neighbors. A breakdown in strictness would inevitably lead to the diminution of Jewish identity. On the other hand, Jesus argues that a theology of compassion and inclusion is more representative of Yahweh's true nature. Compassion trumps cultural identity; and herein lay the source of contention between Jesus and his rivals.

This issue of strictness vs. lenience on cultural identity became a watershed issue between traditional Jews and early Jewish Christians. As emerging Christianity increasingly welcomed Gentiles into its community, it abandoned the ethnic and cultural exclusivism of Judaism and embraced a broader ethic of inclusion. Thus, holiness was redefined from an ancient idea rooted in cultus, ethnicity, and law, to a new Spirit-born movement of repentance and forgiveness for Jews and Gentiles alike (Acts 11:18). The principles underlying such disputes had far-reaching implications for the emerging Christian community in the first century. As Jewish Christians drifted from strict legal practice, the seeds of separation between the synagogue and the church were sown.

Three Modes of Expression in Jewish Religious Discourse: Halakah, Haggadah, and Midrash

Ancient Jewish practice expanded on the basic message of the Bible in three modes. Two were oral and one was written (see Neale 1991, 28-36).

Halakah is defined as "a saying or story about the way something is to be done, a statement intended to have practical effect and carry normative authority, or an inquiry into the logic or legal principle behind such a rule" (Neusner 1971, 3:5).

Halakah was evolutionary because it was a dialogue between rabbis across the generations on how to apply Scripture to the daily demands of life. Eventually, through this dialectic, a solution emerged and attained a measure of a precedent. In this way Judaism adapted the Law to an ever-changing social milieu.

Halakah was legal in nature. It was the Torah expanded to cover many matters of life not specifically addressed there. In the NT, this is generally called the "tradition of the elders," although this phrase is not used by Luke (Matt 15:2; Mark 7:3, 5). The main purpose of halakah was to prevent the breaking of Torah, what Pirke Aboth 1:1 (m. Avot) famously calls to "set up a fence around the law."

The second oral form was haggadah, a term derived from an Aramaic word that means "to flow." Its purpose was to convey "moral and ethical teachings dealing with the problems of faith and the art of living" (Herr 1971, 356). It was a highly adaptive method. It embraced allegory and analogy as basic tools and sought to inspire the faith of ordinary believers rather than establish doctrine. Parables, truisms, stories, and metaphors were the tools of haggadah. Obviously, Jesus was a master of this mode of expression.

The third method of Jewish expression was midrash. It was a written and exegetical method of arriving at halakah and haggadah.

IN THE TEXT

■ **6-11** On another Sabbath, Jesus healed a man with a withered hand. The narrative continues to develop as a hostile conflict with **the Pharisees and the teachers of the law** (v 7). They **lie in wait** in order to **accuse** him (v 7, as in a legal proceeding). They are *filled with rage* and *talk over in detail* what **they might do to Jesus** (v 11). Jesus' action is blatantly confrontational. He commands the man: **Get up and stand in front of everyone** (v 8). Luke omits Mark's description of Jesus' emotional response to his critics. There he "looked around at them with anger" and "was grieved at their hardness of heart," a description consonant with the tone of Luke's setting (Mark 3:5 NRSV).

The crucial point is posed as a question: **I ask you, which is lawful on the Sabbath: to do good or to do evil, to save life or to destroy it?** (v 9). This is a *boruth*, an unanswerable question designed to embarrass his opponents (see 5:23 and 20:22). This has the effect of heightening the tension of the setting. He challenges the opponents to declare their opinion. His question implies, "A man is suffering from a lifelong affliction. How could the relief of this affliction be considered anything but good?" Jesus' lenient stance has the logic of compassion on its side. His anger shows the intensity of the debate.

Günther Bornkamm said of Jesus' wisdom sayings: "Their characteristic is this, that they appeal immediately to the knowledge, experience and understanding of a man, and reject all necessity for outside proof" (1960, 106). The same can be said of this compassionate healing. As in the previous conflict, compassion trumps religious scruple. Most people can see the sense in this, and it astonishes readers that the Pharisees and teachers of the Law do not. In fact, the Pharisees appear somewhat ridiculous in this scene, and this is the narrator's purpose: to reinforce the reader's empathy with Jesus' position by portraying his opponents with a negative caricature. The Pharisees are "paradigms of imperceptiveness." (Darr [1992, 92-95] traces the character development of Pharisees in Luke.)

The narrative has now established a dangerous conflict in which Jesus' opponents openly plot against him. They discuss **what they might do to Jesus** (v 11). This is a somewhat milder form of expression than that in Mark. There they conspire with the Herodians "how to destroy him" (Mark 3:6 NRSV).

FROM THE TEXT

The relationship of Luke's community to its own enemies was no doubt an additional impetus for this negative portrayal of Jesus' opponents. Literary texts can contain history; but they also continue to live in the lives of their readers. These Pharisees, in some way, also represented the opponents of Luke's own community, just as perhaps they do for us today. We rarely see ourselves in the rigidity of the Pharisees and are far more likely to see our opponents as the ones who are blind and hypocritical. The ethic of love can be marvelously deconstructive of dogma or unexamined prejudice. This text comes to life as we inquire about the ways our own belief systems prevent us from displaying compassion.

Religious movements sometimes choose the path of cultural differentiation as a way of establishing and preserving a separate identity. The "otherness" of the movement can be maintained by enforcing cultural behaviors that, in effect, erect a fence around a community. Exclusion is the operating principle that defines such a differentiated community. The NT presents the Pharisees as preferring this kind of cultural correctness over compassion. This prevents them from embracing the inclusive view of God's love advocated by Jesus.

When a community of faith follows a path of inclusion and compassion, the community evolves and changes in unexpected ways. The values of openness and inclusion *are* dangerous for tradition. The path of holiness as exemplified in Jesus' life was (and is) full of both danger and promise. The same is true when the modern church chooses an ethic of inclusion and compassion for those in its society. The path is a danger to outmoded identities based on exclusion as a way of operation. But it is full of the adventure of grace in action.

7. Jesus Chooses the Twelve (6:12-16)

BEHIND THE TEXT

The characterization of the disciples begins here by listing the Twelve. The portrait of Simon Peter is the most intimate and the one that occupies center stage in key events in the narrative (5:4-11; 8:45, 51; 9:20). James and John join Peter at the healing of Jairus' daughter and the transfiguration. So they rank second in importance (on the Twelve see Bauckham 2006, 93-113; and Gerhardsson 2001, 37-40). Most of the Twelve are never mentioned again in Luke (Bauckham 2006, 96). In spite of the Gospel tradition's frank presentation of the disciples as immature and uncomprehending, the group represents an authoritative witness to Jesus' life in Luke (1:2) and in Acts (1:21; Gerhardsson 2001, 96).

Luke also occasionally uses the term "disciples" to describe the larger, nondescript groups who accompany Jesus in his travels. At other times the "disciples" are simply present at various events described in the Gospel (e.g., 9:14*b*; 10:17; 19:37) or taught by Jesus (6:17; 11:1; 12:1; 16:1; 17:1; 20:45, etc.).

IN THE TEXT

■ **12-16** The inner circle of Jesus' disciples is called the Twelve (6:13; 8:1; 9:1, 12; 18:31; 22:3, 28-30). But occasionally the term "disciples" is also used in reference to this group (7:11; 8:22; 9:18, 43*b*). The Twelve are the confidants of Jesus and privy to the secrets of the kingdom (8:10). Jesus promises them a special place in the world to come (18:28-30). Jesus reveals to them his identity and impending death. But they do not understand his meaning (9:18-27; 18:31-34). They will lead the twelve tribes of Israel (22:28-30; see *Pss. Sol.* 17:6).

Jesus' relationship to his disciples has been compared to rabbinic teacher-pupil relationships of the period. The ministries of other rabbinic teachers of the period were characterized by a stable location, a limited period of commitment to a teacher (e.g., Acts 22:3), the transmission of static tradition, and only males as members (Theissen and Merz 1996, 214). Jesus' disciples differed in that they lived an itinerant life, were considered to have made a permanent commitment, experienced the "free formation of tradition," and included women (Theissen and Merz 1996, 214).

C. The Sermon on the Plain (6:17-49)

1. The Beatitudes (6:17-26)

BEHIND THE TEXT

The naming of the Twelve sets the stage for the beginning of Jesus' teaching ministry. A much larger movement is gaining momentum in the narrative. Verses 17-20 serve as both a summary of the ministry to date and an introduction to this new, highly public teaching phase.

Echoes of the crowds, demons, and healings found in previous summaries and introductions are also here (4:40-41; 5:15, 17). In 6:17, people have gathered from all over the region: "from all Judea and Jerusalem, and from the seacoast of Tyre and Sidon" (NKJV). Although the scene is a remote rural area in lower Galilee, the Gospels portray Jesus as drawing people from the major religious center Jerusalem (seventy miles/one hundred kilometers) to the south, and from the Phoenician capital at Tyre (forty miles/sixty kilometers) to the north (Rogerson 1989, 74).

They **come to hear him** (v 18); but the greater emphasis in this introduction is on his healing powers. They want to **be healed of their diseases** and **evil spirits**. Thus, **all tried to touch him, because power was coming from him and healing them all** (vv 18-19). The healing demonstrates his authority (see 5:24) and lends gravity to his teaching. Considering this remarkable setting, the sermon should be understood as an introductory summary of Jesus' most important instruction in Luke. Thus, Luke's characterization of Jesus closely connects his roles as healer and teacher.

The context of the teaching in the Sermon on the Plain is the sectarian conflict that has arisen in the narrative. The broader foreground of the sermon's narrative setting is Jesus' expulsion from the synagogue in Nazareth (4:14-30, material unique to Luke). The immediate foreground, however, is the five conflict stories of 5:17—6:11 (Green 1997, 262). These are derived from Mark, but the sermon material is present only in Matthew and Luke. A common textual tradition underlies the sermons in both Luke and Matthew. Luke's is the shorter version. Both shape the sermon material to their own purposes (Marshall 1978, 243); but Matthew places the sermon at 5:1—7:28, long before his placement of these opposition stories (9:1-17; 12:1-14). Luke, however, inserts the sermon immediately after the conflict stories.

The conflict context of the sermon in Luke creates a significantly different interpretive perspective. The sermon now becomes a treatise on religious conflict, particularly with regard to the Pharisees. The dangerous struggle between Jesus and his contemporaries is continued and amplified in the teaching of the sermon. The words of conflict in vv 22-26 ("hate," "exclude," "insult," "reject," "woe") reflect the growing tension in the narrative with Jesus' opponents.

IN THE TEXT

■ **17-19** Jesus descends from his night of prayer on the mountain to stand on a **level place** (v 17). This has suggested a "second Moses" motif to some (see Exod 3:1-15). Moses brings the Law down from the mountain, just as Jesus descends from the mountain to set out his teachings. But most see this as only nominally present in Luke (see Bock 1994, 562; Fitzmyer 1981, 1:623).

All sought to touch him because *he exuded the power to heal everyone around him* (v 19). The all-night vigil of prayer goes hand-in-hand with his power to heal (compare 4:1, 42; 5:17).

The reference to **Tyre and Sidon** (v 17) alludes to the larger Lukan theme of salvation for the Gentiles (already in 2:31-32; 3:6; 4:24-27), further developed later in the Gospel and Acts. In 10:32 the residents of these Gentile cities are actually cited as examples of the willingness to repent—a scathing critique of Jews who refuse to do so. This reference is a precursor of 24:47 in which "repentance and forgiveness of sins will be preached in his name to all nations, beginning at Jerusalem."

■ **20-26** Two important things are accomplished in the story by the Sermon on the Plain. The first is the stark differentiation between the disciples of Jesus and the opponents of Jesus. The disciples are equated with "true" **prophets** (v 23); the opponents are equated with **false prophets** (v 26).

This is a defining judgment about the identity and solidarity of the emerging community of Jesus, and a defining judgment that becomes a fixture of the story-world from this point forward. The story proceeds on an "us" (the disciples and sympathetic people) vs. "them" (the Pharisees and teachers of the Law) basis. This clarifies the decisions readers must make in interacting with the story.

The second result of the sermon is a far-reaching conceptual redefinition of the social realities faced by the hearers (and later, the readers) of Jesus' words. In the new economy, social structures will be upended, life's hardships will be alleviated, and the experience of suffering will be replaced with joy.

Through a reversal of expectations, Jesus presents a view of life made right by the justice of God. Inequality, oppression and need will be swept away by the reign of God. Retribution will be visited on the wicked (v 25: *you will hunger* and *you will weep*—future tense verbs). The hunger and sorrow of the **poor** (v 20) will be replaced by satiation and joy. The wealth and merriment of the **rich** (v 24) will be replaced by hunger and sorrow. The reversal motif of the new economy redefines the world, by "erecting on this [OT] foundation a new set of dispositions out of which will flourish new practices, perceptions and attitudes" (Green 1997, 261).

These two things together, the sharp differentiation of disciple and opponent, and the radical redefinition of how reality is to be viewed, are ideas that are foundational to the third Gospel's worldview. Building on the purpose statement about repentance in 5:31-32, the chapters to come will show that one moves from opponent to disciple through the doorway of repentance (see the commentary on 7:48-50).

Verses 20-26 form a double couplet structure (see below). Four couplets contrast the disciples with their opponents. These suggest that the former are equivalent to true **prophets**; the latter, to **false prophets** (vv 23, 26). One set of couplets is prefaced by **Blessed are you**. The other set is prefaced by **Woe to you**. Each is further divided into two halves, in which the result of the status is set out. The poor receive the kingdom of God; the rich already have all the comfort they are going to receive, etc. Matthew's treatment of this material does not have the "woes" component. Nor does Matthew explicitly compare false prophets to true prophets. Luke's distinctive representation of this material is thus properly understood in the context of conflict with Jesus' opponents.

The themes of these couplets are consonant with Luke's narrative to this point: poverty and riches (1:51-53; 6:20), filling the hungry (1:53; 6:21), hatred and fear for God's people (1:71, 74; 2:34-35; 6:22), and rejoicing (1:47; 2:29; 6:23). From ch 1 onward these ideas draw on a broad range of sources from the Psalms and the Major and Minor Prophets (see Beale and Carson 2007, 295-96). In Luke 4:16-19 these ideas were placed at the center of attention by Jesus' quotation of Isa 61:1-2 and its underlying reliance on the Jubilee theme—the "year of the Lord's favor." There is an extensive intertextuality underlying the language of the doublets.

Double Couplet Structure

Blessed are the poor	yours is the kingdom of God
Woe to the rich	you have already received your comfort
Blessed are you who hunger now	you will be satisfied
Woe to the well fed	you will go hungry
Blessed are you when you weep	you will laugh
Woe to you who laugh now	for you will mourn and weep
Blessed are you when men hate, exclude, insult, and reject you as evil on account of the Son of Man	for such was the treatment of real prophets by your fathers
Woe to you when men speak well of you	for that is how their fathers treated the false prophets

153

Most scholars assume that a single tradition originating with Jesus underlies the so-called Sermon on the Mount and Sermon on the Plain. Yet, Luke preserves these statements in a form that emphasizes their social and physical significance. He believes the "poor" and "hungry" will be freed from their physical distress. Matthew, on the other hand, believes the "poor in spirit" and those who "hunger and thirst after righteousness" will be blessed. This is an example of how Evangelists shape synoptic material to their own theological purposes. Such differences are sometimes due to the redaction of the sources, but they may also point to complex issues about the nature of the sources from which the Evangelists derived their material (see Marshall 1978, 243-45).

The reference to true **prophets** and **false prophets** (vv 23*b*, 26*b*) adds a practical dimension to the theme of conflict inherent in this passage. How will the faithful recognize the prophet "like" Moses who will "tell them everything" God commands (as promised in Deut 18:15-22)?

Deuteronomy has two tests: First, if the words of the prophet prove to be untrue, that prophet is a false prophet (Deut 18:22; see Neale 1993, 90-94). Second, if the prophet whose "omens and portents" do, in fact, take place, but he encourages Israel to "follow other gods" (Deut 13:1-2), he is also a false prophet. Thus, the test of the prophet is always the test of Israel. Jesus challenges his new community to make judgments about those who claim to speak for Yahweh. He has already been accused of blasphemy by his opponents (5:21) and the charge of false prophecy would no doubt easily follow behind. Jesus calls his disciples to align themselves with him as a true prophet—like Moses (9:33). The burden of discerning the truth in the midst of ambiguity is part of the challenge of discipleship in the new community.

2. Love Your Enemies (6:27-31)

■ **27-28** Jesus promises his disciples more than a new social reality. He challenges them to practice a radical mode of conduct to usher in that reality. Jesus admonishes his followers: **Love your enemies, do good to those who hate you, bless those who curse you, pray for those who mistreat you** (vv 27-28 ‖ Matt 5:44). This radical emphasis on love is not an innovation. Jesus stands generally "within the frame of reference" of Jewish theology and Scripture with his confirmation of the twofold fulfillment of the commands in Deut 6:5 and Lev 19:18 (quoted in 10:25-28 ‖ Matt 22:23-40 ‖ Mark 12:30-31; Chilton and McDonald 1987, 8).

Encouraging kindness toward enemies is not unknown in the OT (Prov 24:17-18; 25:21-22). But it is not prominent, and blessing enemies has no antecedents in Jewish literature (Marshall 1978, 259). Jesus' command to "love your enemies" may merely rephrase the traditional Lev 19:18 command, "love your neighbor," to a far more radical expression (Beale and Carson 2007, 297). Giving enemies the same love as all others is an almost irrational idea in the context of normal human social contracts. It violates every natural instinct.

And yet, we are called to do so by Jesus. His call is not mere passivity in the presence of enemies, but love aggressively pursued.

In Luke, the Sermon on the Plain is set within the context of sectarian disagreement within contemporary Judaism. The narrative structure suggests that Jesus demonstrates the meaning of love for neighbor and enemy in the five conflict stories of 5:17—6:11 (see Behind the Text on 5:17-19). He heals the paralytic, dines with tax collectors and sinners, teaches on the difficulty of embracing change, debates Sabbath piety with Pharisees, and heals a man long disabled. All of this occurs in a context of opposition and disbelief among some of those present.

To **hate, exclude, insult, curse,** and **mistreat** (vv 22, 27, 28) characterizes Jesus' reception since his appearance at the synagogue in Nazareth through these five conflicts. Jesus encourages his disciples to love "enemies" like those responsible for these experiences (see Green [1997, 272], who suggests that the sinners themselves are the "enemies").

This ethic of love follows the path of good for others, regardless of opposition. Jesus does not counsel passive submission to evil. Instead, he urges love as an urgently active force. Luke implies, "This is how you should interpret the things Jesus just did in relation to these five conflicts. This is what this sermon means in terms of human action." Love those who oppose you.

■ **29-31** Three admonitions that have a personal and physical aspect follow. Perhaps Jesus' disciples had already experienced physical violence or been robbed. **Turn . . . the other** cheek (v 29a); **do not stop him from taking your tunic** (v 29b); **give to everyone who asks you** (v 30). This is what disciples engaged in ministry must specifically do to answer the opponents of the Son of Man.

Many of the verbs and pronouns in these verses are plural, indicating a communal responsibility for action. When individuals act nonviolently and generously, it is powerful. But when communities do so, it is even more powerful, leading to the transformation of a culture.

As a summary statement of the ethics of living according to the kingdom, Jesus exhorts his followers: **Do to others as you would have them do to you** (v 31). There are parallels of this in contemporary literature of the time (see Marshall 1978, 262). They are found in both negative and, more rarely, the positive formulation found here. The intertext is Lev 19:18, "Love your neighbor as yourself."

Matthew's treatment of this material (Matt 5:38-42) refers to Exod 21:23-25. This text prescribes proportional restitution in personal injury cases: "eye for eye, tooth for tooth, hand for hand" (v 24). The Law sought to keep restitution proportionate to the damage caused, and thus prevent excessive vengeance. Here in Luke, the exhortation is to forego this principle for the sake of the kingdom (6:27-31).

Some have held that nonviolence as a political way of life was character-istic of the early church prior to Constantine. In modern times, the impetus to pacifism has found expression in the theology of Anabaptists, Quakers, and many prominent figures from Tolstoy to Gandhi to King. Some scholars, such as John Howard Yoder, consider these teachings of Jesus to be at the heart of his message (see *The Politics of Jesus*, 1972).

Israel Abrahams, the great Jewish exegete of the early twentieth century, called the dictum to love one's neighbor the ultimate evidence of the "solidar-ity of the human race" (1967, 20). Treating others with the dignity we desire for ourselves is in harmony with the activist nature of love that has been sug-gested here as an interpretation of Jesus' ethics.

As in the parable of the good Samaritan (10:29-37), the definition of "neighbor" in Jesus' teachings involves a highly proactive "doing." There, lov-ing one's neighbor includes binding, anointing, housing, and feeding (10:25-37, esp. vv 34-35). In this theology, the so-called Golden Rule—doing unto others as we would have them do to us—becomes a fundamental value that guides all human interaction. Maddox describes John Wesley's "relational an-thropology" as one in which loving service to others is "central to true human existence" (1994, 68). Certainly, this activism of love is a central feature of the thought and practice of Wesleyan theology.

3. Love Without Reciprocity (6:32-36)

■ **32-36** Verses 32-36 are an augment to the admonition to love one's en-emies. Jesus explains that there is no moral merit for love, good deeds, or lending when reciprocation is involved (see Deut 23:19-20). The phrase, **what credit is that to you?** is repeated three times (vv 32, 33, 34). Also repeated three times is the acknowledgment: **even "sinners"** love, do good, and lend to those they already love (vv 32, 33, 34). Loving those who love us is good; but there is no healing power in it if reciprocity is its driving force.

The use of "sinners" on Jesus' lips in this negative sense is interesting. These sinners are not the good, healthy sinners who are the characteristic heroes of Luke's narrative (see Behind the Text on 5:1-11). These are the truly immoral and irredeemably lost, more akin to the traditional language of "wick-ed/sinner" language in the OT and LXX (as also in 5:29-30; Neale 1991, 75-95). More specifically, these sinners are those who always seek their own best interests. That is, they love, do good, and lend only when there is reciprocity.

There is, however, a dawning redemption of the sinner in the narrative (5:1-11; 5:27-32; 7:36-50; 15:11-32; 18:1-8; 19:1-10). Those who are held up as the prototypical damned begin to respond to Jesus' offer of forgiveness. These Gospel stories (and this is their proper description) are examples of the transforming power of the ethic of love. It bridges the gulf between the saved and the lost.

4. Do Not Judge (6:37-38)

■ **37-38** Fitzmyer describes the teachings of Jesus preserved in vv 37-45 as directed to those within the community of disciples (1981, 1:630). But this may not fully capture the impact of Jesus' teaching on judging others. The verbs are second person plural, implying a communally shared standard of behavior. They are present tense, implying habitual behavior. And they are imperative in voice, implying a strong demand. Negatively, we must not **judge** or **condemn**. Proactively, we must **forgive** and **give**. But this ethic is directed also to those beyond the community.

In response to refraining from judging or condemning others we will, ironically, receive reciprocation from God according to our actions. We are not to reciprocate, yet God will repay us according to our deeds: **A good measure, pressed down, shaken together and running over, will be poured into your lap** (v 38a). The world can be healed of its cycle of violence only when a community is willing to abandon its claims to retribution, a prerogative reserved exclusively to God. We are to practice unconditional love not just toward fellow disciples, but even toward enemies, trusting the justice of God to make it all right in the end. How different this is from the hope of political/national renewal longed for by Israel (Acts 1:6)!

Ultimately, however, reciprocation *is* fully realized, even in God's kingdom. While acting without selfish regard is paramount, participation in the community of the kingdom also carries with it an immutable law of cause and effect: **For with the measure you use, it will be measured to you** (v 38b). God welcomes the unworthy graciously, but once drawn into a new community of love, its members are responsible to act, and will be rewarded according to their efforts.

Here is the counterbalance to nonreciprocity (see vv 32-36): Disciples are to expect nothing in return for goodness done; but God *does* expect a return for grace given. His reward *is* conditional on deeds. The reward of divine approval depends on our reciprocity toward God.

This is not a "works" theology; it is a theology of responsibility and gratitude demonstrated through actions. To suggest that deeds are not required of true disciples is entirely foreign to the thought and teaching of Jesus. Quite the contrary; our salvation, Luke teaches, requires them. If disciples are called to follow Jesus, they will also be involved in his mission and ministry.

5. The Log in Your Own Eye (6:39-42)

■ **39-40** Under the rubric of telling a "parable," Luke combines two aphorisms (or truisms; vv 39 and 40) and a parable (vv 41-42). The material in Luke 6:39-42 is found in three different places in Matthew (15:14; 10:24-25; 7:3-5). Luke's literary finesse with his sources is usually so seamless it is difficult to tell where a source ends and his own treatment begins. But in this case the compilation of material shows little editorial reworking.

The overarching theme of the three sayings is humility in leadership. Supporting metaphors are based on sight or blindness. First, the physically **blind** obviously make poor guides. They are presented here as a metaphor for the spiritually blind. The physically blind fall into a physical **pit**; the spiritually blind fall into *the* pit, which is a symbol for judgment (Isa 24:17-18; Jer 48:43-44). This story illustrates the humor Jesus often used in his teaching. The blind leading the blind can only lead to a comic end, and the story is rather playful (Phipps 1993, 94).

On the other hand, disciples, when **fully trained** (*katērtismenos*, v 40), will see the truth as well as their teacher. The verb *katartizō* is unusual for Luke. It has a connotation in Paul of "Christian character worked out in the sense of unity of the members of the community" (1 Cor 1:10; Eph 4:12; 1 Thess 3:10; Delling 1964, 1:476). The fully trained disciple is a communal responsibility. That is, disciples exist only within the context of the community, not as independent entities. That the disciple is humble, **not above his teacher** (v 40), calls disciples to be a unifying force within the community, reinforcing the teacher's authority.

■ **41-42** Worse than the blind guide is the hypocrite who claims to see, but is the most blind of all. The mental image of someone with a **plank** in his or her eye trying to remove a **speck** from another's eye, all in a self-righteous attempt to correct another's flaws, is humorous. It is not "intentionally grotesque" (Fitzmyer 1981, 1:642); but it is comically effective (Phipps 1993, 94). The exclamation **hypocrite!** must have been delivered with a wry smile and received with a laugh from the crowd. The point of the stories in vv 41-42 is easily understood. Those who presume to teach or lead must do so in a spirit of humility.

6. Good Fruit (6:43-45)

■ **43-45** Luke and Matthew part ways on how they use Jesus' story of the **good tree** and the **bad tree** (v 43). Matthew uses it in a controversy setting in which the Pharisees charge Jesus with casting out demons by Beelzebub (Matt 12:22-37).

Luke, instead (see 11:14-23), includes it in a more general compilation of Jesus' teachings. As a result, it carries a less pointed application for Luke. The core aphorism is, "For each tree is known by its own fruit" (v 44 NRSV). The principle is reproduction according to its kind. That is, **thornbushes** do not bear figs and bramble bushes do not yield grapes, etc. One important intertext for this principle is the garden of Eden story. Genesis 1:11 says all things are created to reproduce according to their kind.

Figs are considered the most delicious fruit of the region. They serve as a powerful symbol not only of desire but also of God's blessing (v 44; Isa 36:16;

Luke 13:6). Zechariah and Micah both use the fig as a symbol for the future age of God's reign (Mic 4:4; Zech 3:10). The **thornbushes** and the **briers**, by contrast, are often associated with God's curse on Israel (v 44; Exod 22:6; Isa 7:19; Job 31:40).

Jesus applies the analogy of reproduction according to kind to the human heart and the words that proceed from it. The **heart** refers to the center of human thought and will. *The good person brings good things out of the good stored up in the heart, and the evil person brings evil things out of the evil stored up in the heart. For out of the overflow of the heart a person's mouth speaks* (v 45).

Whereas the goodness of a tree is demonstrated by its fruit, the goodness of a person is demonstrated by his or her words and deeds. Goodness flows with ease from within. From that goodness flow the actions of the body and the words of the mouth. This is a simple and wholesome portrait of the holy life.

7. "Why Do You Call Me 'Lord, Lord'?" (6:46-49)

■ **46-49** Again, Luke follows the Q material he shares with Matthew (7:21-27). Matthew 7:22-23, however, is found in Luke 13:25-27. The intertext is Mal 1:6, the prophet's criticism of corrupt priests (see the commentary on 7:24-30 for Luke's reliance on Malachi's rhetorical style). In 1:6 we find a similar formula: a rhetorical question followed by a challenge to loyalty: "And if I am a master, where is the respect due me?" The term *kyrios* (**lord**) appears in both Luke and the LXX of Malachi.

The parable in Luke elucidates the connection between what people *say* and *do*. Jesus warns against a disjuncture between the two. Consistency in word and deed reflects right relationship with our *kyrios*. Hypocrisy is confession without action, and it is compared to being **without a foundation** (v 49).

The marriage of confession (**"Lord, Lord"**) and action is similar to a foundation built upon **rock** (v 48). To hear the words of Jesus creates a responsibility to "do"—to act consistently. An example of the consequences of failure to act appears in 13:25-27. There those who claimed: "We ate and drank with you, and you taught in our streets" are turned away from the householder's door with, "I don't know you!"

Snodgrass calls the story of two foundations "Luke's first parable" (2008, 333). The parable describes the character of those who act on Jesus' words. The aphorisms of vv 39-42 are based on the metaphor of sight and blindness. Here the controlling metaphor is hearing.

Those who "hear" and "do" are like those who build a foundation on bedrock. They are safe from the metaphorical storms of life. Those who hear but do not act consistently are like those who build on sand and are swept away by the metaphorical **floods** and **rivers** of adversity in life.

The point of the parable can be stated simply, *"Anyone who hears Jesus' words and does not do them is a fool"* (Snodgrass 2008, 337). Luke uses hearing as an analogy for spiritual awareness again in 8:4-15, in connection with the parable of the sower.

"Why do you call me 'Lord, Lord,' and do not do what I say?" The question of Jesus strikes a deep chord. Why, indeed, do people call him Lord yet act as though he were not? In his *Essays*, Michel de Montaigne captured the human quandary well, "But we are, I know not how, double within ourselves, with the result that we do not believe what we believe, and we cannot rid ourselves of what we condemn." Regrettably, sometimes even the devout act contrary to their convictions. Jesus' words call for an intimate connection of faith to deed.

Jesus calls for much more than mere obedience. The activist ethic of loving one's enemies is a remedy for the hatred that separates people. It is our *enemies*, Jesus asserts, who must be loved. This radical solution to social malaise is repeated in Luke 10:25-37, in which Jesus identifies our "neighbor" as the hated Samaritan.

There is twofold innovation in Jesus' ethics. First, he radically extends the definition of neighbor to include those we would prefer to hate. Second, he says that our hate, the evidence of our need for God, teaches us who we must love. The principle is timelessly stated: "But love your enemies, do good to them, and lend to them without expecting to get anything back" (6:35).

Reciprocity, which Jesus repudiates in human personal ethical behavior, is God's prerogative alone. The reward for kindness to enemies comes in the form of being called **"sons of the Most High, because he is kind to the ungrateful and wicked"** (v 35). This phrase has programmatic power for the entire story of Luke.

The salvation of **the ungrateful and wicked** becomes the program of the narrative. This brings about a complete reversal of expectations with respect to their identity before God. It will be precisely those who were once **ungrateful and wicked** who comprehend Jesus' true identity. The supposedly "righteous," who remain uncomprehending, are on the outside. The operative factor, the gospel-factor, is the mercy of God to **the ungrateful and wicked**: "Be merciful, just as your Father is merciful" (v 36; compare Matthew's "be perfect" in 5:48).

D. Jesus Teaches and Heals in the Cities and Villages (7:1—8:21)

1. The Healing of the Centurion's Slave (7:1-10)

The healing of the servant of the centurion further develops the theme of Gentile salvation in the narrative. Previously, in the Song of Simeon, the old man described the infant Jesus as "a light for revelation to the Gentiles" (2:32). John the Baptist said that "all mankind will see God's salvation" through the one to come (3:6). In 4:16-30, the rejection of Jesus in his home synagogue was caused by his references to Gentiles—to the widow at Zarephath in Sidon and Naaman the Syrian (vv 25-27). Jesus said that there were many in Israel who were in need; but it was only these Gentiles whom God healed.

Jesus critiques the religious and ethnic insularity of many of his Jewish contemporaries, thus asserting that salvation is available to Gentiles in the kingdom of God. This is the fundamental interrelation between the classical prophetic tradition and the Gospel tradition (see the commentary on 4:23-27).

The inclusion of Gentiles in God's salvation will become increasingly explicit in the Gospel. No longer found on the lips of priests and prophets alone (1:79; 2:29-32), this salvation will be seen in the response of non-Jews to Jesus in the story. Here we have the story of the Gentile centurion (7:1-10). Later in Luke, other stories will reinforce the theme:

- the Gerasene demoniac (8:26-39)
- the ostensible repentance of the residents of Tyre and Sidon (10:13-15)
- the parable of the good Samaritan (10:29-37)
- the description of the messianic banquet (13:22-30)
- the story of the lepers of Samaria (17:11-19)

All these stories are about Gentiles who respond positively to Jesus (or, in the case of the Samaritans, those viewed as apostates by traditional Jews).

The conviction that salvation is for all is further developed in Acts. There the message of the gospel is directed to both Jews and Gentiles (Acts 26:20, 23). The structure of Acts is about the movement of the gospel from its roots in Jerusalem to its proclamation in Rome, the Gentile center of the Roman Empire. Along that path, Gentiles are welcomed into the community of faith of the apostles.

In Luke 7 and beyond, the foundation for the welcome of Gentiles into the community of salvation is laid. By recounting the stories of non-Jews whom Jesus encountered in his ministry, Luke even suggests that salvation will come to the Gentiles to the exclusion of those Jews who repudiate Jesus' mission (13:22-30; also 21:23-24). Speaking to Jewish villagers on the way to Jerusalem, Jesus says that they will "not be able" to enter by the narrow gate (13:24). He adds that many Gentiles will come to the great banquet from east, west, north, and south, but unbelieving Jews like you will be "thrown out" (13:28). The Matthean parallel is even more emphatic: the "subjects of the kingdom"—Jews—will be cast into outer darkness at the eschatological banquet (Matt 8:11-13). This is not a repudiation of Judaism, but an affirmation of a wider reach for the kingdom than some were prepared to accept.

In Luke's theology, membership in the community of Israel is neither an advantage nor a disadvantage in obtaining salvation. All are equal in the new community. Human equality is fundamental to Luke's conviction that only the repentant will attend the messianic banquet, whether Jew, Gentile, or sinner. This equality is the basis of Luke's theological paradigm and makes his Gospel radical to any insular perspective, Jewish or Christian. Thus, the story of the believing centurion is a turning point in the narrative where a wider reach for salvation is introduced.

IN THE TEXT

■ **1-5** The scene returns to Capernaum (v 1) after a period spent in the surrounding towns and villages (4:44—6:49). Capernaum, in contrast to Nazareth (4:20-29), had warmly received Jesus (4:31-37) and continues to be positively portrayed in the Gospel (until 10:15). In Capernaum, **elders of the Jews** (7:3; see 4:36) embrace Jesus' ministry and beg him to aid the God-fearing centurion, citing his good deeds.

This positive portrait of Capernaum's local Jews puts Jesus' opponents in an even more unflattering light. He is embraced by the local population, but opposed by those from afar. The Pharisees and teachers who challenged him earlier (5:21) had "come from every village of Galilee and from Judea and Jerusalem" (5:17). That his opponents travel to spy on him (contrast Matt 9:1; Mark 2:1-2) gives their opposition a darker hue. From a narrative standpoint they are part of a larger, conspiratorial plot against Jesus.

Luke presents the centurion as an exemplary Gentile faithful to God, what Acts calls "God-fearing" (10:2). He is esteemed by his Jewish neighbors and it is the **elders of the Jews** (v 3) who come to Jesus to plead for the centurion: **This man deserves to have you do this, because he loves our nation and has built our synagogue** (vv 4-5; see 8:41).

This is the first time we encounter faithfulness outside of the Jewish community in Luke, but it is also the first time we encounter exemplary faith displayed by *anyone* in the Gospel. This story shows a radical broadening of the reach of Jesus' ministry to include those outside the social and religious propriety of traditional Judaism.

■ **6-10** This centurion is a figure resembling Cornelius in Acts 10:2. Both men were Roman military leaders, devout, supportive of the Jewish community, sought divine help, and received the help they requested. The sidebar below highlights the parallels. The centurion of Acts 10 is the first Gentile confirmed in the Christian faith by the baptism of the Holy Spirit. In a sense, Luke has provided readers with a theological framework of Gentile salvation in these two centurions. The first is a model disciple demonstrating saving faith; the second, an exemplary, Spirit-filled Gentile.

	Luke 7	Acts 10
Description of centurion	There a centurion's servant, whom his master valued highly, was sick and about to die (v 2).	"At Caesarea there was a man named Cornelius, a centurion in what was known as the Italian Regiment" (v 1).
Action of the centurion	The centurion heard of Jesus and sent some elders of the Jews to him, asking him to come and heal his servant (v 3).	"A holy angel told him to have you come to his house so that he could hear what you have to say" (v 22).
Character of the centurion	This man deserves to have you do this, because he loves our nation and has built our synagogue (vv 4-5).	"He and all his family were devout and God-fearing; he gave generously to those in need and prayed to God regularly" (v 2). "He is a righteous and God-fearing man, who is respected by all the Jewish people" (v 22).
Faith of the centurion	Lord, don't trouble yourself, for I do not deserve to have you come under my roof. That is why I did not even consider myself worthy to come to you. But say the word, and my servant will be healed (vv 6-7).	"Cornelius answered: 'Four days ago I was in my house praying at this hour, at three in the afternoon. Suddenly a man in shining clothes stood before me and said, "Cornelius, God has heard your prayer and remembered your gifts to the poor." . . . Now we are all here in the presence of God to listen to everything the Lord has commanded you to tell us'" (vv 30-31, 33).
The miracle for the centurion	Then the men who had been sent returned to the house and found the servant well (v 10).	"While Peter was still speaking these words, the Holy Spirit came on all who heard the message. The circumcised believers who had come with Peter were astonished that the gift of the Holy Spirit had been poured out even on the Gentiles" (vv 44-45).

LUKE

7:6-10

Summary logion about Gentile faith	**When Jesus heard this, he was amazed at him, and turning to the crowd following him, he said, "I tell you, I have not found such great faith even in Israel"** (v 9).	"Then Peter began to speak: 'I now realize how true it is that God does not show favoritism but accepts men from every nation who fear him and do what is right'" (vv 34-35).

Luke 7 idealizes the characterization of the centurion in several ways: (1) His faith is without uncertainty and loving, even under the duress of a servant's mortal illness. His servant is *entimos*—**valued, precious, and highly regarded**—by his master (v 2). He does not need to see to believe, having only **heard of Jesus** (v 3). This kind of faith stands in stark contrast to the kind that requires visible proof and demands signs (see 11:16).

(2) He is humble and trusting: **I did not even consider myself worthy to come to you. But say the word, and my servant will be healed** (v 7). In Matt 8:5, the centurion comes in person to Jesus, but not here in Luke. Here the centurion's humility prevents him from approaching Jesus.

(3) He is a soldier of the Roman occupation, and thus an outcast to Jews. But he is a compassionate man. He asks Jesus to heal a **servant** who **was sick and about to die** (v 2).

He has, in short, all the traits of the ideal disciple. It is ironic that a military leader of the occupying force in Galilee is the most pious individual Jesus has encountered in the Gospel so far. By contrast, his Jewish opponents responded with fury when Jesus healed the man with the withered hand on the Sabbath (6:11). Later they will accuse Jesus of speaking in the name of Beelzebub (11:15). The centurion, and these who oppose Jesus, represent the polar opposites of how people respond to Jesus in Luke. It is, of course, with the former that the sympathetic reader is being not-so-subtly encouraged to identify. Luke urges, "Be like the centurion, not like the doubters."

Ritual Purity and the Centurions in Luke and Acts

The centurion in Luke 7 sends his servants to intercept Jesus when he is "not far from the house" (v 6). This may have been a courtesy, to allow Jesus to avoid contracting the impurity physical contact with a Gentile or his home would have conveyed. In another parallel to the story of Cornelius, his servants also do not presume to come directly to Peter in Simon the Tanner's home. Rather, they stand respectfully at a distance, at the gate, and call out to Peter (Acts 10:17-18).

In Acts 10, both Peter and the centurion know that Jews are forbidden "to associate with a Gentile or visit him." Yet, Peter enters Cornelius' home and says, "But God has shown me that I should not call anyone impure or unclean" (10:28). Likewise, Luke's Jesus presumably intended to enter the centurion's house and would have done so had he not been met outside.

Luke's narrative deconstructs ritual purity as an imperative for salvation in a slow, incremental fashion. Both Gentile centurions, although ritually unclean themselves, display faith and an inner purity not evidenced by ritually observant Jews. From a narrative point of view, both stories build the case for Gentile inclusion in the saved community. Both also point out the narrowness of mind of those who oppose Jesus and Gentile inclusion (see Acts 11). Yet, they do so without making a statement against the purity laws.

While Luke's Jesus shows a general tendency to disregard the rules of ritual purity (5:30; 11:38-41), he does not denigrate ritual observance itself (5:14). His approval of the conduct of the faithful, both Jewish and Gentile, affirms this (5:14; 7:6-7, 39-49; 8:46-48). He does, however, reject the inextricable connection most Jews assumed to exist between ritual purity and personal holiness (see the commentary on 5:12-16; 7:39; and 8:42b-48). And thus, a Jewish attitude that would exclude Gentiles from salvation based on purity issues is progressively deconstructed by Luke.

The centurion says, **For I myself am a man under authority** (v 8). The burden of power seems to unite the centurion and Jesus at a personal level. He knew that Jesus, because of his authority with God, need only speak a word to heal his servant. **But say the word, and my servant will be healed** (v 7). This conforms to Luke's pattern in which presumed sinners, in this case a Roman soldier, are the truly righteous and the supposed righteous, the Pharisees and teachers of the Law, are the actual sinners. The continued reversal of expectations further prepares readers for the concept of a broadly inclusive gospel.

The centurion's faith highlights the lack of faith of Jesus' religious opponents. Jesus says, *I have not found such an exemplary faith, even in Israel* (v 9). The phrase is a comparative one. Jesus lauds the centurion's great amount of faith rather than his faith in anything specific (e.g., that Jesus is the Messiah). His faith expresses his confidence in God as compassionate and powerful. Similarly, in Luke's first use of "faith" in 5:20, he remarks on the faith of those who sought to lower their paralyzed friend through the roof at Peter's house. Their extreme behavior demonstrated that these men had an exemplary, overarching spirit of faith.

In a similar passage on the nature of faith in 17:5-6, the disciples implore the Lord, "Increase our faith!" Jesus refers to faith as small as a mustard seed as sufficient. It is not the object of faith that is emphasized in these stories so much as its quality and quantity. When such faith is combined with repentance (which we shall soon see in the story of the sinful woman), Luke's understanding of the way to salvation becomes clear for readers. Furthermore, it is a kind of faith that rests directly on God rather than on a set of ideas. As such, faith is broadly accessible to those on the margin of religious observance. Luke's sinners are not asked to assume an intellectual position. They are asked to assume a humble posture toward a merciful God.

Faith in Luke and Acts

Faith is prominent in Luke. The word **faith** (*pistis*) is found eleven times in Luke and fourteen times in Acts (in Matthew eight times; in Mark five times). Although prominent, the use of the term in Luke and Acts is not easily categorized.

In the Gospel, the majority of the references to faith are found in connection with healings. Others affirm forgiveness; still other references encourage personal constancy (see below). In only one instance is faith raised in connection with a supernatural event, the calming of the sea, in Jesus' question to his disciples: "Where is your faith?" (8:25).

In general, *pistis* seems to refer to an experiential certainty about God in Luke, a felt belief that leads to action. Luke's use of *pistis* has more in common with the concept of faith in Heb 11 as steadfast endurance, than faith described as the saving mechanism of salvation in Acts and Paul (e.g., Acts 3:16 or Eph 2:8). Luke 7:50 may be the rare exception.

In Acts, the discussion of faith shifts to the content of belief rather than something that is primarily felt and experienced, although the latter is not precluded. In Acts, one is inducted into the faith, holds the faith, has faith in Jesus, is full of faith, or is cleansed by faith. With this broad range of meaning, it is a key concept for Lukan salvation. Without *pistis* one cannot find healing, forgiveness, cleansing of heart, constancy, or membership in the new community.

Occurrences of *Pistis* by Theme

Gospel of Luke

• Faith in relation to healing	5:20; 7:9; 8:48; 17:19; 18:42
• Faith in relation to forgiveness	7:50
• Faith in relation to the miraculous	8:25; 17:5-6
• Faith in relation to constancy in prayer	18:8
• Faith in relation to constancy in commitment	22:32

Acts

• The "faith" as a description of Christian belief	6:7; 13:8; 14:22; 16:5
• Faith in Jesus	3:16; 20:21; 24:24
• Full of faith	6:5; 11:24
• Faith to be healed	14:9
• Cleansing hearts by faith	15:9; 26:18

FROM THE TEXT

The story of the centurion's faith is poignant because faith arises from an unexpected quarter, the Roman military presence in Palestine. There is no overt indication in the story of the complex political and social issues that an occupying force in Galilee raises. Yet, the subtext of social conflict is never far from the reader's consciousness.

As everywhere in Luke's portrait of Jesus' ministry, those of whom faith is least expected have the noblest faith. The centurion's faith is like that of the sailors and Ninevites in Jonah, pagans who display the best in piety, to the chagrin of the chosen (Jonah 3:4-5; Luke 11:32). He is like Naaman the Syrian in Luke 4:27 (2 Kgs 5:1-15), another foreign military figure who approaches the Jewish prophet Elisha for healing.

The interaction between the centurion and Jesus emphasizes humility in one's approach to God, compassion for others in need, and openness to the marginalized. Such traits are sound practice for all Christians, but particularly for Wesleyans, whose theology emphasizes holiness as a way of life. The holiness lifestyle is a personal commitment that should lead to a life of action and social responsibility rather than self-absorption and endless introspection.

The drama of the centurion and Jesus was played out in a context of real social, political, and religious conflict, a context in which the willingness to cross all kinds of boundaries brought healing and restoration. It is to a similar life of courage, decision, and openness that the modern church is called.

2. The Raising of the Widow's Son in Nain (7:11-17)

BEHIND THE TEXT

The story of the raising of the widow's son in Nain is special Lukan material. Nain was a small city about six miles (ten kilometers) south of Nazareth, or twenty-one miles (thirty-four kilometers) southwest from Capernaum. In 1982 an archaeological team located the city walls.

Jesus is accompanied to Nain by **his disciples and a large crowd** (*ochlos polys*). The reference to a crowd is always used by Luke to indicate a public event at a significant juncture in Jesus' ministry.

- A "large crowd" is present at Levi's banquet (5:29).
- Several times while Jesus is teaching (5:17; 6:17; 8:4; 14:25).
- At the foot of the Mount of Transfiguration (9:37).

Now **large crowds** attend this miracle in a remote town of southern Galilee. It seems historically implausible that large groups of people should be found in obscure places such as a tax collector's den, remote mountains, or distant plains. In Luke, these crowds are to be understood as a literary device indicating the public nature of the event.

Although Jesus' activities are largely rural, **large crowds** continue to follow him. This raises interesting historical questions. Who are these people? How many people are required to consider the crowd large? One hundred? One thousand? More? What segments of society do they represent? Do they adopt the itinerant lifestyle of Jesus and his disciples, leaving jobs and families behind? Answers to these questions would reveal interesting information about the nature and substance of the early Jesus movement. Unfortunately, the text contains no historical information on this subject. Luke 8:1-3 calls attention to a particularly interesting feature of Jesus' following: the presence of women on the road with him.

In Luke the public ministry of Jesus is presented as a large-scale, populist, rural movement (see Theissen and Merz 1996, 170-71). If there were, in fact, thousands of people who had suffered social dislocation to follow Jesus, the effect on a rural population would have been significant indeed. And the Roman government would have taken forceful notice. From the outside it would certainly look like a Galilean revolt in the making. On the whole, it seems more historically plausible that those who actually traveled with him on his itinerate ministry were in the hundreds, not thousands.

IN THE TEXT

■ **11-13** The raising of the widow's son at Nain is a turning point in the narrative. It was not the first public miracle (see 5:25; 6:10, 18), but it is the most remarkable in Jesus' ministry to this point. Not only is a **large crowd** accompanying Jesus, but a **large crowd** is present from the city as well (7:11, 12).

The text depicts a visual scene of two large crowds converging, with Jesus, the widow, and her dead son in the center of the frame. From that location emanates a powerful miracle of the resuscitation of a dead man.

There is, in fact, a building pattern of deeds of wonder in the narrative. Demons have been exorcized and the sick healed (4:33-37, 39, 40-41; 5:13, 17-26; 6:6-11; 7:1-10). Now the raising of a man from the dead is an early crescendo in the Lukan narrative. Structurally, this event will lead to John the Baptist's question on the identity of Jesus: "Are you the one who was to come?" (7:19). The identity of Jesus is fully public at Nain and is only clarified by subsequent events as the narrative proceeds.

As Jesus entered Nain, he came upon a funeral procession for a **widow** who had lost her **only son** (v 12; on Luke's concern for widows, see 2:36-40; 4:23-27; 7:1-17; 18:1-8; 20:47; 21:2; Acts 6:1). **When the Lord saw her, his heart went out to her and he said, "Don't cry"** (v 13). Luke tends to refer to Jesus as **the Lord**, a phrase used previously in his Gospel only in reference to God (1:28; 2:15). This is a significant christological statement (compare also 7:19; 10:1, 39, 41; 11:39; 12:42; 13:15; 17:5-6; 18:6; 19:31, 34). Otherwise in Matthew and Mark we have this form of address in only a few places (e.g., Matt 21:3; 24:42; Mark 5:19; 11:3).

Luke's Jesus is usually more stoical than Matthew's or Mark's. They frequently use the stock word for compassion (*splangchnizomai*); whereas Luke usually omits it in shared material (Matt 14:14) or omits the entire story (Matt 15:32-39; 18:27-35). But he does use the word here (translated: **his heart went out**; see also 10:33 and 15:20).

Jesus' compassion for this widow is similar to that Elijah expressed for the widow of Zarephath, who also lost her only son to illness (4:25-26). In 1 Kgs 17:17-24, Elijah raises the widow's son in a similar tender scene. The

Lukan story also echoes the raising of the Shunammite's son by Elisha in 2 Kgs 4:8-37. This occurred just two miles (three kilometers) south of Nain in Shunem (Rogerson 1989, 141). The story of the widow of Nain has the feel of an OT story describing the exploits of a prophet.

■ **14-17** Then he went up and touched the *stretcher,* **and those carrying it stood still (v 14).** Note that Jesus touched the *soros,* a stretcher or litter, rather than an enclosed coffin (Fitzmyer 1981, 1:659). This act would have transmitted ritual impurity to Jesus, something from which he does not shy away in Luke (see above 7:1-10). The continued downplaying of the importance of ritual purity builds Luke's case that faith rather than temple is the adjudicating principle of the gospel. Also, as if in affirmation of the centurion's faith in 7:7, again, Jesus heals with only a word: **He said, "Young man, I say to you, get up!" (v 14;** see 1 Kgs 17:20-21).

The raising in Nain has another point of intersection with the widow of Zarephath. After the raising of her son, the widow of Zarephath said, "Now I know that you are a man of God and that the word of the LORD from your mouth is the truth" (1 Kgs 17:24). In Nain the raising of the man from the dead first causes alarm—"fear seized all of them" (v 16 NRSV; "fear" rather than **awe** is Luke's usual meaning for *phobos*). As at Zarephath, the raising of a person from the dead causes people to glorify God: **"A great prophet has appeared among us," they said (v 16).** Jesus is acclaimed a prophet like Elijah.

In 7:16, the fulfillment of the "visitation" foretold in Zechariah's prophecy (1:68, 78) is realized. There the word *episkeptomai,* "to visit," forms an *inclusio* (i.e., literary bookends) in the song about the coming salvation. The hymn begins and ends with this significant divine "visitation" in the birth of John. In 7:16, this word reappears. **God has** now, in fact, **come to help** [*epeskepsato*] **his people.** The raising of the widow's son in Nain is, thus, direct evidence of the realization of Zechariah's prophecy.

Because of the **large crowd (v 12)** in attendance, word of the miracle **spread throughout Judea and the surrounding country (v 17).** Jesus' ministry has now taken a decisive turn in its public nature. Henceforth, his every action will have public implications in the narrative.

3. Jesus and John the Baptist (7:18-35)

BEHIND THE TEXT

The narrative purpose of 7:18-30 is to bring resolution to the role of John the Baptist. He was a major figure in the early part of the Gospel (1:1-80; 3:1-20). But he now begins his exit from the story. The narrator, always conspicuous in Luke's summaries (see 7:17), is particularly evident here. He is omniscient and gives readers privileged information. The narrator knows what John's disciples did and what John said, even though these events transpire at a different time and place from the narrative setting.

John had center stage in 3:1-20 and spoke there in direct discourse. Here he appears behind the scene, known to readers only through the earlier narrative and the question of his disciples. Subsequently, he fades from the story, appearing only in brief asides (7:33; 9:7-9; 16:16), never to appear again.

John's imprisonment is reported in Luke 3:20. Without mentioning this again, the story has him still there, unable to come to Jesus himself. Josephus (*Ant.* 18.5.2, §119) reports that John was held in Macharaeus, a desolate outpost on the eastern shore of the Dead Sea. John's exit from the story is emphasized by two factors: physical remoteness and narrative distance (i.e., the narrator has John speak only through representatives). Even in his extreme isolation, John carefully follows the ministry of Jesus through his disciples' reports. John's interest in Jesus from a distance functions as an indirect endorsement of his ministry.

IN THE TEXT

a. John's Disciples Visit Jesus (7:18-23)

■ **18-22** John's disciples ask Jesus: **"Are you the one who was to come, or should we expect someone else?"** (v 19). Luke 1:17 reports Gabriel's prediction to Zechariah of John's birth. His pronouncement alludes to Mal 4:5-6 (see the commentary on 1:17). The intimation is that John is Elijah *redivivus* (Webb 1991, 62), brought back to life. He prepares the way for the "Lord" (i.e., Jesus).

John's disciples seem to ask: "Are you the one referred to by Malachi?" (see 1:76; 7:27). From a narrative perspective, John's query becomes a litmus test for Jesus' identity, since John believes himself to be the precursor of the Lord.

The question also indicates the physical and emotional distance between the two, highlighting John's doubts. They were together briefly in the Jordan (3:3, 21; see John 1:29, 35-36), but Luke says nothing about John's later movements (contrast John 3:22-23; 10:40). In Luke's telling, there was no direct communication between them after the baptism and before John's imprisonment. They communicated via disciples (see Luke 5:33).

Based on John's understanding of the coming Messiah (3:15-17), he was not sure Jesus was **the one who was to come** (7:19). John expected an "unquenchable fire" (3:17). Instead, Jesus was a healer and teacher. To emphasize his doubt, John's question is repeated by his disciples in v 20: **"Are you the one who was to come, or should we expect someone else?"** Similarly, Jesus' feats are also repeated in vv 21 and 22 in answer to John's question.

The lists of Jesus' deeds quoted in response to John's question focus on relieving human suffering. First, **Jesus cured many who had diseases, sicknesses and evil spirits, and gave sight to many who were blind** (v 21). Second, **The blind receive sight, the lame walk, those who have leprosy are cured, the deaf hear, the dead are raised, and the good news is preached to the poor** (v

22). The lists describe the redemption of the present human condition, not the establishment of the eschaton, the world to come. But compare Isa 35:5-6, where the two ideas do seem to converge.

Luke informs his readers in chs 1 and 3 that John's role is to prepare the way for the Messiah by calling Israel to the forgiveness of sins (1:77; 3:3). He has done that (3:8). But John expects the Messiah to baptize with "the Holy Spirit and with fire" (3:16). The imagery of harvest implies that he was to execute judgment on the wicked (see the commentary on 3:16-17). The Messiah would usher in a new age, not simply relieve human suffering. Jesus was a different Messiah than he expected. Thus the question, **"should we expect someone else?"** (v 20). This dissonance creates dramatic tension for the reader, who is also grappling with Jesus' identity. But by now, readers will be almost fully convinced that he is the Messiah.

This is a good example of the literary device of defamiliarization. In presenting new ideas, a deconstruction of the familiar must occur. John's expectations were reasonable, given his messianic understanding. They resonate with his readers' yearning for liberation. But Jesus' ministry causes John (and Luke's readers) to reassess their perspective in the light of new information (Darr 1992, 32). John's expectations serve as a foil highlighting their *differences* from the nature of Jesus' messianic ministry.

■ **23** Jesus' word to John's disciples is: **"Blessed is the *one* who does not fall away on account of me"** (v 23). Matthew and Luke use the same Greek phrase, *kai makarios estin hos ean mē skandalisthē en emoi.* It is variously translated in modern Bibles. *Makarios*, as in beatitudes, is always rendered "blessed." The rest of the phrase is handled in various ways: "shall find no occasion of stumbling in me" (ASV), "takes no offense" (NRSV), or "does not find in me reason to falter" (Johnson 1991, 121).

7:18-23

This notion of stumbling is an intertextual reference to Isa 8:14-15. There the Lord Almighty is referred to as the cause of stumbling for a disobedient Israel. Paul quotes this Isaiah text in his discourse on the acceptance of the gospel by Gentiles and its rejection by Jews. The claim that Jesus was the Christ was for them a "stumbling stone" (Rom 9:32). Jesus' language in Luke 7:23 evokes Isaiah's prophetic warning not to be found in this sort of opposition to God.

The NT usage of *skandalizō* is often found in reference to blinding preconceptions. When Peter cannot accept Jesus' suffering as integral to his messianic role, he is called a *skanadalon*, a stumbling block (Mark 8:33; Matt 13:57 || Mark 6:3 || Luke 20:17-18; Ps 118:22). John's uncertainty about Jesus' identity and Jesus' response in the language of Isa 8:14-15 implies that John was in danger of the spiritual blindness Isaiah predicted (Luke 7:23).

b. Jesus Speaks to the Crowd About John (7:24-30)

■ **24-30** In vv 24-35 of ch 7, Malachi continues to be our interpretive template. This is material common to both Luke and Matthew. The source adopts the question-answer rhetorical style of Malachi (‖ Matt 11:7-14). God queries his people and they reply (Mal 1:2, 6, 8; 2:10). But sometimes it is the people who question God (Mal 1:2, 6, 13; 2:17). The two main themes of Malachi are the failure of covenant faithfulness of the priesthood and the coming of the Day of the Lord.

Jesus' soliloquy (Luke 7:24-35), following the departure of John's disciples, assumes the same tone of sarcasm expressed by God in Malachi. The Pharisees and teachers of the Law communicate a similar tone of selfishness and irritability (e.g., 5:21-22, 30, 33; 6:2, 7, etc.; see 7:31-35; see further Neale 1991, 137-38, and the commentary on vv 31-35).

As in Malachi, Jesus queries his hearers (here, about their assessment of John), but answers his own questions. These are rhetorical questions, not dialogue. Also as in Malachi, Jesus questions the covenant faithfulness of the people (in 7:24-36): **What did you go out into the desert to see?** (v 24).

Was John a **reed swayed by the wind** or a man in **fine clothes** (vv 24-25)? Obviously, neither is likely to be found in the wilderness. Luke's readers know that reeds do not grow in desert places; they grow by water. Men in fine clothes do not inhabit the desert; they live in **palaces** (v 25). This is the clear indication of Jesus' sarcastic/ironic comment.

This disparagement of the **crowds** (v 24) seems to challenge their motives for following John. Jesus chides them for their shallowness and curiosity-seeking (as in 3:7-9; see 9:18-19). If not a reed or a man in fancy clothes, what did you go out to see? **A prophet?** (v 26). The repeated rhetorical questions are characteristic of Yahweh's frustration with those who failed to show integrity in priestly duties in Mal 2:4-9.

This is similar to the dependence on Mal 1:6 in Luke 6:46. In Malachi, the phrase, "If I am a master, where is the respect due me?" finds its counterpart in Luke's "Why do you call me 'Lord, Lord,' and do not do what I say?" The effect is the same. It is a prophetic critique of those who are supposed to be the faithful covenant people but display a frustrating nonchalance.

In v 26, Jesus asserts that John is **more than a prophet**. This statement and the following quotation identify John as the figure predicted in Mal 3:1 and 4:5-6, who would usher in the "day of the Lord." From a narrative point of view, John's identity as Elijah *redivivus* is now settled. Matthew includes a direct declaration of this identity: "And if you are willing to accept it, he is the Elijah who was to come" (11:14). The reason for Luke's circumspection is not clear.

Verse 27 quotes Mal 3:1 (see Exod 23:20; Evans 1990, 354): **This is the one about whom it is written: "I will send my messenger ahead of you, who**

will prepare your way before you." The emphasis on apocalyptic resolution in Malachi is the probable root of John's pessimism about Jesus' identity. Jesus focuses on rescuing the **least in the kingdom of God** (v 28). John apparently thought the Messiah would immediately wipe away the faithless priests with "unquenchable fire" (3:17). This was predicted in Mal 3:2b: "he is like a refiner's fire" (NRSV).

The narrator once again steps to center stage in vv 29-30 to give the reader an assessment of the crowd's opinion. The conceptual alignment with Malachi continues. **All the people, even the tax collectors** (v 29) sided with John the Baptist. He was God's messenger to prepare the Lord's way. The "crowd" and "people" can clearly see God's hand at work. The religious elite are blind. The priests in Malachi defend themselves with petulant questions when called to account by God (Mal 1:2, 6, 13; 2:17) and, similarly, the Pharisees refuse to acknowledge what the common people and sinners can see: Elijah has come!

c. The Parable of the Children in the Marketplace (7:31-35)

■ **31-32** This passage is subject to differing interpretations (see Fitzmyer 1981, 1:678-79; Bock 1994, 681; Neale 1991, 137-40). The parable of the children in the marketplace was likely a popular story of the time. It ridiculed selfishness (Herodotus 1.141 and Aesop's *Fables* 27; see Neale 1991, 138). Jesus adopted the story to make his point about spiritual blindness in regard to his identity.

The first question that arises in the interpretation is: Who are **the people of this generation** (v 31) against whom Jesus' criticism is directed? If it refers to the general population, the parable becomes a prophetic critique of "people" broadly understood.

In this reading the population to whom the "Son of Man" (v 34) comes is compared to children playing in the marketplace (v 32). They are confused and conflicted, calling out contradictory tunes (a dance and a dirge) to **each other** (v 32) and generally acting like lost sheep.

This could be a reference to the tension between the followers of John and the followers of Jesus (see vv 24-26). This contrasts the asceticism of John with the celebratory life of Jesus. Are the disciples of Jesus and John like raucous children in the marketplace? Are they taunting one another asserting their respective leader's superiority?

Does **this generation** refer to the religious leaders of v 30, **the Pharisees and experts in the law**? If so, the children in the marketplace refer to them (Green 1997, 305). If this is the intent of Luke, these leaders are like the petulant priests of Malachi. They were engaged in a similar rhetorical dispute with Yahweh. In this reading, the religious leaders criticize Jesus for failing to play by their rules, whether the game is a wedding or a funeral—a dance or a dirge.

Most commentators understand **the people of this generation** (v 31) in terms of the second option. The children in the marketplace are the religious elite who criticize both Jesus and John (for example, Green 1997, 303; Tannehill 1996, 133; Bock 1994, 681; Marshall 1978, 297).

The editorial aside in vv 29-30 seems to portray the general populace in a positive light and the Pharisees in a negative light. This interpretation is further supported by the indirect speech in vv 33 and 34, which only makes sense on the lips of Jesus' critics.

A further irony arises. Jesus and John follow different paths fulfilling their calling—celebration vs. denial, and yet, their religious critics can affirm neither path. When faced with a difficult choice, they are unable to depart from their traditional patterns of thought. To John, they say in effect, "Your fasting is not our style." To Jesus, they say: "Your feasting is not our style." They are incapable of receiving God's messengers, regardless of the lifestyle in which the message is couched. This is what makes their practice of religion seem so stilted to the reader.

The **Pharisees and experts in the law** should be understood as **children sitting in the marketplace and calling out to each other: "We played the flute for you, and you did not dance; we sang a dirge, and you did not cry"** (v 32). The faithless priests in Malachi answered God in insolent terms (1:6, 7, 13; 2:17; 3:13). This parable similarly reproaches the taunting Pharisees for their attitude. They are petulant, self-absorbed, and unwilling to listen. They cannot be satisfied, no matter what game is played. They did not accept John's asceticism, nor would they accept Jesus' more liberal conduct toward sinners. Who can please the fickle and self-centered? To add to the sting of the parable, the fickle children represent the leaders of the people.

■ **33-35** For John the Baptist came neither eating bread nor drinking wine, and you say, "He has a demon" (v 33). A consecutive sense is communicated by *For he came* at the beginning of v 33. That is, it further explains the taunt of the Pharisees about wailing and weeping in v 32c. Similarly, v 34 explains the taunt about flutes and dancing in v 32b.

The fundamental point of the expanded explanation of vv 33-34 is that the religious elite misconstrue the activity of *both* John and Jesus. On the one hand, they misconstrue John's asceticism as demon possession. On the other hand, they misconstrue Jesus' fellowship with sinners as a sign of impiety. Both are exactly wrong! John's asceticism is true Elijah-like piety; and Jesus' association with sinners is, in fact, the evidence of the new kingdom. Ironically, the criticism of Jesus' ministry in v 34 becomes a description of what his life ultimately stands for: he is a "friend of sinners."

With reference to Jesus' table fellowship with sinners, vv 29-30 indicate that the Pharisees and the experts in the Law refuse to recognize John's baptism as from God. But sinners see this clearly (v 29). This validates the propriety of Jesus' table fellowship with sinners: **For John the Baptist came neither** eating bread nor drinking wine, and you say, "He has a demon." The Son of Man came eating and drinking, and you say, "Here is a glutton and a drunkard, a friend of tax collectors and 'sinners'" (vv 33-34). Jesus eats, the text implies, with those who understand the identity of John the Baptist and the Son of Man. In fact, this table fellowship validates their place in the kingdom.

FROM THE TEXT

In Mal 1:6, God caustically asks his priests, "If I am a father, where is the honor due me?" Likewise, here in Luke, the time has come for Elijah to prepare the stage for the Messiah's resolution of intolerable arrogance. John could see no solution for this arrogance other than fire and destruction. But Jesus had a broader conception of the kingdom and its new participants, the sinners.

In Malachi (1:5, 11, 14), the Gentile nations are lauded for their faithfulness. Now, in Luke's story-world, all who have been excluded by the religious elite are once again invited to embrace God's invitation to inclusion. They are sinners, tax collectors, and Gentiles—the last ones we might expect to have spiritual insight into the identity of the Son of Man.

As in Mal 2 so also in Luke: God turns his face toward those that show integrity and righteousness. **But wisdom is proved right by all her children** (v 35). This resolution to the parable captures the idea that wisdom is no respecter of office or privilege—she always sides with the right (see Green 1997, 304).

4. A Sinful Woman Forgiven (7:36-50)

BEHIND THE TEXT

This evocative story continues to attract attention from commentators (e.g., Adams 2008, 140-47; Blomberg 2005, 132-37; Carey 2009, 1-16; Darr 1992, 32-35, 101-3; Mullen 2004; Tannehill 2005, 257-70; Thompson 2007, 84-86). The attention is well earned. The story of the sinful woman is important to Luke's narrative for numerous reasons:

- First, it is one of his major scenes about a sinner experiencing forgiveness. Thus, it is a crucial sequential step along the path establishing repentance as Luke's preferred method of entrance to the new community. Luke has six main figures in his drama of repentance in chs 5—19. (See the overview to ch 5.)
- Second, its portrait of Simon the Pharisee concretizes and consolidates the story of the sinner and Pharisee in the narrative (Darr 1992, 34).
- Third, the story deals with issues of purity and impurity. Thus, the narrative returns to this theme for the first time since its introduction in the leper story of 5:12-16.

- Fourth, it is a continuation of the theme of table fellowship that has been building in the narrative, and provides an open view into this intimate issue. This is first broached at the table of Levi in 5:29-32.

The parable of the children in the marketplace and the story of the sinful woman are connected structurally. In 7:28-35 Luke identifies Jesus' fellowship with tax collectors and sinners as a sign of the kingdom rather than a sin. But the Pharisees and experts in the Law have failed to understand this. The Pharisees in the story continue to view this table fellowship as a serious sin. For them, to assert that Jesus is a "friend of tax collectors and sinners" (7:34, 39) is a criticism of Jesus. That is, they do not see outreach to these marginalized people as an appropriate activity for the properly religious. Perhaps they presume that this is the case of the English proverb, "Birds of a feather flock together."

At the same time, Luke presents Jesus' fellowship habits to demonstrate that he is innocent of wrongdoing in regard to his relationship to sinners. In fact, this table fellowship is the very activity that marks him as a righteous man, in Luke's estimate. Both 7:28-35 and 7:36-50 demonstrate the point. Ironically, he is indeed a "friend of sinners." But far from this being a moral failure, this is the ideal around which his ministry is formed. The story of the sinful woman serves to expand and reinforce this theme; this time through the experience of this particular individual.

In Luke's setting of the story, the last village mentioned is Nain (7:11). But the geographical setting of this event seems unimportant to Luke and he does not mention it. Yet, the transition from 7:24-35 to 7:36-50 is smooth and immediate. This seems to indicate that Jesus moves directly to the home of a Pharisee to eat: **Now one of the Pharisees invited Jesus to have dinner with him, so he went to the Pharisee's house and reclined at the table** (v 36).

Immediately following the charge that Jesus eats with sinners (v 34), Luke places Jesus at table with both a sinner and a Pharisee (vv 36-50). Thus, the present story is something of a thematic parable-in-life in the narrative. As is often the case with the Jesus of the Gospels, he teaches by what he does.

The table setting here is crucial. Simon the Pharisee *embodies* the intransigent Pharisees in Luke (see 5:21, 30; 6:2, 7; 7:29). He fails to recognize true piety when it is seated in front of him. From a story perspective, true repentance (that of the sinful woman) comes face-to-face with false piety (that of Simon); and contempt for the sinner is shown to be the real sin. Luke demonstrates that Jesus encounters the greatest impiety, not as charged, at a table with sinners, but at a table with a Pharisee (for more on Jesus' table fellowship with sinners, see the commentary on 5:29-32).

In terms of the tradition history of this section, a similar story appears in the other Gospels (Matt 26:6-13; Mark 14:3-9; John 12:1-8). The differences, however, are significant enough for Luke's story to be treated as an independent tradition.

In Matthew and Mark the host is Simon the Leper rather than Simon the Pharisee. At issue is the cost of the woman's ointment, not her morals. The setting is the impending passion in Bethany rather than a scene early in Jesus' ministry in Galilee. In Matthew, Mark, and John the woman anoints the head of Jesus rather than his feet, as here in Luke (Craddock 1990, 104). In Mark, the cost of ointment has implications for the care of the poor (Mark 14:5). In Matthew, the ointment is part of the burial ritual (Matt 26:12). By contrast, in Luke, the high cost of the ointment signifies the genuineness of the woman's repentance.

There are four parts to the structure of vv 36-50.

- First, the woman's act of contrition and anointing in Simon's house (vv 36-38).
- Second, the parable of the two debtors (vv 39-43).
- Third, Jesus applied the parable to Simon and the woman (vv 44-47).
- Fourth, the structure is completed by the saying about the authority of Jesus to forgive sins (vv 48-50) and a summary logion.

IN THE TEXT

■ **36-38** Only in Luke does Jesus enter the home of a Pharisee to eat. He does this three times (7:39; 11:37; 14:1; see Thompson 2007, 79-90; Tyson 1992, 64-65). In 7:39, as in 11:37, Luke adds the detail to triple tradition material and adopts a formulaic way of expression. In 14:1 the entire meal scene in the Pharisee's home is Lukan material. The presence of these meals in the narrative highlights the importance table fellowship has to Jesus' relations with the Pharisees in Luke (see further Brower 2005, 54-55).

Jesus is in the **Pharisee's house** reclining at his **table** (v 36), as was the oriental custom. This is a scene of great intimacy. It combines the closeness of the shared meal, the subtleties of hospitality and, more indirectly, reference to the canons of ritual purity.

An underlying supposition of the narrative is that one should be able to expect ritual purity at the table of an observant Pharisee (Green 1997, 307; Thompson 2007, 87-88). The tension of the story arises because this, in fact, is not the case.

The image of the woman at Jesus' feet, uncovering her hair and bathing his feet with her tears, is one of the most emotional scenes in the NT: . . . **weeping, she began to wet his feet with her tears. Then she wiped them with her hair, kissed them and poured perfume on them** (v 38).

The letting down of her hair has erotic overtones, somewhat akin to public nudity in today's society (Green 1997, 310). Thus, her attentions to Jesus may have raised questions in Simon's mind about the nature of the physical contact. She prostrates herself at Jesus' feet (see *Jos. Asen.* 15:11), weeping and pouring the costly ointment. It is a scene of remarkable emotive power.

The woman is not welcome: **she is a sinner** (v 39), says the Pharisee in his heart. She is characterized by the narrator as having **lived a sinful life** (v 37) in the village. But we are left to surmise the meaning of the phrase. The likely complaint against her was that of prostitution (Derrett 1970, 167-68; Corley 1989, 520-21). Others point to a more complex set of social issues that result in her low status (see Carey 2009, 1-15). In any case, her status as a sinner is referred to three times in the story (vv 37, 39, 47). This hints that she was "accomplished in her transgressions" (Mullen 2004, 110).

Wiping the feet of weary travelers was considered a refreshing act of hospitality in Jesus' day. The expensive **alabaster jar of perfume** (v 37), which the woman uses, is symbolic of her act. Perhaps it contained myrrh or frankincense, ointments that were rare and expensive in the ancient Near East (see Mark 14:5). In this case, its rarity represents the depth of her sincerity, an extravagant penance. We can imagine the heady fragrance of perfume filling the room, a potent symbol of her broken and oppressed life.

While such a display would have been a public act of hospitality, in this case her tears, unfurled hair, and prostration make it a scene of shocking intimacy. She seems oblivious to others in the room. Her grief mingled with gratitude is a profound gesture. This is clear even though the woman never speaks. Perhaps an embarrassed silence among the guests greeted the display, especially given her reputation as a woman of low morals. "She enters a home where she is not welcome, disrupts the banquet, and publicly behaves with improper intimacy" (Tannehill 1996, 135). This is how Luke shapes a story to exemplify the ethic of repentance in his Gospel.

■ **39** Here the narrator again demonstrates omniscience by revealing what the Pharisee is thinking. This device is occasionally used by the other Gospels (see Matt 12:25; Mark 14:4); but Luke makes particular use of the method here in v 39: **The Pharisee . . . said to himself, "If this man were a prophet, he would know who is touching him and what kind of woman she is—that she is a sinner."** Normally, no one can read another's mind; and Luke is at his editorial best here (although Jesus *does* seem to read people's minds in Luke [see 9:47; 11:17]). Luke shows Simon's outward cold-heartedness and judgmental inner life in a single verse. This penetration to the innermost thought-life of the story-world is a Lukan characteristic (3:8; 12:17; 15:17; 16:3, 15).

The Pharisee's inner thoughts here are similar to those of the unrighteous Pharisee in 18:11. He stands apart and thanks God in his heart that he is "not like other men." Both are examples of the pride that is the opposite of saving humility in Luke. By contrast, the woman's repentance reaches into the deepest thoughts of her heart and is then outwardly displayed, the body and heart in harmony and humility before Jesus.

Simon is cast as the insensitive representative of the Pharisees. The pathos and sincerity of the woman's act is lost on him; he can see her as only a **sinner**, not as a penitent (v 40). From Luke's readers' perspective, the logic of repentance and forgiveness is beginning to override all considerations of religious propriety. The coldness of Simon sets Jesus' compassion for the lost in high relief.

This makes it apparent that the Pharisees' complaint about Jesus' habit of eating with sinners is morally flawed (5:30; 7:34). Simon the Pharisee appears to be exactly like the child playing in the marketplace: selfish and blind to others.

Simon takes particular exception to the woman **touching** Jesus. To touch is not only an intimate act of social discourse ("what kind of woman is this") but also one with multiple levels of meaning in this Palestinian culture. Jesus touches children to bless them (18:15). He touches to heal (see 5:12-16; 7:14; 22:51). But sometimes people seek to touch Jesus, as though to acquire a blessing by means of *midras* ("pressure"—i.e., conveyed by touch). Note especially the woman with a flow of blood (see the comments on 8:44; 6:19). She resembles the case of the sinful woman here. She seeks to be blessed and bless through the medium of human touch. The basis for Simon's reaction likely involves a complex of reasons (against Snodgrass 2008, 86).

■ **40-43** Some of the most notable moments in Luke are those in which Jesus turns, in personal conversation, to an individual (see 5:10, 14, 27; 7:13; 8:48; 9:20 and others). Such is the case here. In these moments, he deals with the condition of the heart of the individual. Here, Simon is not an evil Pharisee, but a human being who needs instruction (see Tannehill's analysis of the characterization of Simon, 2005, 268-70; also more generally, see Snodgrass 2008, 77-92). The text shows the intimacy of the moment by Jesus' use of his name: **Simon**. Only here and in 22:31 does Jesus use a personal name in direct discourse in Luke. The story of the sinful woman and Simon is, in all its aspects, very personal in tone.

The story of the two debtors is Jesus' attempt to explain the woman's great emotion. The bemused Simon cannot understand what he sees happening before his eyes. He is not portrayed as a sinner, but as one who cannot understand the flood of emotion experienced by a forgiven sinner. The woman is like the one forgiven much; Simon, the one forgiven little (v 47). Luke assumes nothing about Simon's former life as sinful or righteous. His point is that Simon's true error is a failure of gratitude, the most important indicator of a holy life for Luke.

The lesson of the story is based on the proportionality of canceled debt. The story concerns a **moneylender** who **canceled the debts** of two people. One person is relieved of a debt of **five hundred denarii**, about a year and a half's wages for a day laborer. The other is relieved of a debt of **fifty** denarii (v 41), about a month and a half's wages. Jesus asks: **Now which of them will love him more?** (v 42).

This story uniquely connects forgiveness, here analogous to canceled debt, to love. The one whose greater debt is canceled loves more (v 42; greater in the quality and quantity of love, as with faith in 7:9 and 17:5-6). The woman, whose sins are many, **loved much** (v 47). The verbs translated *love* (from *agapaō*, vv 42 and 47) do not refer to affection or emotional attachment, but to gratitude and loyalty (as in 10:27). Jesus explains to Simon that these emotions are the source of the woman's extravagant display (vv 44-46).

■ **44-47** The summary logion in 7:47 sits astride two somewhat contradictory ideas. The woman's act of contrition in vv 36-39 is, in a textual sense, the *precondition* of forgiveness, which is proclaimed in v 47. She displays her lavish love before Jesus announces her forgiveness. In the parable of the two debtors, however, love is the *consequence* of forgiveness. Verse 47 has elements of both sequences. **Therefore, I tell you, her many sins have been forgiven—for she loved much. But he who has been forgiven little loves little.**

On the matter of causality Blomberg says,

Despite centuries of debate among Catholic and Protestant interpreters over verse 47, there is now widespread agreement among scholars of both communities that the causal clause, "for she loved much," must modify the verb "tell," not "have been forgiven." . . . In other words, Jesus is not pronouncing God's forgiveness on the woman because of the love just poured out on him. (2005, 135)

The current consensus may press the language too hard. The matter of cause and effect in human relations cannot be stated so categorically. With people, a chain of complicated circumstances and events always bring about inner change. The text leaves room to consider that the act of repentance and the granting of forgiveness are interdependent in Luke. Whether one loves first and subsequently finds forgiveness, or is first forgiven and then loves, the result is the same: redemption and liberation from sin. In an emotional setting such as this story, the graciousness of Jesus enlivens both possibilities. Here in Luke, repentance, forgiveness, and love are all threads in a single piece of cloth.

■ **48-50** The concluding scene of this story sums up the development of the theme of repentance and forgiveness.

- The theme was introduced by Peter's confession of sinfulness in 5:7 (see also 3:3, 8; 5:32).
- It appears next in the pericope of the healing of the paralytic. There Jesus declares, "Friend, your sins are forgiven" (5:20).

Here in ch 7, in language almost identical to that used in ch 5, Jesus declares the same message to the sinful woman: **Your sins are forgiven** (7:48). As in ch 5, those around Jesus again respond: **Who is this who even forgives sins?** (7:49; see 5:21).

In ch 5, Jesus' appropriation of God's prerogative of forgiveness creates a watershed moment in the narrative. It pronounced the Gospel's thematic statement on repentance, "I have not come to call the righteous, but sinners to repentance" (5:32). That same theme is reiterated and summarized in Jesus' encounter with the sinful woman.

The theme of repentance will receive its clearest expression in the chapters to come. The "heart of the third Gospel" is often considered to be ch 15. There the theme of repentance dominates (15:7, 10, 11-32; see also 13:5; 17:4). Later, at the conclusion of the travel section, in chs 18 and 19, two episodes again highlight the importance of repentance:

- The first is the repentance of the tax collector in 18:9-15.
- The second occurs just outside Jerusalem in Jericho, where the ultimate sinner—Zacchaeus—repents. There Jesus will declare, "The Son of Man came to seek and to save what was lost" (19:10).

It is within this larger context that the story of the sinful woman finds its meaning.

The closing comment of the section is a declaration by Jesus of the woman's status, **Your faith has saved you; go in peace** (v 50). **Faith** has been lauded by Jesus twice in Luke to this point, in 5:20 and 7:9, both in connection with healing (see the sidebar at 7:6-10). Here it functions as the mechanism by which the sinful woman obtains salvation.

In what sense is the sinful woman saved? Luke uses the phrase "saved" a number of times in the Gospel (8:12; 13:23; 18:26; and 23:35). These passages do not clearly answer the question. More broadly in Luke, the themes of salvation and forgiveness often appear together. Both are prominent theological emphases in Acts (3:19, 26; 5:31; 10:43; 13:38-39; see Bock 1994, 707). In the convergence of these two ideas the understanding of Luke's broader concept of salvation is to be found. Certainly, the woman is saved from the guilty prison of her sinful past. She is saved perhaps from future judgment; but more than an individualistic salvation is in view here. She is also restored to the community of faith from which she had been so cruelly excluded (Green 1997, 314-15). Her oppression is lifted and a life of peace finally comes to a sinful woman liberated from her past.

FROM THE TEXT

Theologian and Cambridge Professor C. F. D. Moule explores the causal link between divine forgiveness and the forgiveness of one another on the human level. Matthew's version of the Lord's Prayer seems to suggest conditional terms to God's forgiveness: "Forgive us our debts, as we also have forgiven our debtors" (6:12 NRSV; the perfect tense indicates a present state resulting from a past event). Luke's rendering seems more open to a contemporaneous forgiveness, one that occurs *as* or *after* God forgives: "Forgive us our sins, for we ourselves forgive everyone indebted to us" (11:4 NRSV, in the present tense). Moule's distinction between "deserts" and "capacity" is worth noting:

> The key to an answer to this question lies in distinguishing between, on the one hand, earning or meriting forgiveness, and, on the other hand, adopting an attitude which makes forgiveness possible—the distinction, that is, between deserts and capacity. . . . To make forgiveness condi-

tional on repentance is by no means the same as saying that forgiveness has to be (or, indeed, can be) earned by the recipient. Real repentance, as contrasted with a merely self-regarding remorse, is certainly a *sine qua non* of receiving forgiveness—an indispensable condition. However eager the forgiver may be to offer forgiveness, it cannot be received, and reconciliation cannot be achieved, without repentance. But repentance cannot earn the forgiveness or make the recipient worthy of it, for, by definition, forgiveness is always an act of unearned generosity. (1982, 281-82)

Few will dispute that a life of responsible grace will sometimes bring with it a blurring of the idea of deserts and capacity. Wesleyans understand human volition to provide the capacity to embrace the mystery of the divine and human will in both repentance and redemption.

5. The Women of Galilee (8:1-3)

BEHIND THE TEXT

Jesus continues to travel with his disciples **from one town and village to another, proclaiming the good news of the kingdom of God** (v 1). The term "disciples" was introduced in 5:30-33, and they have been at Jesus' side throughout the narrative (6:1, 13, 17; 7:11). The characterization of his inner circle is now expanded with the addition of **some women** (v 2) of Galilee (see Matt 27:55). There is an unidentified number, but three are named: Mary Magdalene, Joanna, and Susanna (vv 2-3).

Jesus' closest male supporters are described for the first time simply as **the Twelve** (v 1). This specific group of men was chosen in 6:13 (see the commentary on 6:12-16). **The Twelve** also appear in 9:1, 12; 18:31; 22:3 and 47.

The characterization of women is positive in the Gospel tradition in general, but this is particularly true in Luke. There are no female villains in Luke's writings (except perhaps the scheming Sapphira). Women are portrayed as faithful and believing throughout, even those emerging from sinful lives. In contrast, men are often portrayed as disbelieving (Pharisees, Peter, Judas), argumentative and egotistical (the disciples, 9:46; 22:24), and dismissive of the testimony of women as "idle talk" (24:11 ASV). Luke indeed has a gender bias; and it is slanted in favor of women. For Luke, the good news is decidedly countercultural at this point.

Women play prominent roles in Luke. Elizabeth and Mary dominate the infancy and adolescent narratives of the first three chapters (Elizabeth in 1:5-7, 13, 24-25, 36, 40-45, 56-61; Mary in 1:26-56; Anna in 2:36-38). Chapter 1 of Luke is "gynocentric" (Bauckham 2002, 47-76). Later in Luke, the sinful woman and the widow of Nain are prominent figures in the story (7:11-17, 36-50). Now, the women of Galilee assume a key supporting role for Jesus' itinerant ministry. Later, other women will assume this role, all unique to Luke:

- Martha and Mary (10:38-42)

- the crippled woman (13:10-17)
- the woman with the lost coin (15:8-10)
- the widow and judge (18:1-8)
- the report of the women at the tomb (24:22-24) (see Bock 1994, 710)

These stories are a statement about gender and faith in the Gospel. On this issue, Luke is one of the most egalitarian of all the biblical writers. His representation of women, if not a complete deconstruction of patriarchy as a foundation of religious belief, is at least a marked equalization of the sexes as participants in the new community. More than simply egalitarian, Luke's story establishes women as heroines of Jesus' ministry.

In this passage at the beginning of ch 8, women take their place alongside the male disciples as Jesus' closest followers on the road. Women will be at center stage again in the passion, especially in Luke 23:55—24:10. "Unlike Matthew and Mark, where it comes as something of a surprise to the reader to learn, during the passion narrative, that many women had accompanied Jesus from Galilee and had provided for him (Matt 27:55-56; Mark 15:40-41), Luke makes clear that these women disciples were constant companions of Jesus from an early stage of the Galilean ministry" (Bauckham 2002, 112-13; see 279-83).

The women in Jesus' coterie are a mixed group, some were obviously women of means (v 3); but others seem to have been outcasts. For example, Mary Magdalene, as well as others who had been cured of **evil spirits and diseases** (v 2), were beyond the pale of social acceptability. The language of spirit possession likely describes a complex social stigma such women endured. They were deemed religiously and physically unfit for community and effectively excommunicated from healthy society. There were also "many others" traveling with Jesus (v 3). Were they divorced, single, or married? Regardless, the presence of all of them at Jesus' side would have been cause for scandal.

Women, Property, and Patriarchy

Luke's comments on women financing Jesus' work are theologically and historically notable (v 3). In first-century Palestine's patriarchal-kinship society, women had a lower social status than men. The Israelite family unit was the *bet 'av*, or the "house of the father." One role of this social structure was the preservation of land and property at the death of a patriarch; levirate laws were developed to ensure this. A man was obliged to marry the wife of his deceased brother so his land and possessions would not pass out of the clan into that of the bride (see the commentary on 15:11-16).

The dependence of itinerant teachers on women for support was not uncommon in the ancient Near East (Bock 1994, 710). But it would have raised objections about the disposition of property in a kinship culture. Married women produced heirs but otherwise played a subordinate role with limited property rights. The right of the disposition of goods did not, in most cases, lie with the wife in a marriage (Bauckham 2002, 117).

In Luke 8, women travel abroad and use the economic means of the *bet 'av* to support an itinerant teacher. It is not difficult to imagine some of the conflicts this could have produced in the women's families. These issues could be a subtext for some of the opposition Jesus encountered in his itinerancy.

There were circumstances in which Jewish women did have income and property at their disposal. For example, there could be an inheritance from a father or husband, or gifts, such as those pledged to a wife by the husband at the time of the marriage. There could be a dowry, which had to be refunded if the husband died or divorced the woman, or earned income (Bauckham 2002, 121). But it did not become socially acceptable for a woman to travel away from home, spending money without her husband. To do so, particularly in the company of other men, would have been a disreputable state of affairs.

The flow of funds toward the itinerant mission of Jesus from women raises interesting questions about money, power, and sexual politics in first-century Palestine. It also has implications for understanding the roles of women in early Christianity. Given the prominent place women held in the ministry of Jesus, it is difficult to imagine early Christian communities such as Luke's soon returning to entirely patriarchal ways.

IN THE TEXT

■ **1-3** As Jesus moves from town to town he is **proclaiming the good news of the kingdom of God** (v 1; see the commentary on 6:20; on locations in Luke see Tyson 1992, 24-26). This is a reiteration of the phrase "good news," first used in 1:19 and repeated in 2:10; 3:18; and 4:43.

The women who accompany Jesus are named: **Mary Magdalene, Joanna,** and **Susanna** (vv 2-3). The principal figure is Mary, who has been healed of **evil spirits and diseases** (v 2). She is mentioned later among the women who discovered the empty tomb (24:10). Strangely, Luke mentions no women witnesses to the resurrected Jesus (contrast Mark 16:1; Matt 28:1). Is Mary the anonymous woman who anointed Jesus' feet in ch 7? There is no textual indication of this. But some have drawn that conclusion, although no demonic possession is indicated in the story of the sinful woman.

This Mary of ch 8 has been possessed by **seven demons** (v 2). This number suggests her utterly hopeless condition (see 11:26). Ironically, and not unlike the story of the Gerasene demoniac, our story finds the demon-plagued woman healed and seated quietly at Jesus' side. In this case it is further noted that she is helping to fund Jesus' work.

Joanna, the wife of Cuza, the manager of Herod's household (v 3) is the only one specifically mentioned as married (Bauckham calls her "Joanna the Apostle" [2002, 117; see 135-50]). Her presence in the list indicates that so-

184

cially prominent individuals had been won to the itinerant band. Commentators have long speculated that she was a major donor. There is no information about the enigmatic **Susanna**, mentioned only here in the Bible (Bauckham 2002, 117).

The most remarkable thing about the presence of these women in Jesus' entourage is that they share fully in the hardships of an itinerant life. To have female disciples would have been unusual for a rabbi. But to have them traveling around the countryside of Galilee in the company of men would have been scandalous (Green 1997, 318-19: "at the very least their behavior is shameless and quite likely would have been regarded as illicitly sexual").

The question of the status of these women within the traveling community is an interesting one. Influence often follows money, and one wonders if this may have enhanced their status as patrons of the traveling band. While they are not called "disciples," they are **with him** (v 1) just as are **the Twelve**. There is no hint the women enjoy anything less than full participation in the community.

In 10:1 women were undoubtedly included in Jesus' mission of the "seventy-two others." Since they travel in pairs, we might well imagine two women moving about from town to town, spreading the good news of the kingdom. Their presence with Jesus on the road is enough to show the radical nature of his treatment of women.

Motion as a Motif in Luke

A geographic dynamism in the narrative portrays the kingdom of God as the antithesis of static, institutional religion (i.e., temple-based Judaism). The kingdom is instead an energizing force, constantly in motion, similar to the portrayal of the Holy Spirit as a moving force in the broader narrative. The Holy Spirit is always in the midst of the most dynamic scenes (1:15, 35, 41, 67; 2:25, 26; 3:16, 22; 4:1). Verbs of motion dominate the narrative here: "filled," "come," "leaped," "rested" (NRSV), "fire," "descended." Motion, not stasis, characterizes Luke's portrayal of the spiritual power of the kingdom. In 8:16, there is a sense of geography and motion involved in perceiving the light (note "hides," "under," "on," "come in").

6. The Parable of the Sower (8:4-15)

BEHIND THE TEXT

Luke has already reported some of Jesus' brief parables (5:36; 6:39). But the parable of the sower is an example of the genre in its fuller form. It is a familiar story. Reading it is like reading a mystery novel for the second time; all the clues seem so obvious when you know the ending. We know the allegorical interpretation of the parable provided in vv 9-15 and cannot see the parable with any other lens.

Although the meaning seems so obvious, the disciples were puzzled by the parable until Jesus explained it to them. This is one way Luke includes his readers in a privileged relationship. We know things even the disciples do not or cannot know.

The broader history of the parable genre is widely researched. Comprehensive guides continue to be published (see Snodgrass 2008, 1-60, on the background of the parable). Parables were used in both Hebrew and Greco-Roman culture by the time of Jesus, but widespread use of the genre is not found prior to the first century A.D. Rabbinic examples exist, but most postdate Jesus. Of this we can be confident, as a teller of parables Jesus stood apart as an innovator and master of the genre (McArthur and Johnston 1990, 165-66).

The importance of the parable of the sower for Synoptic Gospel studies can hardly be overstated. It is the first substantial example of the genre in all three Gospels. Mark's version is the "middle term," the source from which the others are derived. In all three it contains within its structure an explanation of the interpretation based on Isa 6:9-10. Snodgrass calls it "*the* parable about parables" (2008, 145).

There are actually four existing versions of the parable of the sower. Besides the synoptic versions, the fourth is in the Gospel of Thomas (see Snodgrass 2008, 149; sidebar). Except for Thomas, there is a twofold structure: the parable proper (Luke 8:4-8 ‖ Matt 13:1-9 ‖ Mark 4:1-9) and an allegorical interpretation of the parable (Luke 8:11-15 ‖ Matt 13:18-23 ‖ Mark 4:13-20). Thomas has no allegorical explanation.

The larger narrative context of the parable is the conflict between Jesus and his contemporaries. That setting has the following scenes: the five conflict stories of Luke 5:17—6:11, the unique woe counterparts to the Beatitudes in the Sermon on the Plain (6:24-26), the call to love persecutors (6:27), the conflict with the Pharisees about the baptism of John and Jesus' ministry (7:33-35), and the story of the sinful woman and the controversy caused when Jesus forgives her sins (7:36-50).

This is the context of conflict to which the parable of the sower belongs and which has been building since ch 5. Jeremias considered all the parables "weapons of controversy," which demand an immediate response from opponents (1972, 21; McArthur and Johnston 1990, 171). This is also the role of the parable of the sower in Luke.

Snodgrass lists eight possible interpretations for the parable (2008, 156). There is no consensus among commentators on a "correct" interpretation. But for our purposes, the parable of the sower, and all the parables and aphorisms of ch 8, are to be understood as part of the war of words between Jesus and his opponents. These parables and aphorisms are a response to those who cannot see the sense of Jesus' ministry to sinners, even in the presence of miraculous acts of exorcism, healing, and forgiveness. The allegorical identity of the poor soil is almost certainly his opponents.

The Gospel of Thomas

In 1945 thirteen ancient codices were discovered near Nag Hammadi, Egypt. Among these documents, which date from the fifth century A.D., was a gospel attributed to Didymus Judas Thomas (see Robinson 1977, 117). The Gospel of Thomas has long been of interest to NT scholars since it contains parallels to some of the material of the canonical Gospels.

Thomas contains versions of three famous Gospel parables: the parable of the sower, the parable of the wheat and tares, and the parable of the vineyard. Thomas' versions of these parables all lack the extended allegorical interpretations contained in their canonical counterparts. Some scholars argue that the Gospel of Thomas contains earlier, shorter forms of these parables. Others contend that the Gospel of Thomas removed allegorical material from the original form of the parable for theological reasons (Scott 1989, 30-31).

■ **4-7 A large crowd** was gathered that had come **from town after town** (see the commentary on 7:11-17). Not only does Jesus move from town to town, but crowds follow him from town to town as well. The geographic diversity of those who gather to hear Jesus is a Lukan feature (see 5:17). His location is simply out among the towns and villages, not a particular place (8:1).

Sowing seed is Jesus' agricultural analogy for spreading **the word of God** (v 11; see the comment on 5:1)—preaching. Typically, sowing was done in the fall after the late autumn rains softened the ground. The soil was prepared to receive the seed by means of primitive plows pulled by animals. Seed was broadcast by *the sower* (**farmer**; see Jer 31:27; Ezek 36:9; Hos 2:23).

The Greek text utilizes alliteration in the first phrase of the parable (*ho speirōn tou speirai ton sporon*: "A sower went out to sow his seed" [v 5 NRSV]). It is both rhythmic and rhyming, an almost poetic beginning to the parable. The seed falls on four different types of soil: on **the path, on rock, among thorns**, and **on good soil** (vv 5-8). The first three settings for the seed ultimately yield no crop. In contrast, the good soil yields **a crop** (*fruit*; see John's warning in 3:8) **a hundred times more than was sown** (v 8). Luke's interpretation of this abundant harvest is found in v 15.

> It illustrates the ultimate eschatological success that will attend Jesus' preaching, despite all the human obstacles that will be encountered: ". . . God has made a beginning, bringing with it a harvest of reward beyond all asking or conceiving. In spite of every failure and opposition, from hopeless beginnings, God brings forth the triumphant end which he has promised." (Fitzmyer 1981, 1:701, following Jeremias)

The parable, we know from the allegory, identifies the seed as the "word" (see Jer 17:8). The path, rock, thorns, and good soil represent the four kinds of people who respond to the gospel. It is unlikely that this was a new idea to Jesus' hearers. The Mishnah, a second-century source of rabbinic teaching, has an amusing description that also contrasts four different types of individuals (*m. Avot* 5:10-15). Among disciples there are those swift to hear and swift to lose, those slow to hear and slow to lose, those swift to hear and slow to lose, and those slow to hear and swift to lose. Among those that sit in the presence of the sages there is the sponge who soaks up everything, the funnel who takes in one end and lets it out the other, the strainer who lets out the wine and keeps the dregs, and the sifter who takes out the coarse and keeps the fine.

The parable of the sower has a similar fourfold approach to the characteristics of those who hear Christian preaching. The subtext is that one's response to **the word of God** (v 11) is a matter of personal openness and effort. We could all, the parable teaches us, be swift to hear and slow to lose, a sponge, a sifter who keeps the good, if only we choose. This way of speaking highlights the disciple's responsibility to respond to Jesus' teaching. In Luke's theology it is within a disciple's power of choice to understand and retain the word.

■ **8** **He who has ears to hear, let him hear.** The "explanation" of the parable in vv 11-15 focuses attention on how Jesus' audience hears the **word** and responds to the message. This is the overriding theme in Luke 8:4-21. The word **hear** appears eight times (vv 8, 10, 12, 13, 14, 15, 18, and 21); **word**, four times (vv 11, 13, 15, 21; Scott 1989, 349). Thus, the allegorical interpretation focuses on v 8 of the parable. The visit of Jesus' relatives (8:21) reinforces the point: his true mother and brothers are those "who hear the word, retain it" (v 15).

■ **9-10** **His disciples asked him what this parable meant.** Luke uses a rare optative mood verb to indicate indirect discourse (BDF, 195). Jesus' response implies that he tells parables to divide his audience. Parables unveil **the knowledge of the secrets of the kingdom of God** to his disciples, while they veil that knowledge from *the rest* (v 10).

The disciples' lack of understanding indicates that the parable was a riddle to them. It did not commend itself to their common sense, and its meaning had to be elucidated for them. This seems to run counter to Jesus' mission to seek and to save the lost (5:32; 19:10).That is, if his teaching was, in fact, only understood by the few, it could not at the same time appeal broadly to all who might choose to embrace it.

Here literary method and historical method collide. From a narrative perspective, the disciples' ignorance closes the distance between the narrator and his readers. As readers, we understand what the disciples cannot. This draws us further into a shared truth with the narrator. But did Jesus really hide his meaning from his first audience, even his disciples, through the telling of parables?

The OT reports that God, on occasion, blinded his opponents and hardened their hearts to serve his purpose (e.g., Pharaoh in Exod 10:1; 11:10; 14:8). But it is difficult to think of the gospel story in these terms. This makes the rejection of the good news by Jesus' opponents a matter of divine causation, not human choice. And, if the rejection of the gospel is not by choice, neither those who accept or those who reject are responsible for the consequences—God is.

The crux of the matter hinges on the interpretation of the conjunction *hina* in the phrase **but to others I speak in parables, so that [*hina*], "though seeing, they may not see; though hearing, they may not understand."** Does *hina* denote *purpose*? If so, it was God's intent to blind them. Or does it denote *result*; in which case it was God's intent for them to understand but their obstinacy made them blind (see BDF, §187).

Support for the view that it was Jesus' purpose to veil the truth may be found in the quotation from Isaiah: **so that "though seeing, they may not see; though hearing, they may not understand"** (v 10; Isa 6:9-10). The quotation comes from Isaiah's call narrative and the searing critique of the unfruitful vineyard Israel in Isa 5. In Isa 6:9-10, God said,

> Go and tell this people: "Be ever hearing, but never understanding; be ever seeing, but never perceiving." Make the heart of this people calloused; make their ears dull and close their eyes. Otherwise they might see with their eyes, hear with their ears, understand with their hearts, and turn and be healed.

In this passage God punishes the stubborn and unheeding people by causing them to grow even more dull and blind. So also with Jesus' parable, it can be argued, his opponents' blindness could be seen as their punishment for their obstinacy.

On the other hand, divine veiling of truth does not really fit Luke's theological paradigm. The Gospel of Luke is largely about the obduracy of *self-blindness*. Throughout his Gospel, Luke emphasizes that willingness to accept Jesus' identity and repent of sin grants admission to the new community. Luke's concept of salvation presumes freedom of choice: Repent and you will be saved. Such freedom and responsibility also lies at the heart of Wesleyan soteriology.

Thus, in Luke, the primary characters make saving choices throughout the narrative (e.g., Peter, Levi, the tax collector, the sinful woman, the prodigal son, Zacchaeus). Given this frame of reference, it seems likely that Luke takes Isa 6:9-10 as a caution against hardening the heart to the message of the kingdom, as Pharaoh did (Exod 8:15, 32; 9:34). Willful refusal to acknowledge Jesus as the Messiah is the cause of blindness. To suggest otherwise is inconsistent with Luke's overarching narrative.

The **disciples** (v 9) are those who choose to move toward God by giving heed to Jesus. The **others** (v 10) are those whose volition takes them away from God. And both bear responsibility for their personal choice. The "disciples" have "ears to hear"; the "others" have hard hearts. This interpretation is more in accord with Luke's general theological paradigm.

■ 11-15 In explaining the parable to his disciples, Jesus identifies the seed as **the word of God** (v 11). Luke is the only Evangelist to do so, and he uses the phrase "word of God" several times (see 5:1; 8:21; and 11:28). Matthew identifies the seed as "the word of the kingdom" (13:18 NRSV); Mark, as simply "the word" (4:14). The other Synoptic Evangelists use "word of God" infrequently (only Mark 7:13 ‖ Matt 15:6). In Acts, the "word of God" means the preaching of the church (4:31; 6:2, 7; 8:14; 11:1; 12:24; 13:5, 7, 46; 17:13; 18:11). It is less certain that this is the meaning here.

What does the phrase "word of God" mean on the lips of Luke's Jesus? That is, what exactly constitutes the "proclaiming the good news of the kingdom of God" (v 1; see also 1:19; 4:18, 43; 7:22; 16:16)? If we view it through the lens of the surrounding narrative context, the good news refers to the totality of Jesus' life, including his teachings and acts of wonder in Luke 5—8.

The good news is broadly understood to embrace:
- the call to repentance (3:3)
- relief for the poor (4:18)
- healing of the sick (4:40; 7:10)
- deliverance to the possessed (4:41; 8:36)
- forgiveness for the sinful (5:20; 7:47)

All of this is compressed into the potent phrase **word of God** in Luke's story. It enlightens those who embrace it (8:16) but brings division and conflict to those who do not.

Jesus' interpretation of his own parable then shifts immediately to the soil. The first type of soil has been hardened into a **path** (v 12). Ancient commentators, amplifying the allegory, saw the seed of the word as the catechesis of the church. The devil snatches the church's lesson from hearts hardened through inattention or worldly cares (Ephrem the Syrian, cited in Just 2003, 133).

The seeds sown on **the rock** (v 13) are those who attend the joyful services of the church but, upon leaving the church, immediately forget the lesson (Cyril of Alexandria, cited in Just 2003, 134). The seeds that fall **among thorns** (v 14) are those who are "overgrown by empty occupations" (Cyril of Alexandria, cited by Just 2003, 134).

The various kinds of soils represent the different types of responses to the itinerant ministry of Jesus:
- those who hear but do not follow (e.g., 18:23)
- those who follow for a while but fall away, choked by the cares of the world (12:16-21)
- those who leave all and join the traveling community (5:11, 28)

The latter stand over against all the others as alone the "good soil." They are those who hear the word and hold it fast in a **noble and good heart.** They will **retain it, and by persevering produce a crop** (v 15).

There are twenty-eight parables in Luke (four triple tradition, nine double tradition [from Q], fourteen special Lukan material, and one found only in Mark and Luke; Jeremias 1972, 177). In eight of these an interpretation is provided within the narrative. Only in Luke 19:11 is an explanation provided by the narrator. In the remaining instances, the applications are placed on the lips of Jesus. Of all Jesus' parables in the Gospels, only four have an accompanying allegorical interpretation: the parables of

- the sower (Mark 4:13-20 || Luke 8:11-15 || Matt 13:18-23)
- the wheat and the tares (Matt 13:37-43)
- the net (Matt 13:49-50)
- the sheepgate (John 10:7-18)

Some argue that Mark produced the interpretation of the parable of the sower, which equates the sowing of seed with the preaching of the church (Evans 1990, 374; Green 1997, 327). Most agree that Mark's interpretation was appropriated by Luke and Matthew (Fitzmyer 1981, 1:710; see Nolland 1989, 382).

The failure of the seed to germinate serves as an apology for the failure of the church's preaching ministry (Jeremias 1972, 77-79; Fitzmyer 1981, 1:711; Scott 1989, 343-44; Nolland 1989, 383). That is, the fault lies with those who refuse to hear (the soil), rather than with those who preach (the seed).

Such arguments are based partly on linguistic data. For example, the parable of the sower uses words that appear only infrequently in the synoptic tradition. Most noteworthy are the words *logos* (**word**) and *speirein* (**to sow** in the metaphorical sense of preaching).

The Evangelists, it is argued, create an interpretation that reflects the experience of the church. Thus, parables have a "double historical setting" (Jeremias 1972, 23). That is, parables have a setting within Jesus' ministry and another in the life of the communities of the Evangelists.

This does not mean Jesus never provided interpretations for his parables. Some interpreters contend that agricultural parables naturally call for allegorical interpretations. They insist that Jesus was the originator of both the parable and the interpretation (see Scott 1989, 345). But the parable of the sower clearly has a heightened use of allegory, not found elsewhere in Jesus' parables (see Nolland 1989, 383).

7. Three Aphorisms (8:16-18)

■ **16-18** Luke brings together three brief proverbial sayings that expand on the theme of responding to the word of God as emphasized in the interpretation of the parable of the sower. The saying about the lampstand (v 16; see 11:33) is a "parable in embryo" (McArthur and Johnston 1990, 166). Here it introduces two closely related proverbs (vv 17 and 18), both with a distinctly eschatological slant. All three proverbs elaborate on the nature of good and bad soil from the previous parable.

If the "word of God" (v 11) refers to the totality of Jesus' life and teaching, then the first proverb equates that with the light of the lampstand. **No one lights a lamp and hides it in a jar or puts it under a bed. Instead, he puts it on a stand, so that those who come in can see the light** (v 16). In refusing to curtail his activities, Jesus indicates that he will not accommodate his work to the criticism of his opponents. The public nature of his activities puts the light on a stand for all to see. His activities release those near his revelatory light from the grip of spiritual blindness. Here, this is the blindness displayed by Jesus' opponents in the narrative.

Verbs and prepositions of place dominate the verse:

- *kalyptei*: **remove from sight** or **conceal**
- *hypokatō*: **under, below**
- *epi*: **on** (v 16)

Those who see the light must also change location; they must **come in** so they **can see the light** (v 16). This suggests a geographic location associated with the light. When this is combined with the geographical dynamism of vv 1-3 (see the commentary) in general, the themes of movement and space are evident in the narrative. There is location, movement, and action on the part of those who see this light. If you "come in" to where the light is found, your spiritual blindness will be taken away. Those who "enter" the community of Jesus will see the light. This motif is part of Luke's narrative strategy.

In Luke, entrance to the Christian community requires a willingness to participate in the ultimate form of sacred movement and place—that is, itinerancy. The proverb implies that by entering the itinerant life, disciples will engage in sowing the light of the word. Extending the analogy to the modern Christian life, "the mature Christian, because of his retention of the word of God and his persistence, becomes a light to 'the others'" (Fitzmyer 1981, 1:718).

In the coming judgment, there is **nothing hidden that will not be disclosed** and **nothing concealed that will not be known or brought out into the open** (v 17; see 12:1-3, 35). The claim that things will be **brought out into the open** is another motif of place and motion. It suggests that a day of reckoning will *move* human actions from the darkness into the light. Here again, the light refers to "sacred space."

Jesus' comments here further increase the importance of the decision readers make regarding his identity. The assertion that all will be made known in the judgment should give pause to readers: What type of soil am I? The text implies that the kind of soil we choose to be is known to God. Since he is the Judge, our choices will determine our redemption or judgment.

Thus, hearers are cautioned to give careful attention to how they respond: **Whoever has will be given more; whoever does not have, even what** he thinks he has will be taken from him (v 18; see 19:26). Failure to respond affirmatively to the light will bring the loss of all things.

8. Jesus' True Family (8:19-21)

BEHIND THE TEXT

Luke continues to follow Mark's sequence and general content, as he has since Luke 5:17 (= Mark 2:13). The parallel to Luke 8:19-21 is Mark 3:31-35 and 3:20-21. In Mark, Jesus' family came to "seize" him (*kratēsai*; 3:21 NASB). This strong term elsewhere in Mark is translated "arrest" (e.g., 6:17; 12:12). They plan to do so because they consider Jesus "out of his mind" (Mark 3:21). The NIV correctly assigns this intervention to "his family" (*hoi par' autou*; Taylor 1952, 235-36), rather than "His own people" (NASB, NKJV). Both Matthew and Luke omit reference to this familial intervention, perhaps considering it too awkward to mention.

This family conflict was, no doubt, historical. The church would have been unlikely to create such a theme, "for without the warrant of fact no early narrator would have alleged that the family at Nazareth thought that Jesus was beside Himself and went out to restrain Him" (Taylor 1952, 235; see Metzger 1975, 82). This enforces and expands Luke's conflict theme; it extends even to the intimacy of family.

IN THE TEXT

■ **19-21** **Jesus' mother and brothers** cannot approach Jesus due to the size of the crowd (v 19). More than this, they are **standing outside** (v 20). Not only does this reference to place refer to their physical location, but symbolically it indicates the family of Jesus stood outside his itinerant community.

Jesus declines to bring his family in when they present themselves. This physical and emotional distance is a symbol for the priorities of loyalty that govern Jesus' mission. Familial ties are not simply secondary in importance to discipleship; they are supplanted by its imperatives. **My mother and brothers are those who hear God's word and put it into practice** (v 21).

What does it mean to **put [God's word] into practice**? This translates a single Greek participle (*poiountes*). The NRSV renders is simply: "do it." In the Lukan narrative it means to stand up and move, that is, "follow" Jesus (5:27; 9:23, 61; 14:27; 18:22).

The injunction to **hear** God's word in v 21 reiterates Jesus' plea that concludes the parable of the sower: "He who has ears to hear, let him hear" (8:8). Jesus' true relatives are not those who share his flesh and blood, but those who "hear the word, [and] retain it" (v 15).

That Jesus' family members were exhorted to hear "God's word" (see v 11) relates to their acceptance (or lack thereof in Mark) of his identity. Other Lukan passages address Jesus' relationship to his family (11:27; 12:53; 14:26;

18:28-30; see the commentary on 12:53 and 14:26; for the names of Jesus' family members, see Mark 6:3).

E. Jesus Travels to Gerasa and Back (8:22-56)

BEHIND THE TEXT

In this section Luke reports a natural miracle, an exorcism, and two healing incidents in rapid succession (‖ Mark 5:1-43). These four events have **one day** (v 22) as their timeframe in Luke 8:22-56:

- the trip across the Sea of Galilee with the calming of the storm (vv 22-25)
- the incident with the Gerasene demoniac (vv 26-39)
- the raising of Jairus' daughter (vv 40-42*a*, 49-56)
- the healing of the woman with a flow of blood (vv 42*b*-48)

As a narrative device, this action-packed day has the effect of slowing time and increasing the story's dramatic intensity.

Taken together, these stories further define Jesus' identity and the boundaries of the saved community. The narrative moves from the failure of the faith of the disciples in the calming of the storm, to the redemption of the demoniac among the Gentiles, to the exemplary faith of the leader of the synagogue, to the healing of the unclean woman of Israel. These powerful themes, set side-by-side, demonstrate the reach of the gospel. Chaotic waters and demons obey him (even in Gentile territory); physical death is overcome by a word; and long-standing disease is healed at his touch—all in rapid succession. These stories indicate how one must respond as "good soil" (Green 1997, 343).

I. Jesus Stills the Storm (8:22-25)

IN THE TEXT

■ **22-25** The stilling of the storm is triple tradition material (Mark 4:35-41 ‖ Matt 8:23-27) and the antecedent to Jesus' visit to the pagan Gerasenes. The scene is similar to Jonah's seagoing adventure, which also concerns the evangelization of the pagans (see table below). Original readers familiar with the Jonah story, and who perhaps knew of Jesus' fondness for Jonah's message (see 11:29-32), would draw a connection between these two stories.

As in Jonah, the stilling of the storm sets the stage for Jesus' visit to a pagan land (here, Gerasa). The narrative is about the legitimacy of God reaching out to non-Jews. It also echoes the theme of God's omnipresence outside the Holy Land in Jonah, and the ironic conversion of hated Gentile enemies of Israel. Taken together with the Gerasa event, the stilling of the storm functions as a prophetic critique of a temple-based Judaism that excludes Gentile nations from salvation.

Similarities Between the Calming of the Storm (and Related Lukan Passages) and the Story of Jonah

	Jesus in Luke	Jonah
• violent storm at sea and a swamped vessel	8:23	1:4
• a prophet asleep on the stern/hold	8:23	1:5
• question to sleeping prophet	8:24	1:6
• the calming of the water	8:24	1:15
• the ironic conversion of pagans/Gentiles	1:79; 2:32	1:14-16; 3:6
• petulant rejection of mission of salvation	4:28; 7:28-35	4:2
• mastery of God over nature, esp. watery chaos	8:25*b*	1:15

Jesus saves his disciple from **great danger** (v 23) by calming of the raging sea. This act shows the same dominating power over the chaos of the waters displayed by God in the story of Jonah (1:15; also see Gen 1:2). Jesus' disciples ask, **Who is this? He commands even the winds and the water, and they obey him** (Luke 8:25). The rhetorical question raises an implicit comparison between Yahweh and Jesus, who both command the seas. There is, thus, a subtle allusion to Jesus' divine identity in the comparison.

The disciples do not meet the test of faith posed by their floundering boat. The Gentile sailors on Jonah's ship had faith. The Gentile Ninevites had faith. But when his boat was in danger, Jesus' disciples did not have faith: **Master, Master, we're going to drown!** (v 24). He asks them, **Where is your faith?** (v 25). As so often in Luke, faith is missing where it should be found. And faith is found instead in unexpected quarters, in this case in Gerasa of the Gentiles when the boat lands on the distant shore.

2. The Gerasene Demoniac (8:26-39)

BEHIND THE TEXT

The exorcism of the Gerasene demoniac is narrated in the Markan style (see Marshall [1978, 336-37] for difficulties concerning the name of the region). Luke and Matthew have a somewhat truncated version of Mark's story (Luke omits Mark 5:3-5 and Matthew omits Mark 5:15-20), but the evocative details still come through. Matthew and Luke, usually more dignified than Mark, retain his tumbling style and the chaotic pace of confrontation, first with nature and then the spiritual world.

The account itself is presented as a rather strange event in the life of Jesus. Yet, other features of the story make it almost parabolic, complete with analogy and even allegory. The tombs, solitary places, nakedness, abyss, swine, and drowning all function as religious symbols in Luke's story-world. The story is freighted with layers of symbolic meaning.

The story is unique in another respect. Almost every Gospel passage echoes stories of the OT. Although there are biblical symbols present in the story of the demoniac from Gerasa, it seems to stand largely outside the tradition of the biblical narrative. Its abrupt introduction (v 26), bizarre details, and visceral effect suggest more in common with first-century Palestinian superstitions than biblical tradition (Marshall 1978, 336).

The Gerasene demoniac is the most detailed of the four explicit exorcisms in Luke (4:31-37; 8:26-39; 9:37-43; 11:14-23). There are other passing references to demon possession in Luke 7:33; 8:1-3; 9:49; 11:24-26; 13:31-32, and six summary statements mentioning exorcisms as characteristic of Jesus' ministry (4:36-37; 4:41; 6:18; 7:21; 9:1; 10:17-20; see Garrett 1989, 57-60). These stories demonstrate the authority of Jesus over the spiritual realm and the dawning of the kingdom of God. This struggle "lies at the very heart of Luke's story" (Garrett 1989, 58).

Biblical stories of demons present modern Western readers with an alien, ancient worldview. In Jesus' day, illnesses and psychological disorders were widely attributed to demonic possession. His healing ministry demonstrated liberation from these unseen forces. Disease, plagues, infirmities, and evil spirits are often mentioned together in these summaries. Today, these symptoms would be diagnosed as illness (9:37-43), physical disabilities (11:14), and psychological disorders (8:26-39).

Regardless of the correct modern diagnosis, in Luke's narrative Jesus sets people free from whatever bonds or inscrutable forces entrap them, and the story of the Gerasene demoniac is one of the most powerful in the Gospels. From a tortured existence in a tomb, a whole and restored human being emerges and sits calmly at Jesus' feet (v 35).

IN THE TEXT

■ **26-27** Jesus comes to the dark tombs of a Gentile region and his light heals the most marginalized member of the population. This certainly expresses the far-reaching nature of the theology of salvation in Luke.

The **region of the Gerasenes** is in the Gentile Decapolis, the "ten cities" on the eastern shore of the Sea of Galilee. The region took its name from the city of Gerasa, modern Jerash. The cities of the region were cosmopolitan. Although they had some Jewish populations, they were mostly Hellenistic in ethos and religion (Rogerson 1989, 210).

Jesus' visit here was a rare excursion into Gentile territory. He leaves Jewish country only one other time in the Gospels—to visit Tyre and Sidon (Mark 7:24 ‖ Matt 15:21), a trip Luke fails to mention. Thus, from a narrative perspective this story is paradigmatic of Jesus' attitudes on Jewish and Gentile relations. The text does not say so explicitly, but it seems to assume the demoniac was a Gentile.

To read the exorcism of the Gerasene demoniac as simple history would be to ignore a great deal of textual meaning conveyed by the Evangelists' detailed description of the incident. That the man **had not worn clothes or**

lived in a house, but had lived in the tombs (v 27) suggests the biblical shame of nakedness (e.g., Gen 3:7; Isa 47:3). The uncleanness of the tomb reflects "the lowest place imaginable in contrast to the highest heavens" (see Gen 1:2; Deut 33:13; Isa 7:11; Matt 11:23; Ryken, Wilhoit, and Longman 1998, 349). The demoniac's home among the tombs is also evocative of his spiritual death (elsewhere in the NT in, e.g., Rom 6:4-5).

■ **28-33** The demon-possessed man calls himself **Legion**. He addresses Jesus as the **Son of the Most High God** (v 28; see 4:34, "Holy One of God"). What is unclear in the physical realm is patently clear to Legion in the cosmic realm (recalling "Who is this?" in 8:25). The ascendancy of the kingdom, proclaimed by angels (1:32-33; 2:11) and affirmed by demons (4:34), is proclaimed again by a man held captive by a virtual army of demons.

The name **Legion** indicates that multiple demons possess the man. He was victimized by a plurality of evil **because many demons had gone into him** (v 30, note 4:34 in which the demon asks Jesus why he had come to destroy "us"). Legion serves, as did the demon of 4:33-37, as a cosmic ambassador for Satan and his forces.

The demon often drove the man into **solitary places** (v 29). This seems to symbolize the wilderness where God's people wandered (Exod 14:11) and where Jesus was tested by the devil (Luke 4:1).

Luke describes the demons as beseeching Jesus not to send them to **the Abyss** (v 31; compare Mark 5:10: "out of the area"). Elsewhere in the NT, the term refers to a bottomless pit, the underworld abode of the dead (only in Rom 10:7; Rev 9:1-11; 11:7; 17:8; 20:1-3).

Instead, Jesus sends them into the "swine" (v 33 NRSV). Jews considered these livestock unclean and a symbol of pagan disrespect for Jewish tradition. During the second century B.C., Antiochus IV Epiphanes forced Jews to sacrifice swine and to eat their flesh, one of the factors leading to the Maccabean Revolt (1 Macc 1:47). The exorcised demons, now in the swine, **rushed down the steep bank into the lake** (v 33) and are drowned.

The story as historical event is rather bizarre: Jesus converses with demons through a deranged man and sends them into pigs that drown themselves.

> The biggest problem lies in the demonology presupposed in the story, which is so similar to that attested in popular superstitions of the time that is difficult to believe that it corresponds to objective fact. It may well be that Jesus, while not sharing the man's superstitions, allowed the destruction of the swine in order to convince him that he was really free from the demons. (Marshall 1978, 336)

This story highlights the difficulties in discerning the boundary between an event and its meaning, between an act as history and an act as parable. The lines blur in this story as in few others in the Gospels.

At the narrative level, the destruction of the demonic swine seems to be a symbol of the coming victory of the kingdom of God over its oppressors. The event becomes something of an allegory for the end of the age: the forces of evil are subsumed in the waters of the lake, just as God swept over the waters of chaos on the first day of creation and demonstrated his dominion over all. So also, the coming kingdom brooks no opposition from the cosmic realm. Evil is cast out into the deep, and this Jesus quickly dispatches all evil powers, even when in Gentile Gerasa.

■**34-39** The Gerasenes are **overcome with fear** (v 35) at these deeds and ask Jesus to leave. As with other Gentiles mentioned in Luke (e.g., the widow of Zarephath, Naaman, the centurion), these pagans fear God more than the people of Israel. In Jonah, we recall, the Gentile Ninevites showed the proper fear of God when commanded to repent.

More significantly, the cured Gentile requests to accompany Jesus. But Jesus replies, **Return home and tell how much God has done for you. So the man went away and told all over town how much Jesus had done for him** (v 39). The secrecy surrounding Jesus' identity in Mark, never strong in Luke (only in 4:35, 41), has been fully revoked in the man's testimony to the people of Gerasa. In the two demon possession stories yet to come in the narrative (9:37-43; 11:14-23) secrecy plays no role.

Verse 39 summarizes the Gerasene story. Its Greek grammatical structure is noteworthy. The author places the Greek words for **God** ("Lord" in Mark 5:19) and **Jesus** in parallel at the end of their respective phrases. In response to Jesus' exhortation to tell how much **God** has done for him, the man tells how much **Jesus** has done for him. The subtle christological implication seems to be that Jesus is not merely "Lord," but somehow **God**. This prepares readers for more forthright assertions of Jesus' identity in 9:20-36.

The most notable feature of the story is the intentional expansion of Jesus' ministry into Gerasa—Gentile territory. Jesus exhorts the man to return to his village and spread the news of his healing. This is a command to evangelize the non-Jewish residents of Gerasa. In Mark 5:20, the command is even broader, "the Decapolis." This expands on the assertion of 8:21 that the true members of Jesus' family "hear God's word and put it into practice." His family is now understood to include Gentiles.

3. Jairus' Daughter and the Woman with a Flow of Blood (8:40-56)

BEHIND THE TEXT

This story is based on Mark 5:21-43 (|| Matt 9:18-26). Its "sandwich" structure resembles that of the story of the cursing of the fig tree in Mark (11:12-14, 20-22) where he inserts the cleansing of the temple (vv 15-19) into the middle of the story. The fig tree was a widely recognized symbol for the nation of Israel. The overall effect of the passage seems to indicate the need to reform the nation's central institution.

There is a similar bracketing in the Jairus story. Jesus encounters the leader of the synagogue, Jairus, and raises his only daughter from the dead (8:40-42a, 49-56). Inserted in the middle is the healing of the woman with the hemorrhage (8:42b-48). The juxtaposition of the righteous synagogue leader and the unclean woman shows how Jesus bridges the gulf between them. Both receive his gracious healing, without respect to their status or gender.

IN THE TEXT

■ **40-42a** Jairus is one of the few Jewish leaders the Gospels characterize as pious. Joseph of Arimathea is another (see 23:50-53 ‖ Mark 15:42-46 ‖ Matt 27:57-60). Otherwise, in Luke's special material, the Pharisees who warn Jesus to flee for his life (13:31) get their only positive representation in the third Gospel. Paul was a Pharisee, of course, as were other early Christians. And the representation of the Pharisees in Acts is generally quite positive (15:5; 23:7-9, 26). In reality, Jesus probably had more than a few supporters among the Jewish leadership (e.g., see John 3:1-2), but we find no mention of them in the Gospel of Luke.

Jairus was a leader of the synagogue in Capernaum. He may well have been the one who commended the centurion to Jesus according to Luke 7:3-5. There is a sense of urgency about his faith (8:41). In this he resembles the woman healed of her flow of blood in the next vignette (v 47). Likewise, the details about the sick girl's age—**twelve** (v 42)—and the duration of the woman's condition—**twelve years** (v 43) seem hardly coincidental.

Both Jairus and the woman labor under the burden of ill health: the man for his daughter; the woman for herself. Both are overcome by emotion in their interaction with Jesus. Jairus humbly **fell at Jesus' feet, pleading with him to come to his house** (v 41). The woman at first **came up behind him;** after her healing, she **came trembling and fell at this feet** (v 47). The supplication of sinners in Luke is impassioned and heartfelt (5:8, 12b, 18-19; 7:2-4, 13, 38). Luke's cumulative characterization of the proper approach to Jesus continues to increase in these two interconnected stories.

Jesus' opponents, on the other hand, are characterized by Luke as cerebral and calculating (5:21; 6:3, 7; 7:39). This reinforces readers' perception that those who find healing and forgiveness have the appropriate emotional response associated with penance. This existential unity in what one feels, does, and believes is characteristic of Luke's anthropology of salvation.

This is not a denigration of reason in Luke's theology. But his theology does have a pronounced conception about the relational nature of Christian experience. The connection between human emotions and the experience of God's love and forgiveness is encouraged and celebrated in both the third

Gospel and Acts. Luke's narrative certainly shows us, as no other Gospel, the pathos—the emotional experience—of those who come to Jesus.

■ **42b-48** The size of the crowd following Jesus has been progressively increasing.

- In 6:17 "a large crowd of his disciples was there and a great number of people from all over Judea, from Jerusalem, and from the coast of Tyre and Sidon."
- In 7:11 he is accompanied by "a large crowd."
- In 8:4 "a large crowd was gathering and people were coming to Jesus from town after town."

In the scene of the healing of the bleeding woman **crowds almost crushed him** (v 42; see v 45). Luke portrays Jesus' Galilean ministry as overtly, even chaotically, public. As readers, we are prepared for dramatic events and conflict that reflect this cascading state of affairs.

As they go along the way to Jairus' house they meet a hemorrhaging woman (v 42b). She would not have been welcome at Jairus' house due to the ritual impurity caused by her chronic menstrual disorder (Lev 15:25-33). Her healing on the way indicates that Jesus' ministry extends from the leaders of the synagogues to those categorically excluded from the ritual life of the nation's religion.

Powerful issues of gender, blood, and impurity are represented by the woman's infirmity. She exemplifies not only the marginalized status of women in general, but also one whose physical condition (emission of blood) makes her a source of ritual impurity to all who touch her. This probably explains her attempt to touch Jesus secretly: **She came up behind him and touched the edge of his cloak** (v 44).

In doing so, the woman conveys *midras* impurity, defilement by means of the "pressure" of touch. This transmission of ritual impurity through touch is a private condition known only to those who have it (Lev 12:4; Num 19:11). The woman's knowledge that she is in a state of ritual impurity is, thus, a personal matter. Since the state of ritual purity produces no visible effect, usually no one but the contaminated individual knows of the condition.

Prohibitions associated with ritual impurity are observed on an honor system. This explains why Pharisees, who voluntarily try to maintain the ritual purity of priests, avoid public markets or other ordinary contact with the general populace. One simply never knows who is impure. Thus, the scrupulous order their social contacts so as to avoid those who are "suspect" or whose ritual purity is unknown.

The verb *touch* appears three times in this section (vv 44, 46, 47). Earlier, Jesus had "reached out his hand and touched" the leper (5:13). Now, his casual attitude toward the woman's impurity signals that her condition is not viewed with alarm (see the commentary and sidebar on 5:12-16). It also signals the priority he gives to compassion over ritual purity.

The woman's superstitious and surreptitious behavior hints at her desperation for the healing power of Jesus. She seeks to touch him, even if subversively. Hers is a rogue piety, and Jesus tacitly approves of it (v 48). Like the sinful woman of ch 7, and Jairus in ch 8, she simply *must* have grace to face the next moment of her life.

In many of the sinner stories in Luke, desperate need pushes supplicants into Jesus' presence. In contrast to those preoccupied with rules and regulations, intense need drives some to violate the rules to break through to God's grace. This points to the piety Luke's readers are encouraged to seek—rogue and reckless, not the tradition-bound type.

The woman's condition is graciously healed by the power of God emanating from Jesus, something of which he is immediately conscious. **Someone touched me; I know that power has gone out from me** (v 46). The communication of healing power by touch is analogous, but in reverse, to the spreading of ritual impurity by touch. The **power** of Jesus to heal flows as secretly as *midras* uncleanness (conveyed by touching). It passes naturally and without effort to the woman. This demonstrates that the narrative presents the holiness of Jesus as stronger than ritual impurity. There may also be a subtext that Jesus' authority to cleanse surpasses or even supplants that of temple ritual.

Jesus responds, **Daughter, your faith has healed you. Go in peace** (v 48). Some variation of this declaration is frequent in Luke (5:20; 7:9, 50; 8:25). The woman's faith, fueled by need, is all that is required to receive God's grace. The story implies that the formal structures of religion are not the arbitrating factor for healing grace. Her sense of need and intense seeking makes grace come alive in her life. This is further evidence of Luke's relational theology. In this sense, these stories particularly resonate with a Wesleyan perspective.

■ **49-56** The story of the raising of Jairus' daughter has parallels to the raising of the son of the Shunammite woman by Elisha in 2 Kgs 4:25b-37.

- In both stories the supplicants fall at the prophet's feet and beg for help (2 Kgs 4:27 ‖ Luke 8:41).
- One has an only child and the other an only daughter (2 Kgs 4:14; Luke 8:42).
- Both resuscitations occur in a closed room in the house (2 Kgs 4:32-33; Luke 8:51).
- In both, prophets present the raised child to the amazed parents (2 Kgs 4:36-37; Luke 8:55-56).

It is not difficult to see why stories may have come to Herod that "one of the prophets of long ago has come back to life" (repeated in Luke 9:8 and 19b).

The story of Jairus' daughter also builds on a pattern first seen in the raising of the widow's son at Nain:

- The widow has an only child (7:12).
- Jairus has only one daughter (8:42).

- Jesus tells both parents to stop crying (7:13; 8:52).
- Jesus commands the dead child to rise (7:14; 8:54).
- Everyone is astounded (7:16; 8:56).

What was proclaimed to be true in ch 7 is shown to be all the more true here in ch 8: "'A great prophet has appeared among us,' they said. 'God has come to help his people'" (7:16).

Jesus charges the parents **not to tell anyone what had happened** (v 56). This detail depends on Mark, where this theme is prominent (e.g., Mark 5:43). As already noted (see the commentary on 5:12-16), the element of secrecy is uncharacteristic of Luke in regard to Jesus' healing ministry. In terms of Luke's narrative development of Jesus' identity, such secrecy seems out of place here (see 8:39). Matthew omits the request for secrecy, instead reporting that "news of this spread through all that region" (9:26).

FROM THE TEXT

Three stories in ch 8 deal with powers over which people have no control: the raging sea (vv 22-25), demonic possession (vv 26-39), and debilitating illness (vv 40-56). Luke demonstrates in these stories that Jesus controls nature, spiritual powers, and bodily illnesses. In his identity as the "Christ" (2:11, 26; 4:41; 9:20; 20:41; 22:67; 23:35, 39; 24:46), the "Holy One of God" (4:34), and "Son of God" (4:3, 9, 41; 8:28; 22:70), he commands these powers. And they must yield to his sovereign authority.

Increasingly, all that Jesus does in the story is seen through the lens of this emerging identity. These acts of control over the physical and cosmic realms are possible because of who he is: the Christ, the Holy One of God, the Son of God. By such means, Luke invites his readers to embrace Jesus in this identity and become his obedient followers.

More broadly, the instruments of separation from God are deconstructed in the narrative. Ritual impurity and sin no longer exclude the sinful woman from the presence of the Son of God. Disease, death, and demonic possession, which long separated their victims from God, have their power suddenly overturned and broken. The dead are raised. The sick are healed and the demon-possessed regain their right minds. Jesus' touch overcomes conventional notions of uncleanness, by reversing the flow of impurity, instead making clean those who touch him (5:12-16; 8:42b-48).

The new community has a free-flowing holiness, liberated from the conventions that held it bound before the Messiah appeared. All who enter the community feel its effects in life-transforming and therapeutic ways. This liberating power can inspire modern Christian communities to reach out to those alienated from Christ and the church. As with Luke's sinners, the emphasis on redemptive grace offers an open invitation into Christian communion for the disenfranchised and all in desperate need. Grace and rogue piety trump ritual practice and tradition.

As the identity of Jesus "matures" in the narrative, it becomes evident that he is the one who is in ultimate control of all that is around him. The forces of opposition are mounting, but they cannot stand against his power. Not every storm is stilled, not every demon exorcized, and not every sick person healed. But these incidents show that the light is breaking in and the darkness is being overcome.

As Jesus remarked to the disciples of John the Baptist, "Go back and report to John what you have seen and heard: The blind receive sight, the lame walk, those who have leprosy are cured, the deaf hear, the dead are raised, and the good news is preached to the poor. Blessed is the man who does not fall away on account of me" (7:22-23).

F. Jesus and the Twelve (9:1-17)

1. The Mission of the Twelve (9:1-6)

BEHIND THE TEXT

Jesus now calls the disciples to emulate his own itinerant lifestyle by sending them "out" to proclaim the gospel. Jesus' own itinerancy is first presaged in his journey as an unborn baby from "Nazareth in Galilee to Judea, to Bethlehem the town of David" (2:4). There is "no room for them in the inn" (2:7). This sense of homelessness has continued as a motif in Jesus' life throughout chs 4—9. Jesus begins his ministry in Nazareth, but soon takes his leave saying, "I must preach the kingdom of God to the other cities also, because for this purpose I have been sent" (4:43 NKJV).

The "stage" for Jesus' activities, with their constant and unsettled motion, is the nameless cities, villages, and towns of the Galilee region (5:17; 8:1, 4; 13:22; see Tyson 1992, 24-25). He will declare at the end of ch 9: "Foxes have holes and birds of the air have nests, but the Son of Man has no place to lay his head" (v 58). The Jesus of the Gospels has no place to call home. Luke implies that the same is in some sense also true of Jesus' followers.

The theme of itinerancy is echoed in several other related issues in Luke:
- alienation from family (see 8:19; 12:53; 14:26; 18:28-30)
- detachment from a settled existence and employment (2:6-7; 5:11, 28; 9:57-62; 18:28-30)
- reliance on charity for support (8:3; 9:3; 10:4)
- community polarization, actually encouraged by Jesus in his commission of the Twelve (9:5; 10:10-16)

Such itinerancy and poverty is found in the lives of the Bible's other wandering prophets. Moses, Elijah, Elisha, and John the Baptist all lived without a permanent home during their ministry. The Pharisees of Jesus' day had their wandering preachers as well (Matt 23:15). At least one other first-century

Jewish wonderworker, Hanina ben Dosa, lived in extreme poverty (see Vermes on Jewish charismatics, 1973, 69-80).

Paul of Tarsus was an early Christian evangelist who abandoned the comforts of home and family to roam about preaching the gospel (see 1 Cor 9:5-6). Luke and Acts mention other nearly contemporary exorcists and preachers (e.g., Luke 9:49-50; Acts 1:8; 8:4-5; 10:23-24; 19:13-14).

Some scholars compare Jesus to the wandering Cynic street philosophers described by Epictetus. They were as homeless, unwashed, uncouth, ragged beggars. "Half-naked, filthy, exposed to the elements, and living from day to day—no wonder Epictetus cautioned a would-be Cynic from taking up this manner of life" (Hock 1992, 1223-24). Direct influence of the Cynics on the Gospel tradition, however, has never been established.

Whatever its origins and precedents, itinerancy was a life of extreme hardship and deprivation, and to this Jesus called his followers. Something about the impermanence of this itinerant lifestyle is essential to the kingdom of God in the narrative. Having **nothing for the journey—no staff, no bag, no bread, no money, no extra tunic** (9:3) suggests the immediacy of the kingdom. It is now. In this temporary form, it cannot continue indefinitely. Having no bag, bread, or money is not a sustainable life. Its end—as both goal and conclusion—will come.

IN THE TEXT

■ 1-6 Following a period of intensive preparation, Jesus sends out his disciples to undertake independent activity for the kingdom of God. The Twelve now adopt their own lives of asceticism and itinerancy. In a sense, the disciples come of age in this passage. There is evidence that their earlier lives of itinerancy following Jesus had already involved physical hunger (6:3; 9:13; Mark 8:2). In this new phase of their internship, they are to take **nothing for** their **journey—no staff, no bag, no bread, no money, no extra tunic** (v 3). Perhaps this is how the disciples are to learn compassion for the poor. Perhaps, it is also to teach them to live in total dependence on God's providence.

Total commitment to the kingdom requires the disciples to rely entirely on alms—gracious gifts from others. Self-sufficiency is somehow at cross-purposes with their calling to follow. Perhaps by having nothing, and nothing to lose, they can understand the all-sufficiency of the vision Jesus has laid out for the new economy of God.

What a considerable distance the disciples have come! They have traded the comfort of a livelihood in a fishing village or an authoritative seat behind a tax table for allegiance to a traveling sage. They now find themselves without any predictable means of support, save the message of liberation and healing in the gospel.

The sending of the Twelve involves a new level of public engagement for the ministry. It is no longer one sage with a group of followers. It is one sage and twelve newly commissioned emissaries with independent status (what Theissen and Merz [1996, 217] call "secondary charismatics"). Their commissioning is the beginning of the Jesus *movement*, that tipping point in Christian history at which the words of one teacher begin to take root in a community of activist evangelists. It is no longer Jesus alone against the demons and sickness. It is he and his growing group of followers arrayed against these powers.

The narrative moves from Jesus acting alone against Satan in the testing (4:1-13), to the calling of the Twelve (6:12-16), to the commissioning of the Twelve to fight evil in their own mission (9:1-6), to the commissioning of a much larger group, the seventy (10:1-12). Luke, thus, portrays the substantial growth of the Jesus movement throughout the coming chapters. Then he finds its ultimate extension beyond Palestine in the drama of Acts—arriving eventually in Rome.

Healing and demon exorcism are central to the mission of the Twelve (see Behind the Text on 8:26-39). Here in ch 9, the disciples are specifically empowered to **drive out all demons and to cure diseases** (v 1). This activity is integral to the proclamation of the **kingdom of God** (v 2). The Twelve extend the ministry of Jesus in a new and public thrust. The focus of the Twelve is not only to **preach the kingdom** but to heal and exorcize demons (vv 2 and 6).

Why this emphasis on demons and illness? How is it important in the telling of the story of the Gospel? Why does Jesus not tell his followers to feed the poor and work to banish their suffering, whether by political or religious means?

It is easy to become enamored by the symbolism of the conquest of evil inherent in exorcism and healing (see the commentary on 4:31-37). But, essentially, the result of this activity in Jesus' ministry is the alleviation of human suffering. That is, demon exorcism is an act of compassion in the Gospel as well as a demonstration of hegemony over the sinister powers.

Another feature of the apostolic commission is the emerging political emphasis on the acceptance or rejection of Jesus' emissaries at the civic level. The test of acceptance or rejection begins with the **house** in which the disciples stay (v 4). This refers to the familial unit of a town. But it extends directly to the **town** in which the house stands: **If people do not welcome you, shake the dust off your feet when you leave their town, as a testimony against them** (v 5).

The emphasis is no longer on the response of individuals to the representatives of Jesus. Now it is the response of the household and the town to the representatives of Jesus that matters. This signifies the broadening reach of his mission. Certainly, communities are comprised of individuals. But by fomenting rejection of the Messiah, the community itself becomes subject to rejection by God. It is a **testimony against them** (v 5; see 10:12). This is a new development in the story.

The shaking of dust from the feet represents the disassociation of the disciples from the people of the town and of the town from the growing community of God. The rejection of Jesus in Samaria (in 9:52-53) and in Jerusalem (in 19:41-44) will continue the theme of growing opposition to Jesus and his movement. This issue will be expanded by Luke in ch 10 in the discourse of woe on the cities.

2. Herod Hears About Jesus (9:7-9)

IN THE TEXT

■ **7-9** This **Herod** is not the Herod the Great mentioned in Luke 1:5. This is his son, **Herod** Antipas, the tetrarch of Galilee, nemesis of John the Baptist referred to in Luke 3:1 (also 13:31; 23:7). Luke's characterization of Herod is somewhat equivocal in his Gospel. He is a dangerous figure, as the death of John at his hands indicates. But with Jesus, Herod displays more curiosity than ill-will.

Herod **tried to see** Jesus (v 9). Later, when Jesus is sent to Herod by Pilate, Herod is "greatly pleased, because for a long time he had been wanting to see him. From what he had heard about him, he hoped to see him perform some miracle" (23:8). In Luke 13:31 some Pharisees warn Jesus that Herod wants him dead. But when given the opportunity to have him executed in Jerusalem, Herod merely mocks him, dresses him in an elegant robe, and sends him back to Pilate (23:11).

Luke 9:7-9 is an interesting window into the public perception of Jesus by his contemporaries. Herod had already **beheaded** John. But some were now saying that **John had been raised from the dead** (v 7). Here, Luke acknowledges John's death, although he omits the narrative of his execution (reported in Mark 6:17-29 ‖ Matt 14:1-12). Herod is perplexed by rumors that Jesus is John, who has come back to life, but dismisses them by referring to John's beheading.

There is nothing elsewhere in the literature of the period about a person dying and coming back to life as *another* person. Marshall calls this report about John an "ill-informed piece of popular superstition," but cannot see why "such strange beliefs should not have existed" (Marshall 1978, 356; see 9:19). Three phrases in vv 7-9 make esoteric references to resurrection:

- *ēgerthē ek nekrōn*: **raised from the dead** (v 7)
- *Elias ephanē*: **Elijah had appeared** (v 8)
- *prophētēs tis tōn archaiōn anestē*: **one of the prophets of long ago had come back to life** (v 8)

At the level of the narrative, these references lay the conceptual groundwork for understanding Jesus' resurrection.

The reference to Jesus as Elijah *redivivus* in 9:7 presages the appearance of Elijah in 9:30. John had been identified as Elijah in 1:17 (see the com-

206

mentary on 7:18-23). This suggested identity for Jesus is deconstructed by the appearance of Elijah himself on the Mount of Transfiguration. The question about Jesus' identity is posed poignantly by Herod. If Jesus is neither John nor Elijah, **who, then, is this I hear such things about?** (v 9; note how this echoes 5:21; 7:19, 49; 8:25). The question remains unanswered, but only briefly, since the narrator is about to reveal the truth in 9:20. Green proposes that this question is paradigmatic for the rhetorical purpose of Luke's entire narrative. The question the narrator is at such pains to answer is: Who is this Jesus? (1997, 361).

3. The Feeding of the 5,000 (9:10-17)

BEHIND THE TEXT

Luke's report of Herod Antipas' speculations in 9:7-9 has provided a sufficient sense of time for the Twelve to return from their missions in the narrative. During their travels they have gone hungry and learned to rely on charity for their provisions. Immediately on their return, they are forced to deal with the hungry crowd that has joined Jesus in his travels (v 13). The feeding story is represented in all four Gospels (see John 6:1-14). Mark (6:30-44; 8:1-10) and Matthew (14:13-21; 15:32-39) have two such feedings. The versions of Matthew and Luke are somewhat shorter than Mark's; but all three have the same essential story.

Stories of miraculous feedings are found elsewhere in the Bible. In Exod 16:4-21, Moses mediates God's provision of manna and quail in the wilderness. There Yahweh says, "I am going to rain bread from heaven for you" (Exod 16:4 NRSV). A similar story in 2 Kgs 4:42-44 features Elisha as God's agent. He enjoined a man from Baal-shalisha to distribute twenty loaves of barley to one hundred people. Second Kings 4:44 reports: "Then he set it before them, and they ate and had some left over." The story of the feeding of the five thousand echoes these stories of Yahweh's supernatural provision. In all of these stories the miraculous feeding divinely sanctions the prophet's call.

IN THE TEXT

■ **10-11** Jesus and the disciples continue to be in constant motion. They withdraw **by themselves** to **Bethsaida** (v 10). This is Bethsaida Julias in Gaulanitis, in the jurisdiction of Philip. Capernaum and Bethsaida were just 2.4 miles (four kilometers) apart and were border towns of their respective districts. Bethsaida, Peter's hometown (John 1:44), would have had a more Gentile population whereas Capernaum in Galilee had a predominantly Jewish citizenry (Rogerson 1989, 140).

That Jesus and his disciples withdrew privately is similar to their departure from Capernaum in 4:42. There Jesus attempted to escape **the crowds** but was found by them. He and his disciples seem to have a gravitational pull on **the crowds**. The crowds are drawn to them by the desire to hear good news and the need for physical healing and demon exorcism. An inexorable attraction has been woven into the narrative's story line. Driven by Jesus' movements, the crowds follow him (v 11). When the crowds follow him to Bethsaida his response is warm: **He welcomed them and spoke to them about the kingdom of God, and healed those who needed healing** (v 11).

■ **12-16** Large crowds assemble in a remote place in the evening of the day. There is no hope of finding food or shelter in this inhospitable setting. The sheer impracticality of the logistics creates dramatic tension. The narrative conveys a sense of chaos in the scene, something far beyond the bounds of common sense. Having just returned from their own mission, the disciples find themselves faced with urgent human need on a massive scale. **About five thousand men were there** (v 14). Numbers describing crowds in Scripture are often more symbolic than historical. Even so, including women and children the number of people would have been large.

The disciples, a practical lot, wish to **send the crowd away** in order to **find food and lodging** on their own. They explain: **because we are in a remote place here** (v 12). They quite reasonably suggest that Jesus send them off to the surrounding villages to fend for themselves. Two narrative factors militate against this solution.

First, from a narrative perspective the "gravitational forces" that draw the crowd are inexorable. The crowds have demonstrated the same commitment to itinerancy as Jesus and his disciples. They have adopted the kingdom lifestyle; they cannot be sent away. The dramatic tension would be drained away from the story, and it would be contrary to the characterization of the crowd Luke has been building throughout. Practical matters are not the order of the day in this story.

Second, when sought out, Jesus has reacted consistently with compassion to all in the Gospel; and he does so again here. His own sense of mission mandates that he provide for these crowds who have entered his growing community.

A series of contrasts characterizes the miracle story:

- The asceticism of Jesus and his followers is contrasted to the abundance of the provision made for the crowd.
- The **five loaves of bread and two fish** (vv 13, 16), almost comically inadequate, are contrasted to the **twelve basketfuls of broken pieces** (v 17).
- The practicality of the disciples is contrasted to Jesus' impractical command: **You give them something to eat** (v 13).

■ **17** The **twelve basketfuls of broken pieces** are not just a matter of leftover food. Some commentators have suggested this as an allusion to the Twelve apostles, one basket for each. The baskets may also represent the abundance of God's provision (see also Marshall 1978, 363; Bock 1994, 835).

Other interpreters suggest that the leftover baskets were a *terumah* tithe. This heave offering (one sixtieth of a harvest) was separated by scrupulous observers of tithing (Deut 26:1-4). One scholar asks regarding the food, "Have tithes been paid on it?" (Green 1997, 365). Also, it would have been necessary to separate the so-called first tithe as a gift to the priests (see Neale 1991, 46-49). In fact, it was forbidden that this food be eaten by anyone but priests. This enthusiastic crowd may well have expressed their devotion by meticulous observance of tithing that day. More generally, the growing crowds may have shown their commitment to Jesus by increased observance of the holiness code in *many* ways, moral and biblical.

G. Jesus' Identity Revealed (9:18-36)

I. The Disciples Learn Jesus' Identity and Fate (9:18-22)

BEHIND THE TEXT

Jesus asks his disciples, "**Who do the crowds say I am?**" (v 18). This question brings to a head a series of rumors that have been circulating about Jesus' identity:

- He is a "great prophet" (7:16).
- He is "the one who was to come" (7:19).
- "He has a demon" (7:34).
- This man can't be "a prophet," can he? (7:39).
- "Who is this who even forgives sins?" (7:49).
- "Jesus [is the] Son of the Most High God" (8:28).
- And, "Who, then, is this I hear such things about?" (9:9).

The narrative has primed readers for the resolution of the question of Jesus' identity.

IN THE TEXT

■ **18-20** Jesus challenges the disciples to offer their own opinions on his identity. This is part of their narrative development as followers. That is, they must answer this question "correctly" in order for the meaning of Jesus' identity to deepen in the story. As noted at the beginning of the chapter, there is a coming of age process at work here for the disciples.

Jesus' question comes in two stages. The first is the more impersonal: **Who do the crowds say I am?** (v 18). The **crowds** have been an important and supportive character in the story to this point. But their understanding of Jesus is flawed and unclear. They think he may be **John the Baptist** or **Elijah** or **one of the prophets of long ago . . . come back to life** (v 19).

The second question is more direct. Jesus challenges his followers: **"But what about you?" he asked. "Who do you say I am?"** (v 20). Peter, as chief spokesman, offers the affirmation that Jesus is **the Christ of God** (v 20; NRSV:

"The Messiah of God"). Now, for the first time, the assertion of messianic identity is made by one of his disciples.

The narrative now clearly crosses into a postconfession awareness of the messianic identity of Jesus (see 1:32-33). Henceforth, readers' experience of the story will be shaped by Peter's proclamation (as also in Mark 8:29 ‖ Matt 16:16). It is as if the veil is drawn away briefly and the mystery revealed.

As readers, we are changed by the revelation and suddenly reminded of the assertions at the beginning of the Gospel about Jesus' identity as the Christ (2:11—"Savior . . . Christ the Lord"; 2:26—"the Lord's Christ"; 4:41—"Son of God"). Since these early indications, the issue of Jesus' identity as Messiah has been a matter of rumor, proclaimed by demons, but not explicitly stated.

■ **21-22** Jesus **strictly warned** the Twelve to say nothing of the revelation of his identity as Christ. Different solutions have been proposed to explain this call for silence from a historical perspective. Perhaps Jesus does not wish to create an expectation of a political Messiah. Perhaps he hesitates to move toward proclamation in fear of the misunderstanding about the nature of his role as a suffering Messiah (see Bock 1994, 846, on these and other such attempts).

From a narrative perspective, the reader is drawn to accept the pronouncement. Enlightened readers share something only the narrator and the central characters understand, and this further closes the gap of empathy. We know the secret the public does not (see Behind the Text on 9:28-36). This acts as a persuasive force on readers, compelling them to accept the statement of Jesus' identity. Furthermore, readers who are already well acquainted with the Jesus story find their understanding of the "secret" of Jesus' identity and resurrection reinforced.

The confession of Peter opens the way for Jesus to speak about the future and the prediction of his death: **The Son of Man must suffer many things and be rejected by the elders, chief priests and teachers of the law, and he must be killed and on the third day be raised to life** (v 22; on **Son of Man**, see the commentary on 5:24). This startling revelation is the first of four indications of Jesus' death in ch 9 (vv 22, 31, 44-45, 51; see 2:34-35 and 5:35 for foreshadowed hints about his death). In each passage additional details are revealed. The composite scenario includes:

- suffering (v 22a)
- rejection by religious leaders (v 22a)
- being **killed** (v 22b)
- being raised on the **third day** (v 22b)
- being killed in Jerusalem and that is now their destination (vv 31, 51)
- being "betrayed into the hands of men" (v 44), and this will happen soon (v 51)

Later in Luke, the death march will include being handed over to the Gentiles, flogging, mockery, and insult (18:31-34; also 17:25).

Why must the Son of Man **suffer many things** (v 22)? Just as his true identity has now been unveiled, the idea of a *suffering* Messiah also enters the story for the first time. Actually, the Gospel of Luke never explains why Jesus must suffer. Luke does not, like Mark, indicate that it is "to give his life as a ransom for many" (Mark 10:45). His suffering was predicted by the prophets (Luke 18:31; 22:37; 24:27). Satan was complicit (22:3). His passion is God's will (22:22, 42). But, ultimately, the suffering and death of Jesus is simply a fact for Luke: "Did not the Christ have to suffer these things and then enter his glory?" (24:26).

Looking ahead to Luke's second volume, in Acts the idea of Jesus' death is connected to forgiveness (Acts 2:36-38; 5:30-31; 10:39-43). On the whole, Acts emphasizes Christ's resurrection from the dead as the theological center of the gospel (Acts 4:10; 5:30; 10:39-40), rather than his crucifixion. Christian theologians from Paul onward wrestled with the question of why the Messiah had to suffer. But it is not a question Luke directly addresses (see the commentary on 9:23).

Jesus' intended destination in Jerusalem has been revealed indirectly to the disciples in v 22. It becomes direct in v 31. The journey will now dominate the narrative until the close of ch 19. The journey motif reappears in 9:53; 13:22, 33-35; 17:11; 18:31-34; 19:11, 28, and 41-44. Other ancillary references to Jerusalem are found in 10:30 and 13:4.

Just as the narrative context has been changed by the confession of Jesus' messianic identity, it has now been changed by his prediction of his suffering and death, which must occur in Jerusalem. A great light now illuminates the story because of the revelation of Jesus' identity. But an alternate, ominous shadow is also cast by the revelation of his future suffering.

2. The Life of the True Disciple (9:23-27)

■ **23** Five axioms are found in vv 23-27, one for each verse (‖ Mark 8:34—9:1 ‖ Matt 16:24-28). The death motif from 9:22 is the narrative thread that unites all five sayings:

- cross (v 23)
- lose life (v 24)
- forfeit life (v 25)
- shamed at judgment (v 26)
- taste death (v 27)

Verses 23-27 introduce the notion that in sharing the power of Jesus the disciples will also share in his suffering. There is a progression in the five sayings, from the cross and its living agony, to the actual loss of life, to the finality of judgment, to the tasting of death itself. Verse 23 says, "If any want to become my followers, let them deny themselves and take up their cross daily and follow me" (NRSV; see 14:27).

The cross was the most common form of execution in first-century Palestine (on crucifixion, see Hengel 1977). But the emphasis here is not on the disciples' literal martyrdoms, but the life of obligation imposed by the news of Jesus' impending suffering (v 22). The disciples learn that the "power and authority" (9:1) given them by Jesus comes with a cost—they too will suffer.

Metaphorically, cross-bearing involves "self-denial" and "following." Itinerant ministry, of course, entails a great deal of real self-denial for followers of Jesus. But these ideas are subtly appropriated to describe the *daily* life of discipleship. The "cross" becomes a metaphor for the responsibilities of discipleship, which, in turn, are a form of "death" in relation to their old lives.

The expression **take up** one's **cross** does not predate the time of Jesus as far as we know. This has led some to assert that this language was later placed on Jesus' lips by the church (Fitzmyer 1981, 1:785; Funk and Hoover 1993, 79). In any case, Luke adds the condition that a disciple take up his cross **daily** (‖ Mark 8:34 ‖ Matt 16:24). This makes cross-bearing a matter of routine lifestyle for the postresurrection disciple. From this perspective, carrying a cross is a powerful metaphor for the sacrificial devotion required of disciples.

The Theology of the Cross in Luke

Luke refers to the cross as simply an instrument of death (23:26; Acts 2:23; 4:10). In the present passage, it refers metaphorically to the burdens and responsibilities of discipleship (9:23; 14:27). The cross is not a symbol for Christ's atoning death anywhere in Luke, as in, say, Col 1:20; 2:14. Nor is it a code word for the Christian faith—the "cross of Christ" (as, e.g., in I Cor 1:17; Gal 6:12).

Luke uses the cross to refer to the life of discipleship. It refers "to the attitude of self-denial which regards its life in this world as *already finished*" (Marshall 1978, 373). "For Luke, then, the theology of the cross is rooted not so much in a theory of the atonement, but in a narrative portrayal of the life of faithful discipleship as the way of the cross" (Green 1997, 372).

Paul occasionally refers to "crucifixion" in the life of believers in terms similar to Luke's (e.g., Gal 2:20). Typically, however, Paul refers to the cross as both the instrument of Christ's death and the divine means of salvation.

While no theology of atonement is explicit in the Gospel of Luke, Acts does assign Jesus' death saving significance: They "killed him by hanging him on a tree" (Acts 10:39). To this Luke adds: "everyone who believes in him receives forgiveness of sins through his name" (Acts 10:43). This is as close as Luke comes to an atonement theology. The most well-known and explicit statement of the atonement idea in the synoptic tradition appears in Mark 10:45: Jesus gave "his life as a ransom for many."

■ **24-26** The next three sayings continue the theme of death, that is, the gaining and losing of life. Jesus' words seem ironic: "For those who want to save their life will lose it, and those who lose their life for my sake will save it" (v 24

NRSV). In literal terms, this could mean disciples ought to welcome martyrdom in order to gain eternal salvation. But Luke surely intends this metaphorically. In this sense, cross-bearing means disciples **lose** their lives by expending them unselfishly. Reserving their lives for selfish purposes means losing the spiritual value of life. Giving their lives for God and others will lead to spiritual riches.

This is an idea common to other Eastern religions where "attachment" to physical realities is commonly considered the cause of all suffering. By "detaching" oneself from worldly desires the spiritual life is made possible. The idea in Jesus' axiom is not so different. His call for selflessness does not devalue life, as does martyrdom. Instead, it exhorts disciples to value the spiritual aspect of life above the physical.

Verse 25 expands on this idea. Here, the specific problem is attachment to possessions. Those who **gain the whole world**, will **yet lose** their lives. Those who value the material above the spiritual put themselves at risk. In fact, each will **forfeit** his or her **very self** and will lose his or her true identity. Materialism exacts a mortal toll on the soul. This is why even the "poor" in Luke can have joy (6:20).

In v 26, Jesus warns: Those who are **ashamed of me and my words** demonstrate that they place the opinion of fellow human beings above the opinion of the divine. This is, again, a valuation of the physical above the spiritual.

■ **27** The final saying of this group of five is so enigmatic as to have given rise to various interpretations (see Green 1997, 376; Fitzmyer 1981, 1:786). Jesus predicted: **some . . . are standing here** who **will not taste death before they see the kingdom of God.** Some interpreters suggest that this could refer to Jesus' resurrection and the establishment of the church at Pentecost. Others suggest that the passage alludes to the transfiguration, the narrative of which follows immediately in 9:28-36 (Green 1997, 376; Fitzmyer 1981, 1:786). This presumes that **the kingdom of God** refers to the glory of God revealed in the presence of Moses and Elijah on the mountain. Since the transfiguration was only a few days away, it cannot fully resolve the difficulty (Evans 1990, 412). If **the kingdom of God** refers to the apocalypse, then Luke preserves a failed prophecy of Jesus, since all his immediate disciples died without seeing its arrival. He had predicted: **some who are standing here will not taste death** before they see it. Depending on when Luke wrote, would he have preserved such a problematic prediction?

FROM THE TEXT

The three imperatives of v 23 (self-denial, the daily carrying of the cross, and following Jesus) are the "basis of Christian loyalty" (Fitzmyer 1981, 1:784). Albert Schweitzer once said that Jesus' greatest sayings are like explosive shells found lying around in a neglected corner. When we find one and handle it, examining it closely, it has the power utterly to transform our lives and commitments. The true denial of self is consonant with Jesus' emphasis on forsaking home and family for the sake of the kingdom (8:21; 12:53; 14:26; 18:28-30). This would challenge even the most devout among the disciples to reexamine their priorities. Perhaps few are fully capable of it.

The goal is that disciples should carry their own crosses and follow Jesus. Interpreted through the lens of the broader story, this calls for a lifestyle of humility. As Jesus will teach later in the Gospel: "he who is least among you all—he is the greatest" (9:48); "some are last who will be first, and some are first who will be last" (13:30 NRSV); and "everyone who exalts himself will be humbled, and he who humbles himself will be exalted" (14:11). The command to follow calls would-be disciples to emulate the example of Jesus in his humility and service to others.

3. The Transfiguration (9:28-36)

BEHIND THE TEXT

The story of the transfiguration has a convergence of three themes:
- the progressive revelation of Jesus' identity
- Jerusalem as the goal of the travel narrative (vv 9-19)
- the suffering, death, and resurrection of Jesus

Taken together these themes provide the structure of the remainder of the narrative of Luke.

First, the progressive revelation of his identity has been seen in ch 9 already. The clearer his identity is portrayed in the chapter, however, the smaller the number of people to whom it is revealed. This is a counterpoint to the expanding public profile of the ministry. The "crowds" think Jesus may be **John the Baptist** or **Elijah** or **one of the prophets of long ago** returned from the dead (vv 18-19). But they poorly understand his identity. More intimately still, in the presence of the Twelve he is revealed as the **Christ of God** (v 20). But to his three closest disciples—Peter, James, and John, he is revealed in the presence of Moses and Elijah as the **Son** whom God has **chosen** (vv 28-36). To the inner circle his identity is revealed in **glorious splendor** (v 31).

Second, the centrality of Jerusalem to the story is reaffirmed in the transfiguration. Even Moses and Elijah know that Jesus' destiny lies in the Holy City: **They spoke about his departure, which he was about to bring to fulfillment at Jerusalem** (v 31). Only Luke records the content of their conversation (see Matt 17:3 ‖ Mark 9:4).

Jerusalem appears in Luke's narrative thirty-one times, compared to twelve in Matthew and eleven in Mark. In the Galilean portion of the ministry, Luke refers to Jerusalem fourteen times; Matthew, eight times; Mark, seven. Luke's passion narrative refers to Jerusalem ten times, compared to Matthew's two and Mark's four.

In all three Gospels the journey to Jerusalem is important to the structure of the narrative of the Galilean ministry. But in Luke it is a constant and passionate quest. Luke's unique references to Jerusalem are found in 5:17; 9:31, 51; 10:30; 13:4, 22, 33; 17:11; 19:11, 41; 21:20, 24; 23:7, 28; 24:13, 18, 33, 47, 52. Only in Luke does Jesus say, "I must keep going today and tomorrow and the next day—for surely no prophet can die outside Jerusalem!" (13:33).

In Acts, Luke continues his focus on Jerusalem, with its narrative structure formed around the progress of the gospel from Jerusalem to Rome: "But you will receive power when the Holy Spirit comes on you; and you will be my witnesses in Jerusalem, and in all Judea and Samaria, and to the ends of the earth" (Acts 1:8; also 19:21).

Finally, the third theme is the suffering and death of Jesus. This is reaffirmed in the transfiguration when Moses and Elijah speak about his **departure** (v 31). This signifies that the coming death of Jesus is preordained by God and part of a divine plan, not an accident of history.

Luke's treatment of the transfiguration is more circumspect than that of Matthew and Mark. Those two Evangelists indicate that Jesus was *metamorphōthē emprosthen autōn*, "transfigured before them" (Matt 17:2 ‖ Mark 9:2). Luke departs from such direct language. He instead remarks that *to eidos tou prosōpou heteron*, **the appearance of his face changed** (v 29). This language is more attuned to a vision motif. Notice that the event occurs at night. Only Luke describes the three disciples as **very sleepy** (v 32). Thus, they see the two men with Jesus upon awaking (see Job 33:14-15; Isa 29:7; Dan 7:1-2).

IN THE TEXT

■ **28-29** As with so many of Luke's significant moments, the context for this event is prayer (3:21; 6:12; 9:18). They have withdrawn, once again, to a lonely place for prayer, this time to a **mountain** (v 28).

The transfiguration has numerous allusions to other stories of the OT. As his three closest followers looked at Jesus, **the appearance of his face changed** (v 29). This is reminiscent of the shining glory of Moses' face when he had been in the presence of God (Exod 34:30-35). Jesus' clothes are **bright as a flash of lightning** or "dazzling white" (NRSV), just as God's raiment was "white as snow" in Daniel (7:9 NRSV; see Acts 9:3).

Significantly, the Dan 7:13-14 text next speaks of the Son of Man who is "given authority, glory and sovereign power; all peoples, nations and men of every language worshiped him. His dominion is an everlasting dominion that will not pass away, and his kingdom is one that will never be destroyed" (v 14). This crucial OT teaching on the Son of Man cannot have been far from the mind of the ancient reader, since Luke refers to the Son of Man frequently (twenty-five times) in his Gospel, and recently in his self-identification in 9:22 (see the commentary on 5:24).

■ **30-33** When **Moses and Elijah** (v 30) suddenly appear talking to Jesus, they likewise appear **in glorious splendor** (v 31). The appearance of these two central figures of the OT with Jesus indicates that he is the prophet promised "like" Moses. God promised Moses in Deuteronomy that he would "raise up for them a prophet like you from among their brothers; I will put my words in his mouth, and he will tell them everything I command him" (18:18; Acts 3:22-23). God also promised to hold all "accountable" if they did not heed the words of this prophet (Deut 18:19 NRSV).

In Acts 7:37, Luke specifically identifies Jesus as the prophet to whom Moses referred. Given the controversy with the religious leaders over Jesus' identity in Luke, the allusion to this prophecy here seems particularly relevant. In Deuteronomy, the authenticity of a prophet was said to be proved when his prophecies came to pass (Deut 18:21-22). Since Jesus has just prophesied his death and resurrection (Luke 9:22), the reader knows that Jesus is the true prophet to whom Moses referred. And poignantly, Moses and Jesus stand side-by-side on the Mount of Transfiguration, with Moses himself giving Jesus his imprimatur as prophet.

The omniscient narrator is aware of the topic of conversation between Moses, Elijah, and Jesus: **They spoke about his departure, which he was about to bring to fulfillment at Jerusalem** (v 31). They speak about Jesus' **departure.** In Greek, this is *exodon,* a "powerfully symbolic term" since it was through the Exodus that Moses led the people from Egyptian bondage (Craddock 1990, 134). Here it appears as a circumlocution or euphemism for his death. This exodus is described as something he was **about to bring to fulfillment** (v 31). This indicates that his death is according to God's will. God is in control, and the impending death is neither an accident of history nor a victory for his enemies.

God's sovereignty figures in Jesus' earlier experiences of being tested in the wilderness (4:1-13). It is also at stake in his contest with the demonic powers (4:33-36; 6:18; 7:21; 8:26-39). Just so, the underlying theme of the story is that God's redemptive purposes are never in danger of being preempted by evil. The reference to **fulfillment** also explains, indirectly, why the Son of Man must "suffer" (9:22): it is God's will.

Moses and Elijah also speak of his journey to **Jerusalem** (v 31). This is the first reference to his ultimate destination. Significantly, Luke is the only one to include this information. In a remarkable scene, the normal canons of time and space are set aside. The dead join the living to discuss the future.

The surreal nature of the event is also seen in the experience of Peter, James, and John. They are **very sleepy** (NRSV: "weighed down with sleep"). This seems to indicate a nighttime scene. But after the transfiguration, they **became fully awake** (v 32).

Peter offers to build three *skēnas,* **shelters** (v 33), to commemorate the sacred moment. It seems a weak gesture to memorialize this transcendent event, but it may refer to the Feast of Tabernacles (Exod 23:16; 34:22; Fitzmyer 1981, 1:801). During this annual fall festival, pilgrims joyously traveled to

Jerusalem to celebrate the harvest. Perhaps the act of building tabernacles was inspired by the reference to Jerusalem. But the narrator makes it clear that Peter **did not know what he was saying** (v 33).

■ **34-36** The cloud represents the presence of God in the OT (Exod 16:10; 19:9, 18; 24:15-18). Here, it harks back to God's appearances to Moses on Mount Sinai during the Exodus events. Fear is the typical response (Exod 20:18-20) to such a theophany. Peter, John, and James were **afraid as they entered the cloud** (v 34). Who enters the cloud? The disciples, Jesus and the two OT worthies, or all of them?

A heavenly voice emanates from the cloud: **This is my Son, whom I have chosen; listen to him** (v 35). Mark and Matthew have "my beloved Son" (*ho huios mou ho agapētos*; Mark 9:7 ‖ Matt 17:5). This *Bat Qôl* (= "daughter of a voice") is similar to the occurrence at Jesus' baptism (see 3:21-22). In both experiences Jesus is declared by the voice to be **my Son**. These declarations are the theological center of Luke's Gospel (as also in Matt 3:17 and 17:5 ‖ Mark 1:11 and 9:7). They settle the matter of Jesus' identity by means of divine proclamation.

The reliance of early Christians on this passage would have been controversial among Jews (see the commentary on the baptism in 3:21-22). The voice from heaven in Jewish tradition constituted a divine authority that rational argument could not challenge. The Christian claim of a voice declaring Jesus God's Son usurped the Torah in a matter central to the Jewish faith. Such a claim would have been especially provocative after the destruction of the temple, when Torah stood alone at the center of Jewish practice.

The precise words of the heavenly voice differ somewhat from those spoken at Jesus' baptism. *First*, it is third person now: **this is my Son** (v 35), not second person: "you are my Son" (3:22). This makes it an announcement to the disciples, not a personal affirmation to Jesus.

Second, this time it is accompanied by the modifier, **whom I have chosen,** and the command: **listen to him.** Luke's word **chosen** (*eklelegmenos*, source of the English "election") echoes the language of God's election of Israel from among the nations (Pss 33:12; 65:4; Isa 41:8; Acts 13:17), of the tribe of Judah (Ps 78:68-70), and of Moses (Ps 105:26).

Likewise, Jesus "chose" his disciples (*eklegomai*, Luke 6:13; Acts 1:2). This word is not used in the other Gospels (see Mark 3:13-19 ‖ Matt 10:1-4). This language also echoes Deut 18:15-21 (see above the commentary on 9:30). In Deuteronomy, the acceptance of a prophet like Moses is accompanied by the injunction to accept what he says: "The LORD your God will raise up for you a prophet like me from among your own brothers. You must listen to him" (18:15). Thus, we have here in Luke: **listen to him** (9:35). Jesus is the prophet like Moses, who must be obeyed.

H. Conclusion of the Galilean Ministry (9:37-50)

1. The Exorcism of the Difficult Demon (9:37-43a)

IN THE TEXT

■ **37-43a** A sense of expectancy accompanies Jesus' descent from the mountain after the transfiguration: **The next day, when they came down from the mountain, a large crowd met him** (v 37). We might have anticipated a great miracle or public proclamation following the sublime experience of the transfiguration. Instead, we find Jesus involved in a particularly troublesome exorcism.

A man beseeches Jesus to attend to his only son: **A spirit seizes him and he suddenly screams; it throws him into convulsions so that he foams at the mouth. It scarcely ever leaves him and is destroying him** (v 39). The convulsions and foaming at the mouth are the characteristics of a grand mal epileptic seizure (compare to the Gerasene demoniac who was also "seized" by the demon, 8:29).

The Matthean parallel refers to the child as an "epileptic" (Matt 17:15 NRSV). This condition was associated in ancient times with the phases of the moon. Thus sufferers were termed *selēniadzomai*, **moonstruck**. Ironically, those afflicted with epilepsy in antiquity were considered holy, because of the similarities between seizures and the state of prophetic ecstasy (Sussman 1992, 12).

While Jesus easily healed the boy, his frustration is unlike anything we have encountered in the narrative to this point. The object of his consternation is his disciples. He says to them: **O unbelieving and perverse generation** (v 41). Luke fails to say what occasioned Jesus' comment. According to Matthew's account, the disciples had insufficient faith to drive out the demon (17:20-21). Similarly, Mark blames "unbelief" for preventing exorcisms. The boy's father pleads, "Help my unbelief!" (9:24 NRSV).

Luke concludes without commenting on the cause of the disciples' inability to exorcize the demon. He says only that the people were **amazed at the greatness of God** and were **marveling at all that Jesus did** (Luke 9:43).

2. The Second Prediction of Jesus' Fate (9:43b-45)

■ **43b-45** **Listen carefully to what I am about to tell you: The Son of Man is going to be betrayed into the hands of men** (v 44). This is the second of four references to the impending death of Jesus in ch 9 (vv 22, 31, 44-45, 51). In the first, there is no indication of the disciples' response or understanding. Here Luke notes their reaction as confusion (v 45).

The disciples **did not understand what this meant. It was hidden from them, so that they did not grasp it** (v 45). The disciples were plainly told that Jesus would be betrayed into the hands of men but the meaning **was hidden** from them (*parakekalymmenon;* compare *kekrymmenon* in 18:34). The Greek verb is in the passive form. The disciples were actively kept from this knowledge by Jesus. Is God the unstated cause of their lack of understanding? Is this a literary device to create a dramatic tension for the reader? Or, is this a historical reality?

Taken as an aggregate, the portrayal of the disciples has been positive in Luke. This is much different from Mark, in which the disciples are routinely baffled by Jesus. But as the story becomes more complex and the secret of Jesus' identity and impending death is slowly revealed, the disciples become *less* clear in their understanding. While earlier portrayed as gate keepers for Jesus' wisdom (see 8:10), they are now unable to comprehend the future, although he has plainly told them (9:45). Again, in ch 18, they fail to comprehend: "The disciples did not understand any of this. Its meaning was hidden from them, and they did not know what he was talking about" (18:34). Readers have been privileged to know what lies ahead by the omniscient narrator, but not the disciples. This deepens readers' sense of being insiders to the story.

Historically, Jesus' purpose was probably shrouded in ambiguity, even for his closest followers. The entire drama seems clear enough in hindsight. But these comments by the narrator indicate that the death of Jesus was unexpected by his followers. Although Jesus had spoken about his fate in Jerusalem, his followers, even the Twelve, may have had nothing more than a premonition of tragedy associated with the trip to Jerusalem. Whether historical reality or literary device, the reader will interpret the remainder of the Gospel through the secret lens of Jesus' impending death. A sense of danger and tension will pervade all that occurs. This is a significant device in the story.

3. Argumentative Disciples (9:46-48)

■ **46-48** The disciples show themselves to be normal men by debating their relative merits and arguing over **which of them would be the greatest** (v 46). There is humor in this scene with Jesus, his disciples, and a child. As the disciples quarrel about their own greatness, Jesus gently **took a little child and had him stand beside him** (v 47). Ironically, those to whom the gift of divine wisdom had been given (8:10) now act like children themselves.

In response to the disciples' foolishness, Jesus employed a double entendre, **he who is least among you all—he is the greatest** (v 48). The Greek word for **least** is *mikroteros,* which can also mean **smallest**. Likewise, the word for **great**, is *megas,* which can also mean **large**. With a **little child** standing at his side, he had some fun at the disciples' expense. It is as if he were saying to them, "You think this child is unimportant [*mikeroteros*], because he is physically small [*mikroteros*]. Yet you, who are physically large [*megas*], foolishly debate among yourselves who is great [*megas*]." Judging by human standards such as size and age leads to errors about human value (recall David, small size, big heart for God in 1 Sam 16:7). Personal accomplishment and social

219

standing in the community, the subject of their debate, was not a true measure of greatness.

Luke's is the only account of the incident that highlights the humor of Jesus' remark. Matthew interprets the child's size as a metaphor for humility (18:4). Mark takes it as a metaphor for *lastness*, the apparent insignificance of being a servant (9:35).

4. The Unknown Exorcist (9:49-50)

■ **49-50** The spiritual deficiencies of the disciples are made obvious in a comment credited to the apostle John. These are the only words explicitly credited to John in the Gospels, and Jesus does not approve of them. The disciples had just been instructed in the error of judging by human values. Children, though small, have hearts that believe. Adults, even those to whom the secrets of the kingdom have been entrusted (8:10), and who have just descended from the Mount of Transfiguration (9:28), show themselves to be incapable of faith in action against an obstinate foe (9:41). Although massive crowds had become a part of Jesus' wandering ministry, John still pursues the politics of exclusion by wishing to deny the exercise of Jesus' power to an outsider.

"Master," said John, **"we saw a man driving out demons in your name and we tried to stop him, because he is not one of us"** (v 49). Luke's Jesus has been deconstructing social barriers throughout the narrative. Here, he again offers a new vision of community in which exclusion is *not* the governing principle. By way of contrast, John appears rather pharisaic, wanting to reserve the power to cast out demons to the Twelve.

Jesus' principle of community is broadly inclusive, extending a welcome to all who are **not against you** (v 50). In fact, this renegade exorcist is the first in the Gospel to cast out demons "in Jesus' name." He is a pioneer of the seventy who will soon be sent out across the countryside in pairs to heal and preach, and an example of the renegade piety Jesus has endorsed in the narrative. The seventy will return reporting that "even the demons submit to us in your name" (10:17). The Jesus movement continues to expand its reach into the community.